DATE			

FIRST LADY
OF THE LAW

Florence Ellinwood Allen

Jeanette E. Tuve

UNIVERSITY
PRESS OF
AMERICA

LANHAM • NEW YORK • LONDON

Copyright © 1984 by

University Press of America,™ Inc.

4720 Boston Way
Lanham, MD 20706

3 Henrietta Street
London WC2E 8LU England

Library of Congress Cataloging in Publication Data

Tuve, Jeanette E., 1914-
First lady of the law, Florence Ellinwood Allen.

Bibliography: p.
Includes index.
1. Allen, Florence Ellinwood, 1884-   . 2. Women
judges—United States—Biography. I. Title
KF373.A4T88   1984   347. 73'2434 [B]   84-19506
                          347. 3073334 [B]
ISBN 0-8191-4311-1 (alk. paper)
ISBN 0-8191-4312-X (pbk. : alk. paper)

All University Press of America books are produced on acid-free
paper which exceeds the minimum standards set by the National
Historical Publications and Records Commission.

CONTENTS

PREFACE

Florence Ellinwood Allen (1884-1966) was the first woman to be elected as a state supreme court judge, the first woman to be appointed a federal court judge, and the first woman candidate for appointment to the United States Supreme Court. She made contributions to constitutional and patent law and was among the first in her profession to participate in the mid-century orientation of the courts to more responsiveness to social change and needs. For nearly a half century she was the most distinguished woman jurist in America.

She was a remarkable jurist, but she was an even more remarkable woman. She belonged to a generation of women whose hopes and deeds were shaped by the suffrage movement. She became a zealous crusader for suffrage as a young law student. When the vote was achieved she immediately ran for public office and won with the enthusiastic support of women. A second remarkable campaign elevated her to judge of the Ohio Supreme Court, and a third brought her appointment as judge in the Federal Court of Appeals. Florence Allen went forth and did the things the suffrage movement promised women would do.

She was a pioneer in her profession and a role model for thousands of women to follow. Today more than a third of law students are women, their numbers are increasing among practicing lawyers, the U.S. Supreme Court includes a woman justice, and the women's vote is a factor which every politician must take into account. From the day she won her first election to the day she turned her papers over to the archives, she credited the woman's movement with her success. The goal of this biography is to trace the symbiotic relationship between the life and career of Florence Allen and the woman's movement.

I am deeply indebted to innumerable individuals and institutions for help with this biography. Thanks go to many librarians who helped me find material, and especially to James Casey at the Western Reserve Historical Society, Jacqueline Goggan at the Manuscripts Division of the Library of Congress, and Judith Kaul of the Cleveland-Marshall Law Library. Many staff members went out of their way to be helpful at the Schlesinger Library at Radcliffe Institute, the Smith College Library and the Roosevelt Library at Hyde Park. Lois Applegate of the Cleveland Business and Professional Women's Club made its records available to me.

I am especially grateful to Judge Allen's law clerks, Luke Lyman, Richard Kuhn and Robert Toefler, and her colleague, Justice Potter Stewart, for insights on her professional career. Professors Robert Wheeler and John Cary of Cleveland State University, Professor Marian Morton of John Carroll University, Professor Joan Baker of the Cleveland-Marshall Law School and Professor David Sterling of the University of Cincinnati provided helpful suggestions on the manuscript. A research grant from the Graduate School of Cleveland State University did much to expedite my work.

Several people who knew Judge Allen very generously shared their remembrances with me. I am especially grateful to Helen Lyman, Jane Toefler, Virginia and John Bazeley, Betty Boyer, Charles Hall, Elizabeth S. Denny and Grace Goulder Izant. And, finally, thanks go to my family, whose patience and interest endured through a project that at times seemed to engulf all of us.

Jeanette Tuve

Cleveland, Ohio
March, 1984

JUDGE FLORENCE ELLINWOOD ALLEN
(Photo courtesy Western Reserve Historical Society)

Chapter 1

THE UTAH CONNECTION

One of the remembered pleasures of Florence Allen's childhood was eating the rhubarb that grew in her grandmother's garden. The rhubarb roots had been with the family for more than three centuries, coming originally from Holland, a country from which her maternal ancestors had been banished for inflammatory speeches against the ruling Spanish monarchy. Taking a few treasured possessions with them, the family fled to England where they lived for several generations and became Puritans. One of their number, Samuel Fuller, a surgeon, decided to try the new world and made the trip on the Mayflower; other members of the family followed.

In Massachusetts Bay Colony some of them became disenchanted by the witch trials and moved to Rhode Island to join Roger Williams. From there they went to Connecticut and later joined the westward migration, driving their wagons to Ashtabula County in the Western Reserve of northeastern Ohio. There the rhubarb grew and flourished for succeeding generations to eat and enjoy. Florence Allen used the story often to illustrate the tenacity with which people cling to treasured things. She hoped that for Americans one of the treasured things would be the United States Constitution.[1]

The rhubarb arrived in Ohio in the wagons of the family of Isaac Tuckerman, who came from Sterling, Connecticut in 1839 and established a tannery in Orwell, Ohio. Isaac's son, Jacob, Florence's grandfather, was fifteen when they arrived. Jacob worked in the tannery summers and attended Kingsville Academy in the winter. He was very much interested in religion and joined the Kingsville Presbyterian Church. Later he enrolled in the teacher's course at Oberlin College, the first coeducational college in the United States. Jacob left without graduating because of financial problems at home. He taught for a year in Monroe, Michigan and then returned to the Western Reserve as superintendent of schools for Ashtabula County. In 1848 he moved on to Farmer's College in Cincinnati as professor of mathematics and soon was president of the college.

Jacob Tuckerman married Elizabeth Ellinwood, who, like himself, was "of revolutionary stock and Puritan lineage." Elizabeth was a teacher in the Western Reserve. She began teaching when she was eighteen, received a dollar a week for her efforts and boarded around. As Mrs. Tuckerman she was respected as "a lady of education and refinement, a faithful worker in

1

every good cause, a graceful writer of verse . . . and the inspiration and adviser of her husband in his professional career." The Tuckermans had a large family and Elizabeth managed a busy household, but she was never too busy to read the French classics, Moliere, Racine, Corneille.

Professor Tuckerman stayed at Farmer's College until after the Civil War, retiring at the age of 43, ostensibly because of ill health. He returned to the Western Reserve and took a position as principal of Grand River Institute, a college preparatory institute, where he stayed for fourteen years. From 1882 to 1897, his career climaxed as principal of nearby New Lyme Academy, also a college preparatory school for boys and girls from northeastern Ohio.

Jacob Tuckerman loved teaching and continued until he was 73. Honorary master's and doctor's degrees testified to his scholarship. His obituary in the *Andover Citizen* lauded him as a teacher "in the truest sense of the term" and noted that fathers who had given up all hope of inspiring their sons to greater efforts for higher endeavor had gone to him to enlist his aid. Many men, the obituary continued, considered that the turning point in their lives had been the day they first became students of this beloved teacher.

Many other interests filled Professor Tuckerman's life. He joined the Sunday School movement, organized a state Sunday School Union, and was a delegate to the world convention in London. He was Republican in politics, a 32nd degree Mason and charter member of a Scottish Rite Lodge. He was strongly anti-slavery and a strict temperance man, and gave effective public speeches on these and other issues.[2] So many people remembered him that when Florence Allen ran for judge of the Ohio Supreme Court in 1922 voters were reminded that she was the granddaughter of Jacob Tuckerman.

Among the many interests of Elizabeth and Jacob Tuckerman was the education of their children. Their son, Louis Bryant, returned to New England and graduated from Amherst College, but the question of where to send their three daughters was a more difficult one. Since the days of the early republic there had been argument as to whether young women had the physical stamina, the intellectual capacity or the practical need to master the rigorous curriculum of young men. The Tuckermans wanted an education for their daughters equivalent to that of college-educated young men.

While Louis was at Amherst he met Professor L. Clark Seelye, who was in the process of founding Smith College. Louis hastened to bring his sister, Corinne, who was attending Mount Holyoke Seminary, to Professor Seelye for the entrance examination for Smith. Corinne passed the examination in Greek, Latin, German and other subjects and was the first student to matriculate at Smith. She was a "splendid" student and a good musician, playing the organ or piano at college functions. Her classmates found her fun loving and full of common sense. Above all, the women of the class of '79 felt purposeful. They felt themselves in the forefront of women who were doing something new, getting "a college education like that of men."[3] Several women's colleges were founded in the 1870s. Their establishment recognized and perpetuated the idea that men and women existed in separate spheres, but Smith, among others, denied that education should be different for men and women.[4]

Corinne dropped out of Smith in her junior year to ease the family budget and to marry Clarence Emir Allen. After she married she received a bachelor of science degree from Grand River Institute where her father was principal. The Tuckerman's younger daughters continued at Smith, Florence graduating in the class of '86. Florence returned to Ohio and taught Latin and Greek in Youngstown schools. She expanded her knowledge by traveling to Greece and for many years lectured on the ruins of the Acropolis and impressed her audiences with mounted specimens of wild flowers she herself had collected in Greece.[5]

Clarence Emir Allen, or Emir as he was called by his family, came from an unusually energetic and adventurous New England family. He was a descendant of Ira Allen, who, along with his brother Ethan Allen, had been active in the Revolutionary War and in New England politics. Ethan was remembered as a fighting man who stormed Fort Ticonderoga in the name of the Great Jehovah and the Continental Congress.

Emir's father, Edwin R. Allen, born in 1825, had run away to sea with a friend in his youth and worked as a sailor on a whaling ship. Life on the ship was so unpleasant that they jumped ship and were stranded for some time on a desert island. They were finally rescued and other exciting voyages followed. When the excitement of the sea paled Edwin and his brother Cyrus settled on the tamer shores of Lake Erie at Girard, Pennsylvania, only a few miles from the Ohio border. There Edwin became a farmer and married Helen Anderson, whose family had survived the struggle with the Indians and converted many acres of wilderness into cultivated fields. The family passed along the story of a courageous female ancestor who hid her baby behind a log while she fought Indians. The baby survived but the mother perished in the fighting.[6]

Brother Cyrus Allen founded the Dental School of the University of Buffalo and eventually Edwin became a dentist as well as a farmer. In 1887 he retired from dentistry and became a justice of the peace, an office which he held until his death in 1900. His obituary eulogized him as a man with a very determined mind, his own ideas of right and wrong, and definite opinions in politics, religion and public questions.[7] Florence remembered Grandfather Allen fondly as a distinguished looking gentleman with an immaculate white beard, bushy eyebrows and piercing eyes.

Young Emir worked summers on his father's farm and attended local district school winters. In 1868 he entered Grand River Institute to prepare for college and in 1873 enrolled in Adelbert College of Western Reserve University at Hudson, Ohio. His education was interrupted by frequent times off to earn money to support himself by sawing wood or teaching school. He graduated in 1877 with honors, third in his class, and a member of Phi Beta Kappa.

As a young man Emir was most famous for his prowess in baseball. At first he played on the Girard team which played Erie teams. When Emir played he seemed to be everywhere at the same time, pitching, catching balls at first or second or third or at shortstop or the outfield.[8] Soon he joined an Erie semi-professional team, the Keystone Baseball Club, and played for them during summer vacations. The most remarkable thing about Emir's playing was that he could pitch a curved ball, a technique he had learned from a Pittsburg player.

The curved ball was unknown in Ohio and when Emir Allen returned for his senior year at Western Reserve he pitched the first curved ball in Ohio history. The Western Reserve team won every game that year, catapulting Allen to fame. Some members of the faculty, including world famous physicist Professor Morley, doubted that a curved ball was possible and went out to see Allen prove it. One of the professors finally conceded that the ball indeed seemed to curve.

In the classroom Emir had mastered the classics and after graduation taught Greek and Latin at Grand River Academy. In the fall of 1877 he married Corinne Tuckerman. Two children, Esther and Helen, joined the young couple before tragedy struck. Emir was stricken with tuberculosis. His hold on life seemed very precarious in the north Ohio climate, and his friend Liberty E. Holden, founder of the Cleveland *Plain Dealer*, advised him to go to Salt Lake City. A teaching position was available there at Hammond Hall, one of the New West Congregational Church schools. Emir went to Utah in 1881. No one expected him to live and he was carried into his first Utah home on a stretcher.[9] Fortunately his usual robust health returned quickly, perhaps stimulated by the prospects of an adventurous life in Utah. He took the teaching position and his family joined him. They lived in a three-room house on the school grounds. There a third daughter, Florence Ellinwood, was born on March 23, 1884.

The Allen family moved to Utah at a time of great turbulence and change. Mormon pioneers had established a self-sufficient agricultural economy and organized their community into a territory in 1850. They had purposely neglected the territory's great mineral wealth, thinking its exploitation would interfere with their way of life. Mormon isolation came to an end with the completion of the transcontinental railroad in 1869 and gentiles, like the Allens, began to flow in. The profits to be made from silver and copper mining brought newcomers by the thousands.

4

The citizens of Utah were eager for statehood, but the United States Congress rejected it on the grounds that the Mormon Church's control of politics and the economy was not the proper American way. There was widespread popular antipathy for the Mormon's sanction of plural marriage, a practice which had been approved by the Church to protect unattached women. The Mormons were known to be morally upright, hard-working people, but the idea of polygamy caused a highly unfavorable emotional response among gentiles everywhere.

In 1862 Congress passed an act disincorporating the Church and making polygamy a crime. The Mormons responded by writing a new constitution in 1870 which included the unique feature of woman suffrage. They hoped to prove that they were not unkind to their women and could be at least as magnanimous toward them as the rest of the country had been the year before in extending the suffrage to black men.[10] Congress retaliated by cancelling woman suffrage in Utah territory, two years before Florence was born, but it remained a controversial issue during her childhood years.

Corinne and Emir Allen's interest in Utah affairs expanded steadily.[11] The connection with the Holden family became closer as they became interested in mining properties and Allen mastered the essentials of assaying, geology, and mining engineering. When Florence was two Allen resigned his teaching position and worked for Holden as assayer in the Old Jordan Mine in Bingham. The family, expanded by three more children, Elizabeth, Clarence Emir, Jr., and John, moved to an adobe miner's cabin. The children loved the outdoor western life, and Florence especially loved to ride the mine donkeys. Allen was very successful in locating and managing several good mining properties for Holden and other investors and finally managed nine mines in Utah and Nevada for the United States Mining Company. The company prospered under his direction and so did the workers. Under Allen's management the workers were rewarded with such liberal innovations as workmen's compensation, an eight-hour day, and a six-day week with Sundays off. The Allen family proudly believed in social justice and demonstrated it.

Political affairs were of special interest to Emir. He took up the study of law, passed the bar exam, and successfully ran for the territorial legislature in 1888, 1890, and 1894. Allen was a populist. He stood for benefits for the common man and woman and easy money to benefit the debtor. He credited "the boys" in the mines with sending him to the legislature.[12] One of Florence's earliest memories was of the miners' torchlight parade past their adobe house during his campaign. When he returned from his first session the miners welcomed him with a huge surprise party in Bingham and presented him with a gold watch.[13] As a legislator Allen incorporated workmen's compensation, the eight-hour day, and the six-day week into the territory's laws, putting Utah several years ahead of most eastern states in labor legislation. The legislation was

5

contested in the courts and the eight-hour day was upheld by the United States Supreme Court in the case of *Holden v. Hardy* just before the turn of the century.[14]

In 1890 the Mormons capitulated on polygamy and Utah was on the way to statehood. When Florence was ten her father participated in the convention to write the first state constitution. Woman suffrage was included, making Utah the second state in the Union to have it. The National American Woman Suffrage Association rejoiced at the news and Corinne and Emir Allen were invited to participate in its 1896 convention. Susan B. Anthony introduced them at the opening session and asked them to speak. Emir praised the sun and soil, the mountains and streams and the abundant mineral resources of Utah. Greatness, he added, did not come from material resources alone but from people. He praised Utah for giving women — "that part of the people who instinctively know what is right" — the power to influence the body politic. Corinne spoke of the heroic efforts the women had made for themselves in rallying a thousand workers for woman suffrage.[15]

Allen was a delegate to the Republican National Convention in 1896, but walked out when the party platform advocated the gold standard and rejected silver. He hastened home to run for Congress on the populist platform of bimetallism and campaigned vigorously. According to newspaper reports he was able to speak with superb eloquence for up to two hours before large audiences, dealing mostly with statistics and without the use of notes.[16]

Allen was elected and was among the first delegation of representatives to go from Utah to Washington. The day after the election the Allen children paraded up and down in front of their house shouting "Al-len! Al-len! C.E. Allen!" As a member of Congress Allen's most notable speech advocated the use of silver for currency, but he also helped to establish rural free delivery of mail.

Emir Allen was an enthusiastic American. In an Independence Day speech in Salt Lake City he lauded the day when his countrymen gathered from ocean to ocean to celebrate the past, discuss the present, or "behold with prophetic vision the future glory" of the nation that was the world's leading exponent of government by the people. "History will search the mounds of Asia, the marbles of Athens, the ruins of Rome, the manuscripts of the Dark Age," he declared, "and shall not find wherewith to compare this giant among nations."[17]

Emir's blossoming in maturity might easily have been predicted, but in its way Corinne's blossoming was more remarkable. She was part of a remarkable first generation of American college-educated women. Impressed by their educational opportunities, they felt a responsibility to be of service to humanity, not in small deeds of charity to individuals in need around them as numbers of women had always done, but in larger

6

scope involving social reforms. Unfortunately society was not ready for this new generation and they had to find their own outlets. For many social reform projects provided that outlet, and such women as Jane Addams, Lillian Wald, Florence Kelley and others made a name for themselves in social service.[18]

Corinne Allen became deeply involved in a number of social causes. Most important was the Congress of Mothers, which eventually became the Parent-Teacher Association. While the Allen's were in Washington an organizational meeting of the Congress of Mothers was held. Those attending were encouraged to organize mothers' clubs in their home cities and states.[19] In 1899 the Utah Congress of Mothers was organized for the purpose of studying and discussing topics related to the home, with Corinne as corresponding secretary.

Friction immediately developed over the polygamous versus the monogamous family.[20] Polygamy had been outlawed in Utah, but, according to Corinne, the courts weren't enforcing it. She rose to the defense of monogamy and it became her special cause for the next twenty-five years. She was an easy and forceful speaker and she did not hesitate to speak out. To Mrs. Allen polygamy was adultery and she used the word in that sense. Polygamy weakened the family, she believed, and "the family is the primal basis of our most beneficient institutions."[21]

In 1906 the Congress of Mothers was reorganized without the Mormon women and proceeded to study education and morality as their conscience dictated. Some of their work proceeded through the courts. They sought ways to help juvenile delinquents through the courts, and on one occasion helped to expose "the most famous institution of vice ever founded in any city." The operator was arrested as a result of the women's prodding and convicted. Members of the Congress of Mothers witnessed her trial, and some were suspected of being more deeply involved than as spectators. Five of the mothers were indicted for collusion with the prosecuting attorney to secure the conviction of the accused.[22]

Mrs. Allen was also president of a philanthropic corporation of women which planned and financed Hallock Hall, a home for working girls in Salt Lake City. Citizens were encouraged to tax themselves to assist those who did not have the means to help themselves. The home provided comfortable lodgings for forty young working women so that they would not "fall into a hopeless state of mind and a lower standard of life."[23] It was probably not mere coincidence that a new YWCA residence hall was built on the location of the house where Florence Allen was born.

Mrs. Allen was a charter member and state regent of the Daughters of the American Revolution. The DAR was founded in 1890 in protest to the exclusion of women from the Sons of the American Revolution,[24] and at its inception endorsed progressive reforms, backing conservation, playgrounds for children and opposing child labor.[25]

7

Corinne Allen also helped to establish the Free Public Library in Salt Lake City. She was active in the Ladies Literary Club and was President of the State Federation of Women's Clubs. She was one of the founders of the National Playground Association. Her purpose was reform and she pursued it with dedication. Florence Allen assessed her mother as not afraid of anything in the world, and yet "with all her militant and intelligent activity in public matters, she had a charm of manner which won all those associated with her."[26]

The organizations that Corinne Allen's generation founded provided a means through which middle-class women could play a role in political and social issues. By the time Florence Allen entered politics women's organizations composed a network of millions of women with wide-scale influence on the solution of social problems and the potential of supporting or opposing selected candidates and causes.[27]

Despite her many civic activities Corinne Allen considered her family her primary responsibility. Smith girls, she wrote, were different in that being "womanly" still had a distinct meaning for them and family responsibilities were ever uppermost in their minds, rooted in "the selflessness that comes from a realization of one's place in the eternal scheme of things."[28]

Florence remembered her mother as a good mother and homemaker. She was always there when the children came home from school and supervised them rigorously. She expected them to be on time for meals, sit up straight at the table, and have good manners. Each child had an allowance and chores to do. Esther and Helen helped with the inside chores. Florence was a husky little girl and her special realm was the outside chores, chopping kindling and filling the woodbox to provide for three stoves, and tending the yard. She soon discovered that it was fun to build things out of wood, learned to swing a hammer with ease, and determined to become one of the best carpenters in the world — one of the few ambitions she didn't pursue. The whole family attended the Congregational Church regularly where father was a deacon.

The education of their children was an exciting and pleasant task for Corinne and Emir Allen. At first there were no public schools, only Mormon Church or Protestant denominational schools such as Hammond Hall, and much of the children's education was at home. Father supervised the children's study every evening, and in Florence's opinion no other teacher measured up to him. She was a precocious child, profiting from the attention of her older sisters as well as her parents. Her first recorded poem was written at the age of four with the aid of Helen and Esther, and ended with the couplet

My name is Florence Ellinwood
And I try to be very good.[29]

8

Her first experience with drama also came at the age of four. Esther, Helen and Florence prepared a tableaux for their father's birthday, with the girls dressed in Grecian gowns while Florence recited by heart the Greek alphabet, her birthday gift to her father.

At Sunday School on one occasion Florence won a prize for good attendance. The prize was a book of nursery rhymes. She burst into tears of disappointment, for she had been hoping that the prize would be a book of Homer's poetry in Greek, poetry which her father read to her instead of nursery rhymes. Later on she became so interested in Greek military campaigns that she had all the neighborhood children mobilized and led them with true Greek ardor in skirmishes recalling the Trojan wars. As a child at her father's knee, she learned from the Greeks that ideas are real, that the ideal can be achieved, and that the state is "a great and noble steed" for the conveyance of good in human affairs.[30] The Greeks deified such ideas as wisdom and justice in female form as goddesses, although justice, unfortunately, was blindfolded.

By the age of seven Florence had begun to study Latin. Cicero became real to the Allen children and they proclaimed his political orations, substituting their father's name or that of his political opponents where appropriate.[31] Cicero's conception of justice as a natural right lingered long after his words were forgotten. Florence learned to love the classics and they were a source of joy and reference to her throughout her life.

Books were very important to the family and they had many. Reading aloud to each other was a favorite family pastime. They wrote songs and poems for all occasions, Christmas, Easter, the Fourth of July, birthdays, homecomings and sometimes just for the fun of it. Corinne often played the piano and guided Florence's piano lessons. Esther played the violin, Elizabeth the cello, and the girls played trios together. When she was eight Florence's parents bought her a bicycle as a reward for her good work. It was the first woman's bicycle in Salt Lake City, the first of many firsts for Florence Allen.

In her memoirs Florence recalled her childhood as one of love and understanding from her parents and real devotion among the children.[32] Dozens of times and to thousands of readers and listeners she proclaimed the American home as "the root of everything good." It was her own home that she conceptualized; it was a phrase that her mother used repeatedly. In her later years when many honors came to her, her one regret was that her parents were not present to witness her achievements. It was their image, their sense of morality, justice, and civic responsibility that sustained her for a lifetime.[33]

The whole Allen family went east in the fall of 1896 when Emir was elected to Congress. They stopped in Cleveland to visit Corinne's brother Louis and his family. He was well established as a physician and as an outspoken liberal activist in the city's bubbling politics. He was one of the first to propose that the city should own and operate its own electric power plant to keep the rates of private companies in line. His criticism of private dairy companies for delivering unpasteurized milk to schools had resulted in a court case on the issue.

From Cleveland the Allens went to Girard to visit grandparents. Emir made a speech to one of the largest audiences ever assembled there for a political meeting and it had "quite an effect on many present."[34] His old baseball fans apparently liked him in his new attire.

Emir and Corinne and the younger children — the little three — went on to Washington. The big three, Esther, Helen, and Florence, stayed in New Lyme to attend Grandfather Tuckerman's academy and to live in the girls' dormitory. Uncle Louis Tuckerman's children also attended the academy and his daughter Lois and Florence were roommates. They found their social life somewhat limited by the academy's regulations, but summer was wonderful in their grandparent's big old house, exploring in the woods, and enjoying the rhubarb. Independence Day was exciting in New Lyme with family reunions and lots of ice cream ordered from Cleveland. The night before the Tuckerman boys, Jacob, Will, Warner and Bryant — "a jubilant crowd" — organized a relay of minutemen and fired a gun every hour throughout the night. Sometimes the Allen girls visited Grandfather Allen in Girard and helped him with the chores as their father had done.

Mr. Allen did not run for a second term in Congress and his personal participation in politics thereafter was limited. Utah women continued to play a political role more advanced than women in eastern states. The first women to qualify for jury duty were citizens of Utah in 1898.[35] They were honored at the Democratic National Convention in 1900 when "the lady delegate" from Utah seconded the nomination of William Jennings Bryan, who became the candidate.[36] During the campaign Corinne Allen organized clubs supporting Bryan's candidacy, and managed a meeting of 2,000 club members "in excellent fashion" as if it were a daily occurrence.[37] Women's groups were so well organized in 1900 that they successfully prevented the newly elected Utah congressman, a polygamist, from taking his seat.[38]

On her return to Salt Lake City in 1897 Florence attended Salt Lake College which had developed out of Hammond Hall. Music and Latin were special interests. Under the direction of Miss Gratia Flanders, a teacher Florence felt to be inspired,[39] she studied the piano music of Haydn, Mozart, Beethoven, Bach, Schumann and others. She kept in touch with her piano teacher for the rest of her life, visiting her many times in

California after her retirement. In Latin Florence read Cicero, Caesar, Virgil and Tacitus, all with great delight. She liked to debate and in one debate argued very well for woman suffrage. So orderly and logical was her mind and so forceful her oratory that her father was led to comment that if she were a boy he would make a lawyer out of her.

In 1900, when she was sixteen, Florence went to Cleveland to enter the Women's College of Western Reserve University. The adjustment to college life was not difficult, for sister Esther had attended Western Reserve, graduating in 1900, and Helen was in the class of 1902. Uncle Louis lived near the campus and his household was a center of civic activity.

Florence lived on campus in the girls' dormitory, Guilford House. Dormitory life suited her friendly and vivacious personality. She was never at a loss for friends to go with her to plays, concerts, on hikes, or out for ice cream sundaes, or just to have a good talk. She often played the piano in the dormitory parlor, with or without invitation. She especially lingered over the romantic, sensuous music of Robert Schumann and thought that he towered above other composers.[40] In quiet moments she wrote poetry, not poetry of melancholy introspection, but poetry of the exuberance of life and the world around her.

For fun on weekends she joined other young women at the home of classmate Ruth McKean on East 97th Street where the third-floor ballroom provided ample space for their "Attic Company" to rehearse and perform plays. Louisa May Alcott was a favorite author. Florence reminded the company of Jo March in *Little Women* because of her ability to take over, and some of her playmates called her "Cousin Jo" ever after.[41] Florence and her friends had great fun picnicing together on the shores of Lake Erie or taking in the amusements and rides at Luna Park or Euclid Beach Park.

On campus, she was elected president of the freshman class, as she recalled, "without any desire on my part."[42] She contributed to the college literary magazine, *Folio*, and became its editor. Her final editorial in *Folio* was an attack on sororities as being undemocratic, even though she belonged to Sigma Psi sorority herself. She participated in college dramatics and was a vigorous and uninhibited actress with a voice that projected unusually well. She played a heroic male role in Sheridan's *The Rivals* with such verve that she brought down the house in applause. The epitome of her contribution to dramatics came in her senior year when she persuaded her class to do a play which she had adapted from the work of a fifth-century Hindu poet, with Florence playing the male lead.[43]

Stage productions, operas and concerts fascinated her during her college years and for long afterward. In the terms of the time, she was a "stage struck" young woman. She packed scrapbooks with playbills and programs. In the margins she wrote what she thought of the performances, who she went with, where they sat or stood, how long they had to stand in line, and so on and on. Comments were often in superlatives, with plays and operas following each other as "the best" she had ever seen or heard. She adored the actress Mrs. Patrick Campbell, and, although some people thought Mrs. Campbell vulgar and her plays other than moral, Florence thought her beautiful, her acting inspirational and full of meaning, and her plays good because of the lessons they taught. "I cannot see the standpoint of her detractors," she wrote, " Whatever she is there is not the slightest trace of vulgarity in her acting." She felt "lucky" to have heard Mme. Schumann-Heink during her last concert tour; she thought Richard Mansfield performed "the greatest bit of acting I ever saw," and that Fritz Kreisler played "the most wonderful music I have ever heard." Melodrama did not appeal to her, and she found the play Salvation Nell "too ghastly to be really enjoyable."[44] Going to the theater and concerts was fashionable but many young women were not quite daring enough to go by themselves. An evening with Florence was a great occasion for them, elegant, swank, and exciting.

Her life at Western Reserve was quite within the confines of respectability for an upper middle class young woman at the turn of the century: a woman's college, a major in the humanities, dabbling in poetry and drama, playing the piano. She enjoyed it to the utmost and pursued it more intensely than the average young woman. Her scholarship was recognized by election to Phi Beta Kappa in her junior year and graduation with honors.

In personal appearance she was physically large compared to her peers, taller than average, well proportioned, poised and confident in her manner. She put up her long auburn hair in a soft double swirl high on her head, although a few ringlets always managed to escape. The sweeping curve of her hair in combination with very regular features and a classic profile, as well as her statuesque figure, created a model that an ancient Greek sculptor might have found suitable for a goddess. It was not a figure suitable for an actress in a leading female role.

The summer of 1904 after graduation Florence returned to Salt Lake City for a glorious few weeks climbing mountains, meeting old friends, practicing the piano and playing for friends. The mountains with their trees and flowers and animal life provided endless joy and inspiration. "Why can't we stay always on the heights?" she asked in her new diary. "But then," she remembered, "It was coming down that I found the primroses."[45] Pleasant anticipation of the fall to come enhanced the summer's idyll.

12

FOOTNOTES

[1] Florence E. Allen, "Lectures on the Four Freedoms," *Scripps College Bulletin*, v. XVIII, No. 1, Papers No. 8, 1943, foreword. Florence Allen papers, Western Reserve Historical Society (WRHS), container 29, folder 2.

[2] Information about Jacob Tuckerman and Elizabeth Ellinwood in Allen papers, WRHS, container 1, folder 1.

[3] Information about Corinne Tuckerman at Smith from Smith College Library Archives, 1879, box 80.

[4] Jill K. Conway, "Perspectives on the History of Women's Education in the United States," *History of Education Quarterly*, v. 14, Spring 1974, pp. 1-12.

[5] Allen papers, WRHS, container 1, folder 1.

[6] *Ibid.*

[7] From scrapbooks of newspaper clippings in Allen papers, WRHS, container 25.

[8] Allen papers, WRHS, container 25, v. 1.

[9] Florence E. Allen, *To Do Justly*, Cleveland: Western Reserve University Press, 1965, p. 2.

[10] For an exposition see Alan P. Grimes, *The Puritan Ethic and Woman Suffrage*, New York: Oxford Press, 1967.

[11] Information about the Allen family in Utah from Allen papers, WRHS, container 1, folder 1.

[12] Allen papers, WRHS, container 25, v. 1.

[13] *To Do Justly*, p. 5.

[14] *Holden v. Hardy* 169, US, 366. According to Ronald K.L. Collins and Jennifer Friesen, "Looking Back on *Muller v. Oregon*," *American Bar Association Journal*, v. 69, March 1983, p. 295. In view of the extremely unsafe and unhealthy working conditions of mines, the law was upheld as a valid health law.

[15] Susan B. Anthony and Ida Husted Harper, Eds., *The History of Woman Suffrage*, published by S.B. Anthony, 1902, v. 4, pp. 261-262.

[16] Allen papers, WRHS, container 25, v. 1.

[17] *Ibid.*

[18] See Ellen Condliffe Lagemann, *A Generation of Women: Education in the Lives of Progressive Reformers*, Cambridge: Harvard University Press, 1979.

[19] Sheila M. Rothman, *Woman's Proper Place: A History of Changing Ideas and Practices 1870 to the Present*, New York: Basic Books, 1978, p. 104. Also noted in Sophonisba P. Breckinridge, *Women in the Twentieth Century: A Study of Their Political, Social and Economic Activities*, New York: McGraw Hill, 1933, p. 23.

[20] Letter of Corinne Allen to Mrs. J.H. Reese, September 21, 1924, Corinne Allen papers, Schlesinger Library of Radcliffe Institute, (SL), A-5, folder 26.

[21] Letter of Corinne Allen to L. Clark Seelye, undated 1912, Florence Allen papers, Sophia Smith Collection, Smith College, box 1, folder 1.

[22] In material sent by Corinne Allen to Professor Seelye in 1913. Allen papers, SMITH, box 1, folder 1.

[23] Corinne Allen papers, SL, A-5, folder 0, contains pictures, pamphlets, and correspondence concerning Hallock Hall.

[24] Breckinridge, p. 23.

[25] J. Stanley Lemons, *The Woman Citizen: Social Feminism in the 1920s*, Urbana: University of Illinois Press, 1975, p. 123.

[26] Letter from Florence Allen to Edith N. Hill, March 15, 1938, Corinne Tuckerman papers, SMITH, 1879, box 80.

[27] William H. Chafe, *Women and Equality: Changing Patterns*, New York: Oxford University Press, 1977, p. 28. For the evolution of clubwomen's purposes from self-improvement to public causes see Karen J. Blair, *The Clubwoman as Feminist: True Womanhood Redefined, 1868-1914*, New York: Holmes and Meier, 1980.

[28] From typed article by Corinne Allen "Why Smith Girls are Different," undated, Florence Allen papers, SMITH, box 1, folder 1.

[29] Allen papers, WRHS, container 3, folder 1.

[30] The quotation is from a statement by Allen in *The Women Lawyers' Journal*, v. 48, No. 1, Winter 1962, p. 9. She attributed it to Socrates.

[31] *To Do Justly*, p. 7.

[32] *Ibid.*, p. 10. The account of her childhood is drawn from her autobiography, which was written at the age of eighty, and from speeches and interviews throughout her life. Time may have glorified her memories, but it is clear that she recalled her childhood happily.

[33] In 1948 in acknowledging honors bestowed on her by New York University she said: "I owe anything I have to my family. If we were as good as our father and mother, we would be pretty good in the Allen family." Allen papers, WRHS, container 18, folder 1. There were many such compliments to her parents.

[34] Newspaper clippings in Allen papers, WRHS, container 25, v. 1.

[35] Linda K. Kerber and Jane DeHart Mathews, Eds., *Women's America: Refocusing the Past*, New York: Oxford University Press, 1982, p. 452.

[36] Breckinridge, p. 277. The name of the lady delegate was not given.

[37] From newspaper clippings in Allen papers, WRHS, container 25, v. 1.

[38] Peter Gabriel Filene, *Him, Her, Self: Sex Roles in Modern America*, New York: Harcourt Brace Jovanovich, 1975, pp. 93-94.

[39] *To Do Justly*, p. 17.

[40] *Ibid.*, p. 20.

[41] Many young women of this era identified or were identified with Jo March. M. Carey Thomas, founder of Bryn Mawr College and active feminist, identified so completely with Jo that in her early years she took the name when she wrote in her journal. Marjorie Housepain Dobkin, *The Making of a Feminist: Early Journals and Letters of M. Carey Thomas*, Kent: Kent State University Press, 1979, p. 38. In her autobiography Allen wrote that some of her relatives called her Jo as short for Jove from Greek mythology. *To Do Justly*, p. 14.

[42] *To Do Justly*, p. 19.

[43] *Ibid.*, p. 20.

[44] Quotations from scrapbook in Allen papers, WRHS, container 24.

[45] Diaries in Allen papers, WRHS, containers 3 through 5, for years 1904-1965. This entry July 24, 1904.

Chapter 2

SEARCH FOR A CAREER

Corinne Allen had been invited to give a talk on polygamy in Berlin at the 1904 meeting of the International Council of Women, an international organization for the advancement of women's rights recently founded by Carrie Chapman Catt. All six children went with Mrs. Allen and their stay in Berlin, at first of indeterminate length, continued for two years. Esther, Helen, and Florence studied music at a good conservatory and took courses at the University, and the three younger children enrolled in a private school. Corinne made a survey of German schools during the visit, and the knowledge she acquired was taken back for the Congress of Mothers.

It was in Berlin in her early twenties that Florence Allen began her long search for a career and purpose in life, for by her standards life must have a purpose. Most of the careers she explored were quite conventional for an educated young woman of a good family. The second generation of women college graduates found many more professional careers open to them than had the first generation. Teaching, even at the university level, library science, and medicine, especially nursing, were well within the realm of possibility. The feminist movement and other influences had opened medical schools to women[1] and there were a modest number of practicing women doctors. Social reform work was highly regarded, but most of it was gratuitous. Several women had successful careers in literature, and some had done remarkably well in music and the theater.

The role of homemaker and mother was the first choice of most women and there had been steady escalation of the respect accorded those skills. Prosperity had brought bigger and more beautiful homes to the middle class, entertaining was a gracious art, and the steady flow of immigrant and farm girls available as servants, along with the invention of labor-saving devices, had lessened the drudgery of housework. The development of the science of home economics had improved the image of housekeeping and suggested that a homemaker was a professional.

Motherhood was especially glorified. The urban father saw less and less of his children as his work took him away from home and mother took over the household. The length of childhood had been prolonged as fewer children had to go to work, the years of education had been lengthened, and the horizons of children broadened under the watchful eyes of mothers who stayed at home and guided them. Parenting had become primarily the prerogative of mothers and society had recognized and honored their authority. Mothers were regarded as superior moral beings, pure in heart and mind. It was the heyday of "the cult of true womanhood," and a woman who devoted her life to motherhood could feel that she served a very noble social purpose.[2]

In spite of the glorification of motherhood, the pressure for women to marry was not as great as it would be in mid twentieth century. There were many singles of both sexes and one could feel comfortable without a spouse to cling to. The opening of higher education and a few careers to women had inspired some to choose a career in preference to marriage. So many educated women of Allen's generation chose the new alternative that it became the largest generation of single and childless women in American history,[3] and was most marked among educated women. Although unmarried they did not lack for companionship, for close female relationships were not considered taboo and were regarded as acceptable and appropriate.[4] Some accumulated surrogate families and became heads of household. Others shared a household with another woman and they became as deeply committed to each other as if tied by bonds of marriage.

One of the careers Florence Allen began to explore in Berlin was that of a concert pianist. Her teacher was Mrs. Wilhelm Eylau, a woman from Philadelphia who had married a German violinist. Mrs. Eylau believed she had discovered a new technique which would stretch the hands and greatly improve piano playing. In her first days in Berlin Florence "dreamed foolish dreams" of herself as a famous pianist, but then a few days later, after a bad lesson she confided that she thought "more kindly of some other occupation."[5]

Despite the ups and downs of good lessons and poor lessons and times when she played well or played badly, she continued to study piano and to practice long hours. Mrs. Eylau had frequent evening soirees at her home at which Florence sometimes played. Her playing was found to be "clear and pearly," with a beautiful tone, and most of all, "striking proof of Mrs. Eylau's methods."[6]

Aside from Mrs. Eylau's recitals few opportunities or compliments came to her as a musician. The competition in music in Berlin was undoubtedly formidable, and perhaps it required something beyond talent and good technique to excel. Small physical problems began to interfere with Florence's long hours of practice, tired eyes, a sore arm, a stiff wrist, a headache presumed to be from too much practicing. Sometimes she wished she had never begun to study music. Then she would go to a concert and come home "in a frenzy of hope" and plan all night "to be a concert pianist and earn $50,000 a year! ! !" Next morning her dreams of concertizing would have "vanished" in the cold Berlin dawn.[7] For the rest of her life biographers, publicists, and reporters would say that she started

16

out as a concert pianist, emphasizing that career exploration rather than others. It was a very ladylike beginning.

A more satisfying experience came as a music critic and correspondent. After she had been in Berlin a few weeks she became an assistant to Arthur M. Abell, correspondent for the New York *Musical Courier*. At first the job involved dictation and typing. Florence learned how to type and write Pittman shorthand. The shorthand required considerable practice, some of which she did while writing in her diary. The Pittman, combined with occasional Greek letters and German phrases, would make her diary confounding to later readers.

Allen soon developed her job far beyond ordinary stenography and was writing articles Abell liked and sent along. Reviews were published under her own name, and she was writing additional articles for the *German Times*, a paper for Americans in Berlin.[8] Abell was unstinting in his praise of her articles, predicted a great future for her and offered to triple her salary if she would stay in Berlin.[9] But such temptations could not keep her in Berlin.

Two years in Berlin had taught Florence Allen most of all that she was glad to be an American. In spite of all the excitement about going to Berlin, Florence was bored and disillusioned with the Germans from the beginning. Only things of nature, the birds, the trees, the soft breezes, seemed normal and attractive to her in the new surroundings. She found the Berliners noisy and quarrelsome and thought the women did "unwomanly" things. She was shocked to find this in a country where they had "the pure idea of women and the house."[10]

To Corinne Allen's daughter the cause of this unwomanliness seemed to be "over emphasis on the physical." Constant gesturing and coming up very close to each other in conversation proved the emphasis on the physical. The physical side of marriage, she thought, was emphasized in Berlin while in America it was the companionship side. She planned to write an article about the German life style and its causes,[11] but apparently she came to accept the differences before the article materialized, even though she never learned to like the life style of "Prussian Berlin." Corinne Allen shared Florence's criticism of Prussian life, disgusted, among other things, by the large number of illegitimate children in Berlin, a shocking state of affairs to this determined monogamist. Even the Allen boys, prophetically as it turned out, engaged in physical fights with their German counterparts. Years later, during World War I, Florence Allen blamed the Germans for starting the war and said nothing better could be expected of a country that confined its women to kitchen, church, and nursery.

Florence never felt at home in Berlin, but she made many friends at the American Club which was frequented by college students, many of them also longing for their homeland. They got together frequently to have supper, sing college songs, dance the two-step or just talk. Florence played ragtime, college songs, and Schumann for them and on one occasion gave them "a blast of Mormonism" for their edification.[12] Still time hung heavy on her hands, and she voraciously read English, French and German literature, soon exhausting the American Club library and her own sources. She memorized something almost every day, a piece of music, or a poem, or both. She read the Bible and wrote several pages of analytical notes on the Old Testament.[13]

Occasional trips added some spice to life. In 1905 in Malaga, Spain she went three times to hear the opera "Aida." "It is the most perfect opera I have ever heard," she wrote, "the music bewitching, the theme highly fitting." She was delighted that the baritone was staying at the same hotel and "we all happened to sit at the same table."[14] But all in all it was a happy day when the Allens left Berlin, and Florence wrote in her autobiography that the night before they landed in the United States she had the most intense feeling of joy she ever experienced. Elsewhere she wrote, "No immigrant ever thrilled at the sight of the Statue of Liberty more than I did, after what seemed like a long exile."[15]

After returning to the United States a more conventional career possibility represented itself to her in the fall of 1906 as she took a job teaching at Laurel School, an exclusive private girls' school in Cleveland. For three years she taught Greek, German, geography, grammar and American history, played for chapel every morning, gave frequent lecture-recitals on music, trained the glee club and directed dramatics. She was especially proud of her production of Moliere's "The Doctor in Spite of Himself." She took special pains with commencement ceremonies and initiated the custom of having the girls march into the chapel to the processional of the Dutch hymn "We Gather Together to Ask the Lord's Blessing."[16] In the evening she chaperoned Laurel students at the theater, attended concerts and wrote "Musical Notes," a critic's column, for the Cleveland *Plain Dealer*.

She was a very successful music critic and after she became a lawyer most frequently referred to her previous occupation as that of a newspaper writer. Her youthful admiration for music was so exuberant that it seemed to leap from the pages to infect the readers. She was an expert in the use of superlatives, but occasionally words failed her. "One needs a rhyming dictionary and a catalog of synonyms," she wrote, "to describe the playing of Boston symphony last night — the vernacular is far too pale and thin." The concert of Madame Schumann-Heink raised her to new heights:

> There are just a few moments in life when we come face to face with imperishable art — art so indescribable, so expressive of all the subtleties of feeling, the keenest play of flashing thought, the most onrushing sweep of passion, that we become as worshippers within the inner sanctuary, and surrender ourselves completely to the exaltation of the moment. Such a rare two hours were vouchsafed at the Gray's armory last night, when Schumann-Heink pitted her voice against the Pittsburgh orchestra, and sent her great tones ringing above them all.[17]

A few days later she wrote of another performance so good that "the orchestra seemed to stand on tiptoe and overreach itself."She did not miss the flaws — a grumbling cello, a conductor's uncertain attack, or a tenor's false intonation — but these were trifles in the wonderful world of music. She encouraged Cleveland music "to arise and flourish like the green bay tree."[18] With devotees like Florence Allen, it could hardly fail. In later years she would quip that she gave up symphonies and sonatas for wills and testaments, but she never gave up her love for music.

She lived in a rented room just a few houses from the big Tuckerman household. For Florence it was an extension of her own family. Uncle Louis had died but Aunt Mary continued to preside over the family. Son Bryant had become a renowned physicist and worked in Washington. Three other sons were doctors and shared an office in downtown Cleveland. Dr. Jacob Tuckerman was a surgeon and Director of Glenville Hospital. He was active in the Cleveland City Club and several medical and civic organizations. The only daughter of the family, Lois, had a keen mind, was well educated and a Phi Beta Kappa, but in typically female fashion allowed herself to be outshone by the men in the family and served her doctor brothers as secretary. Lois and Florence were lifetime friends.

At home the Tuckermans read the Greek classics for fun and quoted them often and easily. Conversation sparkled with clever play on words, literary allusions and classical references that challenged the brightest and most nimble mind to keep up. Cleveland politics and civic reforms were important to them. The municipally owned electric power plant that Uncle Louis had supported had materialized and they were discussing new ways the city government could become more efficient.

The Tuckermans loved the outdoors and could survive in the wilderness as well as in the drawing room. Camping, hiking and hunting expeditions were great treats and they went equipped with axes, knives and guns as their pioneer ancestors had done. The family was generous in its support of causes and charitable to individuals less fortunate than themselves.[19]

These were busy years for Florence Allen, busy in many ways that brought her pleasure. She had a host of friends from college days and made many new ones among influential Clevelanders. With her undergraduate friend, Florence Lessick, she often played for university affairs, benefits, receptions, and women's groups. On one occasion she organized and produced a concert, which was a musical success if not a financial success.[20] She continued to act in college plays. In 1908 she played the part of the father in Moliere's "The Affected Young Ladies," while her good friend Bertha Miller played as one of the young ladies.

Her reading ranged from Xenophon's *Anabasis* to the poetry of Omar Khayyam and MacCauley's English history. She wrote poetry and in

1908 published a book of poems entitled *Patris,* the Greek word for homeland. Her poems sang of the majesty and freedom of the western mountains, the wonders and beauties of nature and the joys of friendship. Not many poets write about law, but Florence did:

LAW

Where is our Pilgrim sense of solid right?
Where is our old-time keeping of the law?
Where is our sanity and strength?
　　Rapine pardoned, violence unpunished,
The excellent citizens unheeding!

　　Law thou changest not.
Our heritage it was to know thee.
Do we sell thee for a mess of potage?[21]

Corinne and Emir occasionally visited in Cleveland, New Lyme, and Girard, and Florence went home to Salt Lake City during summer vacations. There she renewed acquaintance with her sisters and brothers and family friends. Life was no less vigorous in Utah than in Cleveland as she climbed mountains, rode and cared for horses, mowed lawns, and participated in the Allen family musicals which were regular Sunday afternoon events.

These were pleasant years but not cloudless years. There were annoying physical problems, with pains in her arms and neck, trouble with her eyes, which she attributed to the glare of lights in concert playing, and "horrid" headaches which often lingered for two or three days. Frequent trips to doctors brought no relief. And she was putting on weight. She noted the gain in weight and feared becoming "fleshy," was pleased when friends told her she looked thinner, and chagrined when a medical examination for insurance reported her overweight — "too fat."[22] She tried dieting, but found it one of the few things in which she did not excel. Part of the problem was that she loved to eat and was a good patron of local restaurants. Hiking and a regular routine of exercise kept her in trim but not thin.

Then there were her "fast-developing psychological conflicts" noted in her autobiography.[23] What these conflicts were was not elucidated and perhaps they were not clear in her own mind. She noted sometimes in her diary that she "felt blue," a feeling most uncommon to her. She had found no satisfying purpose in life, no great cause for being.

Her friends were rapidly marrying and anticipating joyous fulfillment of their purpose in life. Florence was not yearning for marriage and her diary records no succession of prospects or intimate men friends. She was not the model of "dainty femininity" and domesticity which, if the literature is to be believed, men sought in a wife. She neither cooked nor sewed and was too exuberant to appear retiring or submissive. She was not petite. She did not assume a graceful carriage as young ladies in finishing school were taught, but strode along like a woodsman on the way to work. On the other hand, surely she could have married if she had wanted to and put her thought and efforts into it. Marriage and a career were not considered possible in those days. The decision to marry closed the exciting new option of having a career.

Part of the psychological conflict was making the decision as to what career. She felt that her technique wasn't good enough to become a concert pianist,[24] and maybe it wasn't. This was probably a wise decision, for it would seem that playing the piano was for her either a personal escape or a pleasant avenue of sociability. Her mind was not truly absorbed in the sounds of music; her real talents were in words and ideas. She felt that she did not wish to devote her life to musical criticism and lectures on the history of music, although obviously she was very good in this field. She did not record her feelings about teaching except for the boredom of teachers' meetings and the presence of "millions" of papers to grade.[25] But teaching had not absorbed her totally and had presented even fewer tantalizing challenges than the life of a concert pianist.

A partial resolution to her career problems came from one of her college professors. In her second year of teaching at Laurel she went back to Western Reserve University to enroll in a masters program in political science. She especially enjoyed Professor Augustus B. Hatton's courses in international law, comparative governments, and municipal law. Hatton had also helped to write the Cleveland city charter, which was of interest to her, and supported many liberal and philanthropic undertakings. While she was taking his course it came to her "like a flash out of the blue"[26] that she wanted to be a lawyer. She talked with Hatton about it and he encouraged her to go ahead.

The prestige of the law profession had been steadily escalating for half a century, and the prestige of the profession was attractive to Florence Allen. Lawyers had become more professionalized, law schools formalized their training, and going to law school was one of the best routes to honor, acclaim and financial success. Only the ministry equalled law in prestige in these days when skill in oratory was much admired. Besides, Papa was a lawyer and the Allen family regarded law with reverence as the embodiment of the ethics of the American people and their English ancestors — the Puritan sense of right.

Ambition for prestige and financial success was unladylike, but Florence could rationalize that lawyers also advanced social causes. In the same year she decided to go to law school, 1908, lawyer Louis D. Brandeis, later to be a confidante of Woodrow Wilson and a Supreme Court Justice, had brilliantly defended the ten-hour day for working women in the case of

21

Muller v. Oregon and it became part of American ethics. Brandeis' evidence to prove the weakness and delicacy of women and the need for protection was based on research done by two idealistic young women reformers.[27] *Muller v. Oregon* was considered a liberal, landmark decision in 1908. It paved the way for a body of protective legislation for working women, legislation which women's organizations approved and supported.

There were very few women lawyers when Allen made her decision to go to law school. In the early days when one became a lawyer through apprenticeship with a practicing lawyer, there had been a few women in the profession. The first woman lawyer in Cleveland started practice in 1885 after serving an apprenticeship with a law firm. As law schools developed and lawyers became more professionalized women were squeezed out because law schools were not open to them.[28] Women doctors had suffered a similar fate, but by 1900 they had begun to crack the profession as it could be argued that caring for the sick and dying was a natural occupation for women. But the law remained a male fortress, with lawyers concerned mostly with aspects of private property, business incorporation, crime, and legal affairs with which women supposedly were not and should not be concerned. Even in 1920, when the proportion of women in the professions reached a peak, less than three per cent of the legal profession was female.[29] It was this male fortress that Florence decided to penetrate. Her previous career explorations had been traditional ones for women; this one was not.

Western Reserve University was her first choice, but it did not accept women in its professional schools. She applied to the University of Chicago Law School and was accepted. She had moments of indecision during that summer vacation in Salt Lake City, but in the early fall decided to go to Chicago. It was an excellent law school with a very distinguished faculty, including Roscoe Pound. Pound thought law was no profession for a woman and the four women students in the school thought he discouraged them from practicing law. Florence was sometimes the only woman in a class of a hundred men and found it an embarrassing "ordeal." Her discomfort did not affect her grades, and by the close of the winter quarter she was second in the class. A few fellow students congratulated her for having "a masculine mind,"[30] an observation she regarded as a compliment and one that would come to her often in her lifetime. A masculine mind was one that was considered to be ruled by reason rather than feelings, emotion, or intuition.

Florence was not happy in Chicago. She often felt blue and even "hated things."[31] Although her parents enthusiastically supported her, money was short and she needed a job. At first the only job she could find was as a housemaid, scrubbing floors, washing dishes, cooking and preparing food. She was rescued from that unsuitable occupation by finding a job cataloging French and German legal treatises for the university library, which was probably no more exciting than grading papers at Laurel. Her physical problems continued. Her eyes bothered her frequently and an operation in which a muscle was cut resulted in wearing new glasses but not in total relief from eye trouble. Friends were far fewer than in Cleveland, but she became interested in Jane Addams and the Hull House Settlement. The young women there were dedicated social reformers. Among then was Sophonisba Breckinridge, an ardent feminist and outstanding scholar.[32] The settlement house movement was in its heyday. Smith College graduates of Corinne Tuckerman Allen's generation had been pioneers in the movement, and by 1910 more than 400 settlement houses had been established,[33] of which Hull House was the most illustrous.

Florence left Chicago, without regret and with no plans to return, in June 1910 for the usual vacation in Salt Lake City. According to her autobiography, she had been "induced" by Frances Kellor[34] through connections at Hull House to go to New York in the fall to take a job in social work. Kellor was a lawyer and head of the New York League for the Protection of Immigrants which dealt with matters of employment, education, naturalization and living standards for newcomers.[35] Kellor devoted her entire life to social causes, never taking any salary at any time. Allen came to admire her greatly, treasured her friendship, and sought her advice over the years. She also became acquainted with Kellor's lifelong companion, Mary Drier, who was president of the Women's Trade Union League.

For the League for the Protection of Immigrants Allen went to Ellis Island to meet immigrants and to protect them from being taken advantage of. She was also part of the Henry Street Settlement on the teeming lower east side of Manhattan and became acquainted with Lillian Wald, the founder and director. The Settlement, like Hull House, was financed by private philanthropy and the staff was composed of dedicated reformers, mostly young women, who were expected to live in the neighborhood, improve the life of its people on a person-to-person basis and become part of the Henry Street "family." Florence found a room in the neighborhood with an Irish landlady. By the end of August she was acquainted with her work and was ready to look for a law school.

There were two important law schools in New York, Columbia and New York University. She had her heart set on going to Columbia, but that was a hopeless dream since it did not admit women. New York University Law School did admit women and in the fall of 1910 Allen began taking evening classes. The NYU Law School was one of the largest in the country. In the years when Allen was there it was fifth in size among law schools, surpassed by Georgetown, Harvard, Michigan and Columbia, having about 650 students of which about 80 were women. Out of a total of 606 women enrolled in all law schools in 1914, 82 were at NYU.[36]

Education in law was being upgraded rapidly in the early years of the century, with the best schools requiring a three-year course of study. NYU included the three-year requirement and provided it in both day and evening courses. The curriculum was similar to that offered by other leading law schools, requiring such courses as Contracts, Torts, Real Property, Equity and Evidence, and a wide range of elective subjects. Courses were taught by the new case method, which had originated at Harvard and was adopted by the best schools because it forced students to analyze cases and articulate their legal reasoning.

Several law schools had begun to require two or three years of college before entering law school; NYU still admitted students with a high-school diploma. Those who entered with a high-school diploma were awarded the LL.B. degree on graduation; those who entered with a bachelor's degree were awarded the J.D.[37] Among her professors, Allen paid great tribute to Dean Frank H. Sommer, an outstanding teacher who also donated his skills to community service.

Life for Allen immediately became very involved, with long hours at the office of the League, errands all over the city in connection with her work, attending classes in the evening and studying. The law classes were very satisfying, but the social work was less satisfying. She didn't like her accommodations in the Henry Street neighborhood. A few nights she sat in a chair all night rather than share the bed with its insect occupants, and quietly she planned to move, hoping that one one would notice she was leaving the neighborhood.[38] Lillian Wald sought increasing commitment from her but Florence by choice stayed on the periphery of the Henry Street family, although she participated in many social events at the settlement house and made contributions playing the piano or speaking.

As she wrestled with the complexities of her future, physical problems returned to haunt her. Most distressing was the trouble with her eyes. Muscle spasms bothered her, even though the muscle had been cut and she had new glasses. Using her illness as a pretext — as her father and grandfather had done in similar situations — she resigned her position with the League, shedding her career in social work forever. She had decided to give law school first priority. Financial reasons were crucial: social work was largely gratuitous and she must make a living for her family was not wealthy. She was not burdened with the guilt of being able to lead a life of leisure or devoted to philanthropy on family riches exploited from the less fortunate. Social work had lost some of the thrill of a new adventure which it had had for an earlier generation, but it was not yet a recognized profession. Law was a recognized profession and its practice a real challenge for a woman.

Another pair of glasses corrected the problem with her eyes, and moving out of the Henry Street neighborhood into an apartment with her friends Bertha and Marie Miller from Cleveland ushered in a new era of surprising and joyful domesticity. Bertha was also attending NYU Law School. What fun they had buying furniture, making curtains, fixing up their apartment. Cooking became a new pleasure, with menus recorded along with culinary successes and failures. Brother Emir came often from Yale for week-ends filled with apartment dinners for him and his friends and the Millers and their friends. Emir helped out with small tasks of carpentry in the apartment and Florence and Emir enjoyed the wonderful sights and sounds of New York together.

Florence was happily back in law school, taking full-time day classes, after only a short absence with her eye problems. Her days were filled with studying and making new acquaintances with other students, especially women. She refused, however, to join a legal sorority because an able Jewish girl was not invited to join.[39] Among her friends was Inez Milholland, a Vassar graduate who had organized students there for suffrage, and who, like Allen, had come to NYU Law School because it admitted women. Milholland picketted with women strikers in the shirtwaist and laundry industries, and "gallantly captained" a suffrage parade down Fifth Avenue.[40]

Women students had an organization which met regularly and listened to speeches relevant to their particular needs. One of the problems of women lawyers, they were told, is their narrow range of general information. Most women can't read and understand a broker's statement, for example. Women lawyers must be willing to pay the price for success. They must be willing to put every drop of vitality into their work and not into "some side issue." They must work the clock around day in and day out and be at the beck and call of business when it comes. They must compensate for the fact that the voice, physical appearance and attire of the average woman lawyer does not produce the impression of authority and aggressiveness which are characteristic of the average male lawyer.[41]

The Law School was seemingly free of prejudice against women on the part of faculty and male students. In 1911 the women's organization arranged for English suffragette Mrs. Philip Snowden to speak in the biggest classroom in the school. On this occasion women students were surpised and angered by the prejudiced and insinuating questions male students asked the speaker. In an excited session after the speech the women decided that although men might hold women back in other professions it could not happen in law. After graduation they were confident that there was no way men could keep them from having clients and representing their clients in court.[42]

Florence was self-supporting in law school, knowing that the Allen family budget was burdened by the expense of having Emir and Jack at Yale, and thinking that her parents had paid enough for her education. Interesting work for a woman law student was hard to find. In the spring of 1911 she gave a few lecture-recitals for the New York Board of Education and occasional lectures on current events at a private girls school on Park Avenue. She was paid five dollars for each public school lecture and ten for the current events lectures. Unfortunately her appearance demanded a more impressive wardrobe than she ordinarily possessed. She bought a suit with a fashionable hobble skirt, but found it inconvenient because she couldn't sit down in the skirt and had to stand on the street car on her way to schools as well as through her talks.[43] It was her only venture into high fashion.

A job with the National College Women's Equal Suffrage League brought in $40 a month. A tight food budget prevailed in the apartment and the girls made the best of the scheming necessary to make ends meet. During summer vacation Florence worked doggedly on a series of lecture-recitals and had circulars printed to advertise them, with Bertha Miller as her agent. Florence hoped for a broader audience for her lecture-recitals, but the Board of Education was her only regular patron.

Although law school was her primary concern, it was the woman suffrage movement that gave special direction and purpose to Allen's life. Woman suffrage had been a staple of her life since childhood when it was a burning issue in the exciting politics of Utah. In her college days she had attended many suffrage meetings, discussed the issues often, and paraded with the sisterhood. But it was her association with Maud Wood Park that turned her life dramatically to the cause of woman suffrage. Park was executive director of the National College Women's Equal Suffrage League and picked Allen from a number of candidates to be her assistant secretary in 1911.

To the twenty-seven year old Allen, Park was the epitome of the finest American womanhood and an admirable role model. Park was a Radcliffe graduate in the class of '98, a Boston Brahmin matron, a social reformer, a purposeful woman. She was also beautiful and blond, always perfectly groomed and poised, and had "a look of caste."[44] Florence especially admired her intellectual qualities, her charming and persuasive speaking ability, and her plan to organize college women for the suffrage. Part of the admiration was for Park's intuitive sense of tactfulness and her ability to soothe and persuade men who were hostile to women's rights, to appease men rather than confront them, talents which Florence felt she lacked. Her admiration never faltered from their first meeting in 1911 to the day in 1960 when she spoke at the Radcliffe College celebration of forty years of woman suffrage commending Park's contribution to the movement.

As Park's assistant Florence corresponded with college suffrage leagues all over the country and planned the schedule for speaking engagements. It brought her into the inner workings of the suffrage movement.

FOOTNOTES

[1] For an exposition see Mary R. Walsh, *Doctors Wanted: No Women Need Apply*, New Haven: Yale University Press, 1977.

[2] Mary R. Ryan, *Womanhood in America*, New York: New Viewpoints, 1979, pp. 75-80.

[3] Ryan, p. 142. According to Elizabeth Kemper Adams, *Women Professional Workers*, New York: Macmillan, 1921, p. 23, 75% of female professionals were unmarried in 1920.

[4] Carol Smith-Rosenberg, "The Female World of Love and Ritual: Relations between Women in Nineteenth Century America," *Signs*, v. 1, No. 1, Autumn 1975, p. 27. For a historical exposition of women's friendships see Lillian Faderman, *Surpassing the Love of Men*, New York: William Morrow and Co., 1981.

[5] Diary, August 12, 1904. Entries in her diary in the early years include her thoughts and feelings. As time passed entries became more or less an account of where she was or what she was doing and seldom reveal her thoughts and feelings.

[6] From newspaper clippings in Allen papers, WRHS, container 25.

[7] Diary, October 13, 1904.

[8] Scrapbooks in Allen papers, WRHS, container 24.

[9] *To Do Justly*, p. 22.

[10] Diary, August 29, 1904.

[11] Notes in Allen papers, WRHS, container 3, folder 1.

[12] Diary, November 12, 1904.

[13] In notebooks in Allen papers, WRHS, container 3, folder 1.

[14] From notes in a scrapbook, Allen papers, WRHS, container 15.

[15] *To Do Justly*, p. 22, and Allen papers, WRHS, container

[16] *Ibid.*, pp. 22-23.

[17] All quotations from newspaper clippings from the Cleveland *Plain Dealer* in Allen papers, WRHS, container 25, v. 1. The article on Schumann-Heink was dated November 22, 1906.

[18] *Ibid.*

[19] Information about the Tuckerman family from personal interviews. Names withheld for privacy.

[20] Florence Allen letter to Mamma, undated 1906, Allen papers WRHS, container 6, folder 1.

[21] Florence E. Allen, *Patris*, Cleveland: World Publishing Company, 1908, p. 11.

[22] Diary, January 22, 1907.

[23] *To Do Justly*, p. 23.

[24] *Ibid.*

[25] Florence Allen letter to Mamma, October 7, 1906, Allen papers, WRHS, container 6, folder 1.

[26] The *Chicago Sunday Tribune*, September 17, 1939, feature interview with Allen, in Allen papers, WRHS, container 27, folder 4.

[27] Florence Kelley, founder and President of the Consumer's League and Josephine Goldmark provided the evidence that women workers suffered physical and moral harm from excessive hours of labor. Clark A. Chamber, *Seedtime of Reform: American Social Action, 1918-1933*, Minneapolis: University of Minnesota Press, 1963, p. 6.

[28] See Francis R. Aumann, *The Changing American Legal System*, New York: DaCapo Press,

1969, pp. 94-119.

[29] William Henry Chafe, *The American Woman: Her Changing Social, Economic, and Political Roles, 1920-1970,* New York: Oxford University Press, 1972, p. 58. Ryan gives a lower figure: 1.4% of lawyers were female in 1920, p. 141. Breckinridge gives a figure of 2%, p. 189.

[30] *To Do Justly,* p. 24.

[31] Diary, March 3, 1910.

[32] Noted in Women's Rights Collection, SL, box 1, folder 4.

[33] Ryan, p. 139.

[34] *To Do Justly,* p. 24.

[35] Helen C. Bennett, *American Women in Civic Work,* New York: Dodd Mead, 1915, pp. 163-179.

[36] Information from Alfred Z. Reed. *Training for the Public Profession of the Law,* New York: Carnegie Foundation, 1921, p. 452, and Beatrice Doerschuk, *Women in the Law,* New York: Bureau of Vocational Information, 1920. pp. 114-124.

[37] Leslie Jay Tompkins, *The New York University Law School,* New York: np, 1904, pp. 51-52.

[38] Diary, October-November, 1910.

[39] *To Do Justly,* p. 27; Allen papers, SMITH, box 1, folder 5.

[40] Anne F. Scott and Andrew M. Scott, *One Half the People: The Fight for Woman Suffrage,* Philadelphia: J.B. Lippincott, 1975, p. 30; Women's Rights Collection, SL, box 1, folder 4.

[41] As reported in *75 Year History of National Association of Women Lawyers, 1899-1974,* Ed. by Mary H. Zimmerman, Lansing: NAWL, 1975, pp. 27-34.

[42] *To Do Justly,* pp. 27-28.

[43] *Ibid.,* p. 26.

[44] *Ibid.,* p. 30.

Chapter 3

FINDING A CAUSE

The women's rights movement was born in 1848, after several years of gestation, when Elizabeth Cady Stanton and Lucretia Mott called the first women's rights convention in Seneca Falls, New York. The idea of women's rights had grown out of the anti-slavery issue which gripped the country as it occurred to some reformers that women as well as black people were exploited and subordinated in our society. Characteristically the women who participated were upper middle class, of north European heritage, and Protestant. The convention called for a variety of equal rights for women and based the ideas on the argument that under God and the American Constitution men and women were equal. The assembly closed with a declaration of sentiments and resolutions proposing economic, political and social equality for women, and an exhortation to local•women to create state organizations.

By and large the public greeted the first stages of the women's rights movement with laughter and derision and newspapers panned their efforts. Even those who didn't laugh said the women were obviously out of their sphere and should go back home. The movement was greatly strengthened when Susan B. Anthony joined its forces, contributing her great legal and organizational skills and indeed her entire life to the cause.

The Civil War blasted the budding women's movement. A few women thought the Fourteenth Amendment gave women as well as black men the right to vote. Anthony had the courage to try voting and to take her case to the courts, only to go down in defeat. The women's organization was in great disarray, bickering over issues and methods. Meantime women were making small advances, particularly in property rights. Higher education was available and a few professions were slowly and painfully opening. For working class women there were plenty of jobs in domestic service, textile mills, and the sweatshops of the clothing industry at long hours and low pay.

The disparate elements of the women's movement were pulled together in 1890 with the organization of the National American Woman's Suffrage Association, but no workable strategies were devised. After 1896 many years passed without any new suffrage states being added. There was no national headquarters for the NAWSA except for the files and records which were stored in Warren, Ohio at the home of the treasurer, Harriet Taylor Upton. The women's rights movement was in the doldrums.[1]

In 1901 Maud Wood Park, just out of Radcliffe, formed the College Equal Suffrage League to organize college women for suffrage.[2] The idea was attractive to women educators and in 1908 President M. Carey Thomas of Bryn Mawr, President Mary E. Woolley of Mount Holyoke, and others founded the National College Women's Equal Suffrage League. These women believed women's rights could be achieved a step at a time. They thought women had won the right to higher education and economic independence and the next logical step was the right to vote.

About the same time Carrie Chapman Catt began to reorganize the NAWSA along political district lines. Bold and dramatic new tactics produced dynamic and very visible campaigns. The new tactics were learned from English suffragettes who had found that parades, mass demonstrations and soap-box oratory paid off in publicity. Philadelphia and New York women had copied their methods with great success, and a similar campaign had won the vote for women in the state of Washington in 1910.[3]

As the movement gathered momentum, public laughter ceased and the NAWSA acquired powerful allies: millions of members of women's clubs and organizations that were flourishing across the land, male voters of progressive inclination, most of the Protestant ministry, liberal newspapers and socialists.

The NAWSA also acquired powerful opponents. Politicians who had learned to deal with the status quo and industrialists who were wary of women reformers were opposed. Neither of the major political parties supported the NAWSA for twenty-five long years. Also opposed were those involved in the liquor industry either as producers or consumers who had noted the size and aggressiveness of the Women's Christian Temperance Union and didn't want its membership at the polls to vote for prohibition.

Ohio was one of the bloodiest battlegrounds in the fight for woman suffrage. Its women were among the first to organize, a state meeting having been called in the village of Salem in 1850, two years after the Seneca Falls Convention. Other meetings followed in Akron and Massilon before the trauma of the Civil War ended activities. Ohio women had reorganized in the 1880s and achievements had been modest but consistent with advances in other states. In 1880 women were given the right to their own earnings; in 1887 they acquired the right to control their own property, engage in business and make contracts. In 1893 they were allowed to act as guardians, and in 1894 as executors and administrators of estates. In 1896 they were enabled to vote for and become members of local school boards.[4] Several bills had been introduced in the legislature for broader woman suffrage and had failed to pass, but each time more legislators had favored passage.

After 1899 the Ohio movement was revitalized when Harriet Taylor Upton became president. Upton had spent several years in Washington while her father was a senator and had learned very well the working of politics and the men in politics. She had been treasurer of the NAWSA for several years. With the aid of her husband, Upton had become a prolific editor and publisher of NAWSA literature, including its weekly newspaper, the *Journal*. She dominated the Ohio organization until suffrage was achieved in 1920. Her band of ardent workers called her "the General" because of her courage, salty humor, and ability to drum up morale.

Elizabeth J. Hauser was Upton's executive secretary. Originally from Girard, Ohio and a newspaper woman, she had unlimited enthusiasm and unusual talent in writing, editing, and public relations. She had been secretary to Tom L. Johnson, Cleveland's outstandingly liberal mayor, and in 1910 was delegated by the Ohio Suffrage Association to organize women for suffrage in Cleveland. In the same year Inez Milholland and Maud Wood Park organized a Cleveland chapter of the National College Equal Suffrage League.[5]

The Progressive Era was in full swing in Ohio in 1910. For some time society had been suffering from the evil effects of growing industrialization: crowding of the cities, abominable living conditions for the urban poor, exploitation of labor, shady commercial practices, weak and corrupt politicians. The progressive movement combined a fight against corruption and inefficiency in government, an effort to regulate and control big business, and a movement for social welfare regulation.

Prodded by the progressives, the voters of Ohio had decided in 1910 to write a new constitution to make their government more responsive to their demands. A constitutional convention was called in Columbus in January, 1912 to propose a series of amendments to modernize the old constitution. The women's organization proposed an amendment to eliminate the words "white male" in voting requirements and to replace them with the words "every citizen." Elizabeth Hauser and her crew got 15,000 signatures for the amendment and presented them to the convention. The women opened suffrage headquarters across the street from the capitol and it was said no better lobby ever haunted the capitol corridors.[6] The amendment became No. 23 in a list of 41 proposed. A special election was called for September 3 to vote on the amendments.

The campaign for amendment No. 23 was launched by Maud Wood Park. She arrived in Cleveland on April 12 and spoke at a public meeting at the New Knickerbocker Theater at East 84th Street and Euclid

Avenue. Six hundred women in their Easter finery and a lone man attended the meeting, it was reported.[7] Typically, the newspapers commented on the ladies' attire, noting that Park looked very elegant in a black dress with white gloves and a black hat with a white plume. After this opening event Park attended numerous teas in Cleveland homes where the talk was about organizing the campaign. Precinct captains were chosen and the women, with considerable fear and trembling, since they had never spoken in public or participated in politics before, practiced their arguments on each other.

Florence Allen arrived in Cleveland in June 1912 after law school closed to work on the campaign. Through the suffrage organizations she immediately met a number of women who, either through their own activities or their families, were influential in Cleveland affairs. Elizabeth Hauser was in charge; Zara DuPont of a distinguished family was one of her organizers. Zara persuaded Lucia McCurdy McBride, a brilliant socialite herself and wife of a well-known philanthropist, to join in. She in turn enlisted the support of Belle Sherwin, daughter of one of Cleveland's wealthiest industrial families and herself a graduate of Wellesley and founder of the Cleveland Consumer's League and director of the Visiting Nurse Association. Minerva Brooks, a Vassar graduate and daughter of an outstanding lawyer and wife of another was in the group, as well as Edna Perkins, a professor at Western Reserve University.[8]

It was Maud Wood Park, however, who started Allen on the project that would spread her name and fame across the state. The women had decided to use the new English methods. Successful campaigns in western states had extended these tactics beyond the cities to rural areas and that was what Park and Allen had in mind. On a bright Sunday morning with forty young women and a sympathetic young newsman, Louis B. Seltzer, they set out for Medina in a rented trolley, the sides covered with "Votes for Women" signs. Mrs. Park did most of the talking; for the others it was a learning experience.[9]

Florence Allen learned many things that summer. She learned how to organize a campaign within a county and she learned how to speak extemporaneously and effectively. She learned how to deal with hecklers, for heckling suffragists was great sport that summer.[10] One evening in the small town of Seville, as they spoke from the bandstand on the public square, a crowd of boys began to hoot and catcall Mrs. Park. Florence was "so furious at their treatment of this high-bred lovely woman" that she "excoriated the boys" sharply. That night, in their hotel room, Park told Florence that sharp words were not the best approach and that "you catch more flies with honey than with vinegar."[11] Mrs. Park also counselled her never to let a man get himself in the position of saying flatly that he was against woman suffrage. It would be too hard for him to retract that statement without losing face.[12]

Most of the women Allen met, organized, and worked with were upper middle-class women, living in domesticity. Most had led very sheltered lives and shrank from the thought of public oratory or even of trying to persuade their acquaintances of the virtue of woman suffrage. At the outset few could articulate their political views publicly. Lack of oratorical skills was one of the greatest handicaps for women as they began to enter public life.[13] By September many of the suffragists could speak out, even in the face of catcalls and heckling. Allen regularly counselled them not to be emotional as the men expected them to be, but to fight the issues on the facts.

Allen worked on committees and at headquarters. She attended rallies, luncheons, and garden parties. She travelled the length and breadth of the state and spoke to women's clubs and steel workers, to associations of lawyers, teachers, and ministers, at churches and county fairs, band concerts and farmers' institutes, circuses and Chautauquas, on street corners, court house steps, and standing in the back seat of automobiles. She declared her willingness to speak as long as anyone would listen. When she counted up at the end of the summer, she had made 92 speeches,[14] and had found it a stimulating and satisfying experience. She made personal friendships with women in the movement that would continue for years and developed a "fine acquaintance among forward-looking Ohio women"[15] that in the long run would have productive political rewards.

She also made acquaintances with suffragists from other states, about fifty of whom, including Jeanette Rankin of Montana, came to help the Ohio women. Rankin in 1916 was the first woman elected to the U.S. House of Representatives. Rose Schneiderman, an executive officer of the National Trade Union League, came from New York and gave talks at noon-time among factory workers, but recruited very few for the cause.[16]

Illustrative of the friendships Allen made was that with Vadae Meekison, who practiced law with her husband in Napoleon, Ohio. Vadae and Florence campaigned together in 1912 in Henry County. They traveled by horse and a buggy with fringe on the top. Florence did most of the driving because Vadae had a baby in her lap. They carried a soap box in the back of the buggy to stand on to speak. In one town it was not needed for the proprieter of a traveling medicine show allowed them to use his stage for their speeches. Vadae later campaigned vigorously for Florence at every opportunity and was utterly indefatigable in her efforts to have Florence nominated as a justice of the United States Supreme Court.[17] Another equally loyal supporter was Eva Epstein Shaw, a lawyer in Toledo, who campaigned with Florence for woman suffrage and remained a loyal friend.

Allen's chief argument for woman suffrage was the old and logical one of Stanton and Anthony that the vote was woman's right under the supreme law of the land, the Constitution. She spoke about the great inequity which denied women the right to vote, about the justice of their demands for enfranchisement, the right to hold public office, and the right to equal opportunities.

Much newer and more in line with the times and the cult of true womanhood was the argument that women's purity and morality, their skills and efficiency in housekeeping would be extended by the right to vote to the public domain and would end corruption in politics and clean up the political mess that had been made. Allen also subscribed to this idea and believed the suffrage would temper public affairs with womanly compassion. The newer argument proved to be more persuasive with the voters than the argument based on justice.[18]

The irony of the special sphere argument was that both sides were using it. Anti-suffragists argued that the role of women is in the private world of the home and family while the role of men is in the public world of business and politics, that women did not really want to vote, that it would be an added burden to them to take on political responsibilities, and that their intrinsic purity might indeed be besmirched by such activities.

When the votes were counted in September 1912 the woman suffrage amendment lost by a vote of 295,000 to 335,000.[19] Cincinnati had rejected it most emphatically and Cleveland was not far behind. Out of the 41 amendments only eight had been defeated. and more votes had been cast on the issue of woman suffrage than on any other.[20] The Ohio suffrage remained limited to white males even though the Fourteenth Amendment had long since negated the "white" restriction. The suffragists, least of all Florence Allen, were not discouraged, believing that their message had not reached enough people and that once voters learned of the merits of woman suffrage it would carry. At the end of the summer Allen hastened to take the train back to New York for her senior year in law school.

During her senior year speeches and trips for the cause of suffrage continued. In October she went to Syracuse to make a speech at the NAWSA convention; in November she spoke at Swarthmore College; in January 1913 she went to Ithaca to speak at Cornell, then to Cleveland to speak at the City Club, and on to Mt. Holyoke and Barnard. In February she and Bertha Miller joined the suffragist march to Washington, the purpose of which was to present President Wilson with a petition seeking his support for suffrage.

Throngs of people greeted the marchers along the way. The streets of Philadelphia, Princeton, Baltimore, and Washington were lined with spectators. As many as 45 newspaper reporters accompanied them. At the last moment the board of the NAWSA decided not to have the marchers present the petition they were carrying to the president, but to have it presented later by the board itself. Allen returned to New York by train to try to persuade the board to change its mind, but she was unsuccessful. In

Washington the leader of the march was presented with a huge bouquet of flowers and the marchers disbanded. The petition was never presented to the president.[21]

From a historical perspective, the most important development in the woman's movement in 1913 was the formation of the Congressional Union, out of which the National Woman's Party developed under the leadership of Alice Paul. Paul's group agitated for more radical methods than those of the NAWSA to achieve suffrage.[22] Allen was never attracted by the NWP, but became steadily more involved in the NAWSA, and in the summer of 1913 was elected to the executive board of the Ohio Woman Suffrage Association.

While the woman's movement focused on the struggle for the vote in these years state legislatures were passing laws in profusion to protect women from long hours, night work or heavy work or in jobs considered hazardous to their delicate female constitutions and maternal potential. The courts had struck down such legislation for men, but, following the *Muller v. Oregon* decision, approved it for women.[23] Women's organizations were pleased and approved this relief for working women. Suffrage campaigns and speeches highlighted Allen's life, but her basic business was law school. Most days and most evenings were spent going to classes or the library or studying. She graduated *cum laude,* second in the class, with a LL.B. degree in June 1913.[24]

Overall in law school she had spend more time studying the law codes of New York state than any other single subject, preparing her to be a lawyer there. In spite of that she decided to take her bar exams in Ohio and to practice in Cleveland. Why Cleveland and not New York which she loved, where she had a law degree and there were many law offices? She said it was because of her stimulating experience with the Ohio suffrage movement and her many acquaintances in it.[25]

Beyond that Cleveland in 1913 had many attractions. Unusually well located on transportation routes for communication and natural resources, it had experienced tremendous development in heavy industry and this was the golden age of heavy industry. Great companies in mining, in iron and steel, in transportation equipment, in petroleum were centered in Cleveland. Its society was the equivalent of any big city and more glittering than most, its families living in pretentious mansions vying for grandeur, and celebrating their new-found wealth with gorgeous extravagances. It had demonstrated its charitable magnanimity by being the first city in the country to launch a united fund for the relief of its poor and underprivileged. Its street lighting was famous and so was its street car system, the latter for its extensive public control, brought about by an outstandingly progressive mayor, Tom L. Johnson. The city was in the process of building a municipally owned electric power plant to provide competition for private companies and to keep their prices in line. Newton

D. Baker, Johnson's protege, was mayor and nationally known for his constructive idealism in politics. There were political bosses in Cleveland but their power was slight compared to that of Tammany Hall in New York. A sympathetic observer might easily conclude that Cleveland's promise for the future was equal to that of New York.[26]

Cleveland had problems, too, most of them concerned with how to house, educate, and otherwise accommodate a burgeoning influx of European immigrants, attracted by jobs in the steel mills. Cleveland was not at all a poor choice for an ambitious young lawyer.

Allen did not intend to take up the practice of law immediately for she had still to pass the bar exams and find a job, and she was eagerly looking forward to the challenge of another suffrage campaign. The suffrage organization was actually her best legal client. She was retained as its attorney until 1920, although she may well have contributed more money to the cause than she was paid by the organization.

Florence quickly renewed old friendships. Had she needed a refuge the Tuckermans would have provided it. Zara DuPont and Florence became very good friends, Sally (Zara) quickly becoming the boon companion that Bert (Bertha Miller) had been in New York. Sally, also on the executive committee of the woman suffrage organization, came from a more than adequate household which provided great hospitality, an abundant and delicious cuisine, good conversation, and transportation if need be, for they had a car. The DuPont's red Winton was a feature of many suffrage parades. There were many lunches and conferences with Minerva Brooks, now president of the Cleveland Woman Suffrage Party, and with Grace Treat, executive secretary, to plan the coming campaign.

Ties were renewed with Laurel School, where Mrs. Lyman was still headmistress and was pleased to have Florence return to play for chapel and give lectures on current events. She called on President Charles F. Thwing of Western Reserve University, and was happy to find that "Prexy" still believed in her. In a letter of recommendation he had written that "in birth and in breeding Miss Allen represents the noblest elements of life."[27] President Thwing was a member of the Woman Suffrage Party, as was Professor Hatton.

The amended Ohio constitution included provision for initiative and referendum, a newly honed device of the progressive era to enable the people to bring issues directly to the voters. The executive committee of the suffragists, still convinced that the people were for them, started a campaign to have a petition initiating a woman suffrage amendment. There were several months of delay while the legislature worked out the details of initiative and referendum, but by early 1914 the way was clear. Again Allen travelled the state, organizing a crew of women to circulate petitions among the male voters and get the ten percent of signatures required. No longer were the suffragists meek, shy, and sheltered women. They aggressively

36

went out seeking signatures, no number too small. Allen's speech in Mt. Vernon, for example, brought 50 signatures, in New Lexington 27 signatures and so the total grew[28] and in three months was filed with the secretary of state.

The secretary of state gave some signal of what the campaign might be like for the suffragists. In the morning he jovially accepted the petitions for a referendum, a "wet" referendum ending local option to prevent the sale of liquor, and called the press in for interviews and pictures. A few hours later when the suffragists arrived, 176 strong (two from each county), and paraded around the capitol to deliver their petitions, the secretary refused to appear. Messengers failed to bring him forth and after much delay it was the president of Ohio State University who went inside and delivered the petitions to an office assistant.

The suffragists continued to be largely educated middle class women of the older European migration, some, like Florence Allen, descendants of the New England puritan migration. They considered the vote the key to democracy and good government, as their ancestors had thought back to the days of John Locke. Women in the suffrage movement met with little resistance in their own homes. Their men supported women suffrage because their women wanted to vote and it might double the vote of the old-line migration[29] in face of the incoming new migration from southern and eastern Europe.

The magnitude of the problem for the old-liners was spelled out in the *Woman's Journal*.[30] It identified Cleveland as the center of the newer immigration, and reported that of its 560,663 inhabitants 223,908 were of foreign parentage and 195,703 were of foreign birth. Only 140,672 were so-called natives, of which 8,000 were black. The article indicated that this foreign group might retain some old-world ideas about women, but did not add that most of these immigrants had escaped the rigors of puritanism and regarded consumption of liquor as a pleasant libation. Nor was it mentioned that the right to vote was not necessarily part of their cultural heritage. Many of them were family oriented rather than community or state oriented. Many were Roman Catholics and had not been influenced by the Protestant ministry.

The opposition was very interested in the 1914 campaign and well supplied with funds to wage a counter campaign. The liquor question was of primary importance. Three issues were to be voted on; two were concerned with wet-dry options and were highly controversial. The suffragists tried to separate themselves from the liquor question, but it was impossible for the Anti-Saloon League supported suffrage.[31] And a large segment of wealthy industrialists opposed it,[32] not wanting the protective legislation for women and children that the suffragists advocated. They favored the Association Opposed to Woman Suffrage.

The women's campaign started with a sentimental pilgrimage to

Salem honoring the old timers of the 1850s. In Salem they re-adopted the original Salem resolutions and consecrated themselves anew to the cause, linking the past and the present. In Cleveland a beautiful pageant, "A Dream of Freedom," featuring hand-made classic Greek costumes and including the wife and children of Mayor Baker, drew a large audience at a fashionable downtown theater. Mrs. Upton sat in a box and wiped away a tear as she told a reporter she didn't see how anyone could deny woman suffrage after seeing that.[33]

Educational campaigns were renewed, suffrage tea parties, garden parties, college parties. Florence Allen again covered rural Ohio. This time the crowds were larger and the places better known. No longer was it necessary to set up a soap box on a street corner or stand in the back seat of an automobile. In Ashland, for example, Allen spoke to a Chautauqua audience of 2,000 and got "good applause." In Wooster she spoke from the grandstand at the county fair. In Mansfield she went to a "whopping meeting" of the Federation of Woman's Clubs and received their endorsement.[34]

Cleveland newspapers and newspapers generally were supportive of the suffragists. Their editors were also part of the old migration. Photographs of the women speakers and committee members pleased the suffragists. Their activities were fully and regularly reported, and not on the society or women's pages. Hal Donahey of the Cleveland *Plain Dealer* did a series of sympathetic cartoons, and the *Cleveland Press* was outright prosuffragist. Everywhere Protestant ministers and their congregations opened their doors to the suffragists.

For Allen the climax of the campaign came in October when she debated with Lucy Price, first at the Men's City Club and then in Gray's Armory in Cleveland. Financed by the Association Opposed to Woman Suffrage,[35] Price offered $100 for any question from suffragists she could not answer. Florence Allen responded to the challenge. In the debate Price argued that woman's place is in the home and that is where she wants to be. She claimed that division of labor occurs in the family as well as in the factory and that women's specialty is the home and men's specialty is business and politics. Burdening women with politics would take them out of the home to its detriment and in the long run "endanger the human race."

Few events in her life made Florence Allen as nervous in anticipation as her debate in Gray's Armory with Lucy Price. The cavernous hall was packed and President Thwing presided. Allen based her argument on two ideas: that without the vote women are taxed without representation and governed without their consent. Thus the state is very skimpy in providing money for child welfare but spends it like water in taking care of the potato bug and looking after the welfare of hogs. Both debaters could quote published statistics: that the tax rate and the divorce rate had gone up in states where women vote; that the crime rate and the infant mortality rate had gone down in the same states.[36]

Who won the debate remained undecided, but when it was over Allen was pleased with her presentation and happy with the complete newspaper coverage. Thwing wrote next day that her speech was "a noble effort in every way."[37]

A mammoth parade in Cleveland was one of the features of the campaign. Several thousand men, women, and children marched, with Florence Allen, Minerva Brooks and Lucia McCurdy McBride in the front ranks. It was hoped many young business women would participate, but only a few came, fearing that such activities were job threatening. A few black women joined, notably Jane Hunter, founder of the Phillis Wheatley Association. Fifty or so industrial women showed up, a disappointing turnout because of the effort spent recruiting them. Except for a handful of Czechs, most ethnic women did not come.[38]

Allen wrote that in this campaign the suffragists did *everything*,[39] and it was true that the women involved worked hard and courageously and did everything themselves, even to making their own parade gowns — white for purity. They had pathetically little money, most of it coming from their own donations and augmented by bake sales and bazaars, They moved their headquarters to cheaper rooms on the second floor and sold lunches to workers and friends for extra cash. Some of their husbands contributed to make ends meet.[40]

The opposition had a few enticements the women couldn't match, designed to appeal to voters the suffragists didn't reach — working men. There were picnics at Euclid Beach Park with free beer for all comers, the only cost listening to politicians speak. Trolley cars on which most working men travelled were festooned with posters against the twin evils of prohibition and woman suffrage. Sample ballots instructed ignorant voters exactly how to vote against woman suffrage. After it was all over the suffragists conceded that the opposition had conducted a slick and expensive campaign. It was also a successful campaign and again woman suffrage was defeated, even more overwhelmingly than in 1912.

During the excitement of the woman suffrage campaign Allen reviewed her law courses for the bar examinations. The only thing she recorded that made her feel blue during the early months of 1914 was the prospect of the exams. She looked at old exams at Western Reserve University Library and felt certain that she could not pass. But she continued to review and felt relieved when the news came in June that she had passed, placing seventh among the participants.[41] She was quoted as saying on the day she became a lawyer, "If more women entered the competition for jobs now held exclusively by men, women would show their capability of running the government and a woman would be nearer the White House."[42]

No position with a law firm was forthcoming. Allen had introductions to several lawyers in Cleveland through family connections, but for one excuse or another not one would give her a position. One said, pointing to a few snow flakes floating past the window, "Why, I wouldn't think of sending a woman down to the Court House on a day like this."[43] Employers undoubtedly detected at first interview that Allen was not motivated by the profits to be acquired as a lawyer but by the social justice that might be achieved.

Law firms generally were proving to be more hostile to women peers than law schools were to women students. And northern Ohio was apparently below the national average in numbers of practicing women lawyers. A biographical index of lawyers of the area compiled in 1921 included about 1400 men lawyers and judges and only four women.[44] The introduction to the index said that if anyone was left out it was because of lack of space; it is possible that more women lawyers existed but found themselves spaceless in this compilation. It is also possible that there were fewer women lawyers in northern Ohio because there was little opportunity for education; a large segment of the men were products of Western Reserve University Law School which did not admit women. In any case, women lawyers were not being taken seriously.

On the other hand, law schools were opening to women, Harvard and Columbia being the major hold outs, but women were not applying for admission. There is evidence that midwestern university law schools had fewer women students in 1912 than they had had in the 1880s and 1890s.[45]

By September 1914 Allen had decided to open her own office and to volunteer for the Cleveland Legal Aid Society. The Society had been established some ten years previously through private philanthropy to provide free or moderately priced legal services to persons who might not otherwise be able to hire an attorney. Allen's first case was that of an Italian woman who was suing her husband for divorce because he had deserted her and their children. The woman's brother paid Allen $15. In her first year she made $875.[46]

The young lawyers who managed the Legal Aid Society were idealists like Allen and believed the law should serve all the people. They were friendly and helpful to her and within a few months her office was combined with those of Bartholomew, Leeper and McGill. Robb O. Bartholomew was about the same age as Allen, his roots were also in the Western Reserve, and his degree from Western Reserve University Law School. Allen and Bartholomew became good friends and colleagues and Allen often sought his advice and trusted it. Inevitably she referred to him as "Barth."

More cases soon came to her: men whose wages had been garnisheed, mothers who wanted to keep their children out of the Industrial School, people who had been defrauded by smooth-talking sharks, poor people with all sorts of human problems. Allen represented cases at court and became acquainted with the judges. Visits to the police court were sometimes unpleasant, and on at least one occasion the "vile, stinking place"[47] made her sick. Fees were small and slow in coming. Fees from lectures at Laurel and for the association of nurses augmented her small income.

It continued to be the suffrage movement that was stimulating. In 1915 she went to Boston to help with the campaign there. The Boston association had sent speakers to Ohio for its campaign and Allen reciprocated for the Ohio association. She felt that she should be properly clothed to speak in Maud Wood Park's home town, and Sally and Minerva made a proper black dress for her, finishing the last touches in the railroad station as the train came in. [48] She spoke at Fanieul Hall, at factories where she found the unions surprisingly favorable to woman suffrage,[49] and at a huge street rally. Emir joined her in Boston and they went to New York for fun together. It was like old times. Emir had graduated from Yale *magna cum laude* and was attending Columbia Law School. Although Florence had been frustrated in her desire to go to Columbia, she and the whole Allen family rejoiced in Emir's success.

During the same summer Allen arranged for a speaking tour for the English suffragette, Emmeline Pankhurst, whom she had first met in Chicago in 1909 and again in New York in 1912. The American woman suffrage movement had learned much about political action from their English counterparts, but the violent behavior of the English women had been something of an embarrassment to the Ohio suffragists in their 1914 campaign. English suffragettes had chained themselves to the doors of Parliament, attacked guards with axes, and went on hunger strikes when jailed.[50] Ohio suffragists were confident they would not have to use such violent means.

The women had given up on amending the state constitution as the route to suffrage and had turned to municipal affairs. The new state constitution had given cities the right to frame their own charters and determine their own officials. The women thought that a city charter could, therefore, give women the right to vote for municipal officials. In Illinois in 1915 the courts had decided favorably on that issue.

East Cleveland was chosen as a test case. It was writing a charter in 1916 and was a prosperous middle-class suburb where there was considerable sympathy for woman suffrage.[51] The suffragists conducted a house to house survey and found that the majority of women wanted to vote. Allen spent many days in her office and in the library reading law books on constitutions and charters, reviewing specific charters, election laws and laws concerning women. She spent evenings at committee meetings and talking with influential people. In June the voters of East Cleveland adopted a charter including woman suffrage for municipal officials. Then the Board of Elections announced that it would not permit women to vote. The Woman Suffrage Party initiated a taxpayer's suit to test the right of women to vote in a charter city, with Allen as the party lawyer.

While the case was pending, Allen visited her family in Utah. The war was the main topic of conversation, but Emir and Esther were there and they had a fine time hiking and mountain climbing. Esther had married Ralph Gaw and they lived in Salt Lake City. Florence prided herself on being able to keep up with the men in mountain climbing. Inevitably her weight accumulated in spite of strenuous exercises before breakfast and climbing mountains in the afternoon.

She also went to Atlantic City as a delegate to the NAWSA Convention. Both political parties had endorsed woman suffrage, but would leave legislation up to the states. Presidential candidates Woodrow Wilson and Charles Evans Hughes both spoke favorably for the cause of suffrage. The NAWSA Convention was big and optimistic about the future but split on policy toward the political parties. Florence Allen urged the women to adopt a policy of neutrality since the suffragists had maintained for years that they were issue oriented rather than party oriented. Members for the National Woman's Party wanted to campaign against Wilson's reelection because the Democrats had been in office four years and had failed to pass the suffrage amendment. When the NWP announced that it would campaign against Wilson in the western enfranchised states Allen volunteered to campaign for him in Montana.[52] The Montana tour was arranged by Homer Cummings of the Democratic National Committee, an Allen family friend. Montana women were voting for the first time and Jeanette Rankin was running for Congress. Allen's campaign was a great success as she travelled to Glendine, Niles City, Billings, Bozman, and Helena. In Billings, for example, there was a dinner and reception for her at the Grand Hotel, followed by a speech before a packed house in the Majestic Theater. Many were unable to secure seats and stood during the speech.[53] Many must have though of her as C. E. Allen's daughter.

As she travelled around Montana she kept in touch with Ohio friends about the charter case. Finally a wire came that the case would be heard before the Ohio Supreme Court in six days. Allen hurried back to Cleveland, studying her charter briefs in her berth on the way. She had done her homework well and the Supreme Court upheld the right of Ohio women to vote in municipal elections.[54] The court delayed announcing its decision until the following April, however, and as a result East Cleveland women voted separately that fall and their ballots were held until the court's decision was announced.

So encouraged were the women by their success in achieving suffrage in municipal elections that they looked for other possibilities. Several states had granted women the right to vote for presidential electors, the U.S. Supreme Court had found it constitutional, and the Ohio suffragists decided to try that route. Allen spent most of the fall of 1916 working on the bill and she and her co-workers personally talked with every legislator to explain its purpose. Representative James A. Reynolds introduced the bill and in early February it passed both houses by a comfortable majority and was signed by progressive Democratic Governor James A. Cox.[55]

Antisuffragists immediately began to circulate petitions calling for a referendum on the bill. By July the suffragists began to suspect that many of the petitions were fraudulent. Allen again travelled around the state checking petitions and finding that many signatures were obviously written by the same hand and with the same pen. Saloons were favorite places to circulate petitions and the women, although they never personally frequented saloons, were very suspicious of what went on in them. Florence spent much of the summer of 1917 checking petitions.[56] She would need more money to continue this work, she told Upton, and again the women's organizations raised the money to challenge the petitions and to defend presidential suffrage in the coming referendum election. Allen spoke at one fund raiser for the campaign, asking for $1,000 and getting $4,000.[57]

Lawsuits were initiated in selected counties to challenge the petitions. Some courts refused to hear the cases, in spite of "a good deal of scrapping"[58] on the part of lawyer Allen, but four eventually did and threw out more than ninety percent of the signatures as fraudulent.[59] Fraudulent petitions could only be challenged by boards of elections and in 65 counties they failed, or refused, to do so. The suffragists tried to take the issue to the Ohio Supreme Court, but it declined to hear the case, and their old political friend, Newton Baker, refused to take a stand.[60]

Even time was not on their side. The courts which did examine petitions delayed action so long that they failed to make the forty days before election deadline in challenging petitions. The fact that Alice Paul and ten of her National Woman's Party workers were arrested in October for picketing the White House did not help the suffragists' cause, although the NAWSA stoutly denied any sympathy with Paul. The referendum went on as scheduled, and the legislature's extension of the suffrage to women in presidential elections was recalled by a large 144,000 majority.[61]

At this point the suffragists gave up on Ohio and directed their faith and their efforts to the United States Congress to pass a national amendment. Even the General was exhausted from the Ohio campaign and sent a handwritten note to Flossie that she was "sick of life. . . so tired." She confided that she dare not say this to her husband or Elizabeth Hauser and so was "unloading it" on Florence.[62]

FOOTNOTES

[1] The history of the woman suffrage movement can be found in Eleanor Flexner, *Century of Struggle,* Cambridge: Harvard University, 1959; Aileen Kraditor, *The Ideas of the Woman Suffrage Movement, 1890-1920,* New York, 1965; William L. O'Neill, *Everyone Was Brave: The Rise and Fall of Feminism in American,* Chicago: Quadrangle Books, 1969; Scott and Scott, *op. cit.*

[2] Scott and Scott, p. 29.

[3] *Ibid.,*p. 29-30. As early as 1905 Emmeline and Christobel Pankhurst had experimented with "dramatic tactics."

[4] Florence E. Allen and Mary Welles, *The Ohio Woman Suffrage Movement,* Cleveland: Committee for the Preservation of Woman Suffrage Records, 1950, p. 40. Edna Perkins, "Ohio Women and the Ballot," p. 2, in Belle Sherwin papers, Schlesinger Library, scrapbook v. 2, microfilm reel 1.

[5] Virginia Clark Abbott, *The History of Woman Suffrage and the League of Women Voters in Cuyahoga County, 1911-1945,* Cleveland, 1949, pp. 11-16.

[6] *Ibid.,* p. 18.

[7] Cleveland *Plain Dealer,* April 13, 1912.

[8] Abbott, pp. 11-16.

[9] *Ibid.,* p. 19.

[10] *Ibid.*

[11] From Allen's speech at the Radcliffe College celebration of 40 years of woman suffrage, NAWSA papers, LC, container 37, microfilm reel 25.

[12] *Christian Science Monitor,* November 14, 1960, NAWSA papers, LC, container 37, microfilm reel 25.

[13] So President M. Carey Thomas told Bryn Mawr Students, according to Dobkin, foreword, p. vi.

[14] Diary, September 18, 1912. *To Do Justly,* p. 32.

[15] *To Do Justly,* p. 32.

[16] Abbott, pp. 22-23.

[17] information from Vadae G. Meekison papers, Ohio Historical Society Library. The suffrage amendment did not carry in Vadae's county, but Florence wrote Vadae that was only to be expected in the "German wet" county.

[18] Kraditor, p. 50.

[19] Diary, September 23, 1912.

[20] Hoyt Landon Warner, *Progressivism in Ohio, 1897-1917,* Columbus: Ohio State University Press, 1964, pp. 340-341. According to Abbott, p. 27, the suffrage amendment got the second largest vote of all the amendments.

[21] Diary, various entries. Ida Husted Harper, *History of Woman Suffrage,* v. 5, New York: Arno Press, 1969, p. 453. Allen had apparently not fully learned Park's admonition about hecklers. As they marched through Philadelphia she picked up a young heckler by his

collar, hauled him over to the curb, put him across her knee and spanked him, according to the *Cleveland Press*, January 20, 1922, Allen papers, LC, container 8.

[22] Scott and Scott, pp. 31-32.

[23] Lemons, p. 138, 143. The heyday of protective legislation was 1911 to 1921.

[24] *To Do Justly*, p. 28.

[25] *Ibid*.

[26] The best history of Cleveland is William Ganson Rose, *Cleveland, The Making of a City*, Cleveland: World Publishing Company, 1950.

[27] Thwing letter in Allen papers, WRHS, Container 6, folder 1.

[28] Diary, various entries.

[29] This is the thesis of Alan Grimes.

[30] *The Woman's Journal*, v. XLV, No. 40, October 3, 1914, p. 270. Upton's *Journal* had been renamed *The Woman's Journal* and was the official organ of the NAWSA.

[31] Abbott p. 28-29.

[32] *Ibid.*, p. 30, says "most" of the wealthy industrialists opposed it, but the statement is not documented.

[33] Cleveland *Plain Dealer*, May 24, 1914, p. 1.

[34] Diary, August 10-15, 1914.

[35] Abott, p. 32.

[36] Cleveland *Plain Dealer*, October 29, 1914, p. 10. Allen's "research notes" for the debate contain a statement that in Wyoming woman suffrage had aided in banishing crime, pauperism, and vice, that it secured peaceful and orderly elections, good government, and a remarkable degree of civilization and public order: From Resolution of Wyoming House of Representatives of 1893 as printed in *Woman's Journal*, v. VI, No. 3, May 1893, Allen papers, LC, container 3.

[37] President Thwing's letter in Allen papers, WRHS, container 6, folder 1. Allen's feelings about the debate from diary entries October 1914.

[38] Abbott, p. 39; Cleveland *Plain Dealer*, October 4, 1914, p. 1l

[39] Allen and Welles, p. 45.

[40] Abbott, p. 35; Allen and Welles, p. 49.

[41] Diary, June 21, 1914 and various entries.

[42] Rose p. 722.

[43] Allen papers, WRHS, container 15.

[44] William B. Neff, *Bench and Bar in Northern Ohio*, Cleveland: Historical Publishing Company, 1921, pp. 260-739.

[45] Information from Elizabeth Kemper Adams, *Women Professional Workers*, Chautauqua: Chautauqua Press, 1921, p. 72. The information is not well documented, but was probably from Carnegie Foundation reports. Adams was a professor of education at Smith College.

[46] From Allen interview with Allan Harding from "The First Woman to Set on a Supreme Court Bench," *The American Magazine*, v. XCV, No. 4, April 1923, pp. 18-19, 198-202. In another interview she said that in her first law case she represented the plaintiff in an argument over possession of a featherbed. *Cincinnati Post*, February 24, 1934, Allen papers, LC, container 3.

[47] Diary, February 9, 1915.

[48] *To Do Justly*, p. 31.

[49] Diary, November 15, 1915.

[50] Accounts of English suffragette activities were on p. 1 of the Cleveland *Plain Dealer,* June 4, 1914, June 5, June 8, and June 19.

[51] *To Do Justly,* pp 35-37; Allen and Welles, p. 49.

[52] Abbott, p. 51; Scott and Scott, pp. 33-36.

[53] Newspaper clipping, paper not identified, October 24, 1916, Allen papers, LC, container 5.

[54] Allen was paid $100 for her work on the East Cleveland charter. Letter from Grace Treat to Allen, February 17, 1916, Allen papers, WRHS, container 6, folder 1.

[55] Allen and Welles, pp. 50-51.

[56] *Ibid.*

[57] Abbott, p. 55.

[58] Diary, October 21, 1917.

[59] Allen and Welles, p. 51; letter of Allen to editor *New York Evening Post,* Allen papers, WRHS, container 6, folder 1.

[60] According to letter from Frank Davis to Allen, October nd, 1917, Allen papers, WRHS, container 6, folder 1.

[61] Allen and Welles, p. 51.

[62] Upton to Allen, January 22, 1918, Allen papers, WRHS, container 6, folder 1.

Chapter 4

JUSTICE IN CUYAHOGA COUNTY

Nineteen seventeen was a distressing year for the American people as well as for the Ohio suffragists. It seemed inevitable that the United States would be drawn into the war in Europe, and finally President Wilson led the country into it with the rationalization that allied victory would serve the cause of justice, humanity, and world peace. On that basis the Allen family could support it and sons Jack and Emir were soon in uniform, although Florence noted feeling "terrible" about Emir being in uniform.[1] Emir had finished his law degree and had been admitted to the bar in California early in 1917. Jack was a student at Yale.

By midsummer Emir was stationed near Syracuse, New York where, as he wrote, he was taking up his "new profession" as an infantry officer. Sixty-five recruits, he reported, were under his direction and he had a good set of non-commissioned officers, but equipment was lacking and the men were sleeping twelve to a tent "packed in like sardines."[2]

At Christmas Florence went to the Tuckerman's country place in Westerly, Rhode Island for a bittersweet reunion with Emir. They walked by the sea and around the pond, flushed patridges in the cranberry bog, dragged up trees and sawed wood for Aunt Mary, roasted rabbits and chickens on a spit, ate plum pudding and toasted marshmallows. They sang and danced and admired Emir's calisthenics, but it was a sad day when he left. On New Year's Eve Florence went to New York to visit Bert and say a final good-bye to Emir.[3] Shortly after he sailed for Europe and she learned that he had reached "the other side" safely.

Papa and Mamma pleaded with Florence to come to Utah for a vacation that summer, but with her law cases, petition problems, and a multitude of speaking engagements, she regretted that she was too busy to go. She escaped to Florida for a few days to visit Jack before his departure for Europe, and her sister Helen was a regular Cleveland visitor, sometimes for weeks at a time. Helen, like many women, was having serious difficulty finding a satisfying and continuing job worthy of her qualifications. Esther and Ralph were proud parents of a little boy named Emir to whom Florence often sent gifts.

During the war the suffragists toned down their drive for the vote and turned their efforts to winning the war. Headquarters was transformed into a Red Cross Center. Belle Sherwin coordinated the efforts of all the women's organizations as Ohio Chairman for the Council of National Defense. Massive efforts were undertaken by women to conserve food, recruit service men and workers, and raise money for Liberty Loans.[4] Florence Allen was on frequent call from the speaker's bureau. She didn't talk much about suffrage, but she sometimes told her listeners that the war would not have occurred if women of the world had had the vote for the twenty previous years.

Society was more open to women during the war, and Allen and her friends took the opportunity to open Western Reserve University schools of law and medicine to women. President Thwing replied favorably to Allen's inquiry, but felt that the problem of rest rooms would present some difficulties.[5] With Allen's prodding that problem was resolved and the schools were opened to women.[6]

There were no quiet years in Florence Allen's life, but 1918 was more bated than most. Helen lived with her until April, when Mamma came. After a quiet reunion with Aunt Mary and Aunt Florence, Mamma and Helen left for Salt Lake City. Florence was busy with her law practice and with many talks for the war effort. She walked a great deal, practiced the piano every day, and looked for letters from Emir and Jack. On July 20th she read her last letter from Emir, and few days later a telegram from Papa came telling her that Emir had been killed in action in France on July 15th.[7] Emir was 27.

The day after receiving the telegram Florence took the train to Westerly. Bert hastened to be with her and together they shared sentimental remembrances as they walked along the shore and around the pond. When Florence returned to Cleveland the DuPonts showered her with flowers and extended more than their usual hospitality. Sally hovered over her, took her for rides, entertained her with gramophone records, and invited her for breakfast, lunch and dinner. Word came from Emir's fellow officer that he had been killed instantly by an exploding shell while trying to rescue four of his wounded men.[8] He received the Distinguished Service Cross for Extraordinary Heroism.

In spite of her sorrow, Florence believed that the war was a just war and continued to speak for Liberty Loans. In October, 1918 she spoke at a huge rally on Public Square in Cleveland, the goal of which was to raise a million dollars. Mrs. Baker led the singing, Sarah Bernhardt, who was performing at the Hippodrome, put in an appearance, and the featured speakers were Harriet Taylor Upton and Florence Allen.[9]

The saddest time of all was her Christmas trip to Utah. The train was miserably crowded and delayed by returning soldiers whose persons and baggage overflowed all accommodations. Jack had been injured in action and was still in Europe. Jack was 23. He had been a balloon observer and was shot down and parachuted out four times. The last time he was caught in a tree and hung there fifteen hours before being rescued. The experience had incapacitated him. Mamma was feeling very depressed and discussions with Papa were not lively. Esther was there and she and Florence kept up the Christmas spirit as best they could for the sake of little Emir.[10]

Up to this point, Florence Allen had lived pretty much in a woman's world. As her suffrage work tapered off she began to move into the world of men. Her settlement house and legal aid work had given her a liberal education in the seamy side of life which otherwise would have been remote from her own experience. Her legal work for the suffrage association had given her a chance to work for human rights and to defend the beliefs to which, as she said, her heart and soul were dedicated.[11]

A case of special interest to her from the point of view of working women and human rights developed as the war ended in the case of *Employees v. Cleveland Railway Company.* Men street car conductors had been hard to find during the war and in the summer of 1918 the Railway Company hired about 300 women in spite of the objections of the National Amalgamated Union of Street Car Conductors. The women were willing to join the union but the men refused to admit them.[12] One hundred seventy-three of the women became conductors, and, although the vast majority of them had been working women before the war, these were better jobs than they had had before.[13]

When the men began to return they wanted their jobs back, but many of the women were unwilling to retire voluntarily. The union objected to the continuance of women as conductors and when the company refused to fire them the men went out on strike, paralyzing Cleveland transportation for three days. The company settled the strike by agreeing to the union's demands.

Florence and her suffrage friend Rose Moriarity, who was interested in labor welfare as well as women's rights,[14] became deeply involved in the case,[15] had many conferences with the "conductorettes" and defended the women. They appealed the case to the National War Labor Board, directing the complaint against both the company and the union. The board immediately ordered the company not to fire the women until they could investigate. A preliminary hearing was held in which the women were allowed to present their side of the case. Thereafter, without the presence of the women, but with the advice of the mayor that men were increasingly available, the board issued an order recommending that the company employ no more women and replace them by January 3, 1919 with men.

The National Women's Trade Union League protested the decision as "unjust, undemocratic and unAmerican,"[16] and hired counsel, including Florence Allen, to demand a rehearing on the grounds that the women had not had their day in court with reference to the order. Before the hearing the company fired the 64 women who were still working. When the board met Allen argued that the women had not had their day in court on the dismissal order, that there were enough positions to keep them all, and that the original terms of the women's contracts had justified them in believing that their employment would continue until they voluntarily retired or proved incompetent in their duties Her arguments were convincing and the board recommended reinstatement of the women with full seniority and other privileges.[17]

It was a victory for women, but a barren victory. The company honored its strike settlement with the union and ignored the recommendations of the War Labor Board. There were no more women conductors on Cleveland street cars, but Allen was the first woman lawyer to present a case before the War Labor Board.

The experience of the Cleveland women was not an isolated one. Similar cases occurred in Detroit and New York. In New York 1,500 women conductors and ticket agents protested their dismissal at the end of the war. Nevertheless, 800 lost their jobs and 700 were demoted.[18] All over the country working women were being demoted or expected to retire when the men came home.

Florence Allen, like her mother before her, had faith in women's organizations as a means of promoting social action. She joined many and eventually they provided a means of communication to millions of members. She worked very hard for the organizations as a speaker, as an adviser on policy decisions, and as a delegate to conventions. During the course of her life she spent an incredible and exhausting amount of time and a considerable portion of her income attending conventions. Without women's organizations Florence Allen's life and career would have been entirely different.

One of the first organizations to be interested in her was the Daughters of the American Revolution, of which her mother was a charter member. When Florence was in law school Ruth Bryan Owen, daughter of William Jennings Bryan, was executive secretary of the DAR. Mrs. Owen visited Florence many times in New York and they discussed the organization.[19] There is no doubt but that Florence might have been a more active member, especially since Mrs. Owen had married an Englishman and planned to live abroad. Florence retained her membership, she spoke occasionally for the DAR, but she held no offices. The DAR remained largely supportive of her career, although their viewpoints diverged as the DAR, originally liberal in its policies, became more conservative.

Allen was enormously loyal to alumnae associations, that of New Lyme Institute, the Women's College of Western Reserve University, and the Law School of New York University. She held no offices but made contributions attending meetings, often as a speaker.

50

It was to be expected that she would join legal organizations. The Ohio Bar Association was very generous in welcoming her as soon as she passed the bar exams, a gesture for which she expressed her gratitude many times over the years. Soon she was urging the membership to vote for woman suffrage and assuring them that Ohio women wanted to work with men in the future development of the state. The American Bar Association was less generous and prohibited women members until 1918. Allen joined it as well as other legal organizations.

More important in her life was the National Association of Women Lawyers. Before women lawyers were admitted to the ABA they had formed their own women lawyers' clubs. The first one started in New York in 1899. By 1911 there were enough clubs to begin publication of the *Women Lawyers' Journal*. Florence Allen joined in 1915 and was on the plenary committee when the NAWL was formed in 1923.[20] The NAWL was a bulwark of strength and support to her for a lifetime.

Federations of women's clubs — the Cleveland Federation, the Ohio Federation and the General Federation of Women's Clubs — shared her life in a variety of activities. During the winter of 1918-1919, for example, Allen gave a series of lectures on citizenship for the Cleveland Federation for Women's Clubs. The lectures were primarily on current events and world problems and were held at the Statler Hotel. They proved to be very popular. On the average 600 people attended, paying fifty cents per lecture. Her arguments must have been persuasive, for after her lecture on the League of Nations she took a vote of the group and found that they unanimously favored American entrance.[21] The General Federation's endorsement of a policy or a candidate spoke for millions of women.

She was a charter member of the Cleveland Woman's City Club. It was founded in 1916 to provide a central meeting place for women, an open forum for discussion, and to promote the general welfare of the city. It had a charter membership of 1,200.[22] One of the Club's major projects was providing school lunches for poor children. Working on such palliative projects was not Florence Allen's style, but she was many times the speaker for the club's forum for discussion.

Allen was more active in the Young Women's Christian Association than the Woman's City Club. Her mother, too, had been very interested in this organization designed to provide young working women with a comfortable and wholesome environment in the city. In Cleveland Marie Wing was executive secretary of the YWCA, and she and Allen were very kindred spirits. Marie was a Bryn Mawr graduate, active in the Consumer's League and in the struggle for protective legislation and the minimum wage for women. The YWCA provided ten-cent suppers for working women and educational lectures thereafter, often lectures by Florence Allen.

Florence and Marie planned the establishment of the Cleveland

Business Woman's Club, an extension of the YWCA for the advancement and welfare of business women, mostly secretaries, clerks and telephone operators.[23] Business women's clubs grew rapidly in membership and in 1919 were organized in the National Federation for Business and Professional Women's Clubs with the purpose "to plan so that young women of the future might come into business and professional fields better able to cope with conditions and with fewer handicaps to overcome."[24] The largest segment of membership continued to be clerical workers, but a fair proportion were teachers and nurses and, occasionally, lawyers.[25]

In February 1920 the Ohio Federation of Business and Professional Women was organized and immediately urged Governor Cox to appoint Allen to a vacancy on the common pleas bench.[26] The project failed because suffrage had not been ratified and a woman could not be appointed to an elective position. According to one account, the Ohio Federation was organized for the specific purpose of supporting Allen's candidacy.[27]

The NAWL and the NFBPWC were the most influential organizations in support of the career of Florence Allen. She clearly perceived that, altogether, these organizations represented the voice of concerned, progressive women everywhere. With the coming of woman suffrage they represented an enormous potential for political as well as social reform.

In 1920 the NAWSA disbanded and was replaced by a much smaller organization, the League of Women Voters for the purpose of political education on issues. It did not endorse candidates, but did support a myriad of liberal causes: maternity and child protection, federal regulation of food and marketing, the cooperative movement, prohibition of child labor, aid to education, hours and wages laws.[28] Special to the Cleveland League was its support of the city manager plan. Allen was an active participant. At its second annual convention in Cleveland in 1921, for example, a huge audience assembled in Masonic Hall to hear the speakers: Judge Florence Allen, war correspondent Will Irwin, and Carrie Chapman Catt.[29]

Allen's political affiliation was with the Democratic Party. In 1919 she became a national committee woman for Ohio and worked with Bernice Pyke of Lakewood who was in charge of the local women's organization. Allen family friend Homer Cummings was Chairman of the National Democratic Committee. The party greatly appreciated Allen's speaking talents. She spoke at the committee meeting in Syracuse in 1919 on woman suffrage and the publicity director wrote a glowing letter telling her that the audience had been "tremendously impressed" and that personally he thought it was the best talk he had ever heard by man or woman.[30] Allen was as enthusiastic as Wilson about the League of Nations and promotion of it began to share her speaking time with women's rights.

In Cleveland she became acquainted with Burr Gongwer, formerly Tom Johnson's secretary and after his death Democratic Party boss in Cuyahoga County for twenty years or more. While Allen was in the midst of the streetcar case he asked her to become assistant prosecutor for Cuyahoga County. This was her first substantial and financially rewarding job offer, and it is not surprising that it was in the public sector. Professional women have found the public sector more open to them than the private sector.

Allen accepted Gongwer's offer immediately, and was the first woman in the country to hold such an office. Yellow roses, symbol of the woman suffrage movement, bedecked her office when she arrived, reporters interviewed her, photographers took pictures. The county prosecutor was reported as saying, "I consider that Miss Allen will do a man's job in our office. I rate her as the equal of virtually any male attorney in Cleveland."[31] Allen replied that she would do the same work men did and try every case assigned to her.

One of the shocks of the first day at the office was to learn that she would "be slung into cases without preparation." The court was so backlogged that perhaps there was no alternative to handing the file to the prosecutor as the case came up. At any rate, it was good legal experience, although she felt that her cases were "rottenly prepared."[32] She learned the working of the prosecutor's office and the Court of Common Pleas, became acquainted with the judges, and within a month someone suggested that she should run for a judgeship. Forty years later a young newsman of the time who became editor of the *Cleveland News* remembered her first trial as an assistant prosecutor and the excitement of Baker and Gongwer over the higher standards that she, one lone woman, had brought to that very average prosecutor's office.[33]

Democrat Stephen M. Young was her immediate supervisor and much mutual respect developed between them. Young was on the threshold of a brilliant political career. Elected to Congress at the age of 27, he had stepped down to enter the military service. When discharged he had immediately been appointed to the prosecutor's office. Young recognized Allen's talents and put her in charge of the grand jury where she was responsible for preparing indictments returned. Young was interested in preventing delays, insisted on long hours, and Allen was his willing supporter.[34] From September to December 1919 the grand jury returned more than 1100 indictments,[35] a record accomplishment.

Allen liked the idea of running for a judgeship and her friends encouraged her, but women were not eligible before the passage of the Nineteenth amendment. The amendment was passed by Congress in 1919; all that was needed was the ratification of thirty-six states. In Ohio, Reynolds had introduced another bill for the presidential suffrage and it and the Nineteenth Amendment were ratified by the legislature on the same day, making Ohio fifth in line to ratify the woman suffrage amendment. It was a joyous and festive occasion when the legislators escorted women into the sacred chambers of the capitol. Liquor interests immediately initiated a referendum on the Nineteenth Amendment and the Eighteenth, hoping to stop the implementation of woman suffrage and prohibition. The Ohio Supreme Court and the United States Supreme Court ruled that there could be no referendum on constitutional amendments,[36] and thus the voters of Ohio never approved either prohibition or woman suffrage.

It was not until August 1920 that the 36th state, Tennessee, ratified the Nineteenth Amendment, after a long battle, and woman suffrage was promulgated. Allen had spent many sleepless nights during the Tennessee delay, but now the way was clear for her to declare her candidacy for judge of the Cuyahoga County Court of Common Pleas. Lawyer friends suggested to her that a juvenile court judgeship might be more appropriate for a woman, but she preferred the court of general jurisdiction.[37] It was only ten weeks before the election in which two Ohioans, Democrat James A. Cox and Republican Warren G. Harding were competing for the presidency.

Allen decided to run on a non-partisan ticket for several reasons. One was that she had had a falling out with the National Committee of the Democratic Party over Secretary of War Baker's universal military training bill. She wrote Homer Cummings resigning her committee position because she was "unalterably opposed to compulsory military service in peacetime," believing that the system of conscription "as established in Prussia . . . induced the world war."[38] A few newspapers were critical of her action in defiance of the party. The *Cincinnati Enquirer,* for example, advised that "the ladies must learn, like the men, that resignation carries away all the political chips in front of the player."[39]

Another reason for non-partisan candidacy was that the public had long been calling for the separation of politics from the courts and for non-partisan judges. Legislation provided that candidates for judgeships must be listed on a separate ballot without party affiliation, but most candidates found that they could not swing a campaign without party support.

Most important for Allen was that she hoped women would vote for her. Theoretically there should be a large constituency of women from both parties who had campaigned for the right to vote and for women to be in public office who would welcome the opportunity to vote for a good female candidate.[40]

News of her candidacy came as no surprise for talk of it had been in the wind for at least six months, the idea promoted primarily by the Cleveland Business Women's Club. The primaries were long past and it was necessary to file by petition, but many of her old suffrage friends had been enlisted to help.[41] The day after woman suffrage was promulgated she phoned her petitions committee and the campaign was on. Women workers left no stone unturned in getting petition signers, some climbing high scaffolding to get signatures from carpenters and other construction workers.

The pace for Florence was gruelling with grand jury cases every day and speeches at lunch and after work. She could not afford to quit her job for personal family expenses at the time were heavy. Few people would have had the physical stamina to endure the grand jury duty and as many as four or five personal appearances a day, many involving speeches.[42]

Dozens of people spoke for her, men and women. Now that suffrage was won her women friends could channel their fervor to her candidacy. They feared she wouldn't win, remembering the suffrage campaigns, and thought that getting the message to the voters was critical. Maud Wood Park, national president of the League of Women Voters, came to Cleveland to speak for Allen's candidacy. Belle Sherwin, president of the Cleveland League, explained that although the League did not support candidates they had made an exception in Allen's case because she was a non-partisan candidate.[43]

The Consumer's League, Lakewood Civic League, Lakewood PTA, Women's Protective Association all boosted her candidacy. The Business Women's Club published and distributed campaign literature. A group of nearly seventy five lawyers and representative citizens endorsed her on the front page of the *Cleveland Press*.[44] There were those who opposed a woman in public office and a few of her posters were torn down, but there was no organized resistance. Woman suffrage had ceased to be a political issue; it was prohibition that was a smoldering national problem.

Those who supported Allen praised her thorough qualifications, her sound knowledge of law, her good common sense, her strong character, her sense of fairness and justice, her interest in the individual and the community, and claimed there was need for a woman in the court because so many cases affected women and children.

All the political organizations, women's organizations, and newspapers made a concerted drive to encourage women to register to vote and told them where and how to do it. Newspapers had political editors for women to call to answer questions and ran columns of instructions. The YWCA gave a regular course of instruction in voting for women. There was some fear that women would not register because they would have to reveal their age. It was suggested that a law be passed so that a registrant would need to say only "over 21." Florence Allen did not hesitate to reveal her age, and started a major speech by announcing that she was thirty six and a half.[45] The audience applauded so much that she had to wait until the clapping died down to continue.

For the instruction of women voters Elizabeth Hauser edited a series of newspaper articles on parties and issues, featuring interviews with Harriet Taylor Upton, who defended the Republicans, Rose Schneidermann, who defended the Farmer-Labor Party, and Maud Wood Park, who told women to vote for individuals who would protect women and children, education and political reforms. Women did not register in great numbers, however, and the county registered many more men than women to the disappointment of suffrage supporters. Over the country as a whole only about one-third of the eligible women voted in 1920, compared with two-thirds of the eligible men.[46]

On the day before the election the *Cleveland Press* made its final plea for votes for Allen. A sample ballot was centered on the front page with large black arrows pointing to the name of Florence Allen. The message was brief and succinct: There is only one woman on the ballot, we need women in office, you are to vote for four common pleas judges, save one of your votes for Allen, make it unanimous.[47]

The Cleveland Bar Association, which had recently begun to rate judicial candidates for the edification of the voters, did not rate Allen highly; she was their sixth choice out of ten candidates.[48] The voters apparently ignored that evaluation, for when the votes were counted Allen led the ticket by a generous margin. When interviewed she said she did not consider it a personal triumph, but that she was "the beneficiary of the entire woman movement."[49] Through the years she remembered this election as the most wonderful experience of her life.[50] After the election her fellow judges proposed that a separate divorce court should be opened with Allen as presiding judge. She firmly refused, not wanting to be relegated to domestic affairs.

The Common Pleas Court to which Allen had been elected was a glaring example in 1920 of an institution in need of the kind of housekeeping reforms that the suffrage campaigners had promised women would bring. More than 6,000 cases were backlogged and awaiting trial.[51] Excessive delays made it possible for the accused to jump bail, while the facts of cases were forgotten, muddled or concealed in the lapse of time. Victims of crimes were kept in jail for their protection until their cases came up, often for months, while the accused were free on bail. There was no administrative head of the court. The twelve judges rotated from criminal to civil cases without regard to experience or continuity.[52] Women's organizations and the press took up Allen's cause that the courts needed an administrative head and advocated a bill, providing for a chief justice to administer common pleas courts in the counties of Ohio, which was passed by the legislature.

Local critics claimed that some of the judges were loafing on the job and some were downright lazy, that most of them were playing politics to the detriment of justice, that they were spending more time at weddings and picnics, wakes and funerals than in the court room, and that many of them were beholden to pressure groups and political parties. Critics said there was no dignity in the courtroom, judges didn't bother to wear robes, came and went without announcement, and fraternized freely with whomever was there. During interesting cases, spectators jammed the courtroom and followed the proceedings like a sporting event. One critic said that "the courts are run like bar-rooms" but another said that was an exaggeration, but that "in dignity of atmosphere" the courtroom "does not rise above a salesman's display room in a hotel."[53]

The people of Cleveland and Cuyahoga County were up in arms about the efficiency of their courts. Newspaper editors, the Cleveland Bar Association, the Chamber of Commerce, the League of Women Voters and other women's groups were demanding reform. In response the Cleveland Foundation funded an investigation of the problems and made recommendations for improvement which in 1921 were presented to the public in an 800-page report.[54]

While the public eye was on the courts Judge Allen was performing her duties in her own energetic and efficient way. Her court started at nine o'clock promptly. Jurors were scolded for being late. Attorneys who were not on time were replaced. At first attorneys could not decide whether to call the new judge "Miss," or "Mrs." or "Ma'am," or "Your Honor." The new judge insisted on being called "Judge Allen" at all times. Requests for special favors were ignored. She prided herself on the number of cases that were heard in her courtroom — 579 in the first twenty-one months. She was reversed in three instances, but sustained in all of the important cases.[55]

Judge Allen was very concerned about victims of crime, especially those who were held in protective custody while the accused were free on bail. In one case a man who had been robbed of a few dollars was imprisoned for 106 days while the robber was out on bail. She saw to it that cases of this kind were the first to be heard in her courtroom.[56]

One of the most serious criticisms of the courts was that skilled criminal lawyers successfully persuaded judges to "pass" far too many cases until the next court term. Passed cases were less likely to result in a verdict of guilty when tried because of the loss of evidence with the passage of time. The responsibility of being presiding judge rotated, and in April, 1921 when Allen became presiding judge she issued an order requiring an affidavit of due diligence on the part of the attorney and the presence of the defendant in court before passing any case.[57]

As for decorum in the courtroom, Judge Allen was observed as being always in her robes, completely attentive to the testimony of witnesses and the arguments of attorneys, and giving carefully prepared instructions to juries, which, for the first time, included women.[58]

Sensational criminal cases brought Judge Allen special publicity and demonstrated her ability to dispense speedy and certain justice. One was the case of Frank Motto. Motto was the leader of a gang that shot and killed two Cleveland business men and robbed them of their company payroll. Motto was apprehended and tried in Allen's court. As the trial opened suspicious looking characters came into the courtroom. They were searched and found to be carrying concealed weapons, jailed, and the trial continued. A letter was received threatening to murder Allen and the members of the jury if Motto were executed. But the trial continued and Motto was found guilty of murder in the first degree and Judge Allen gave him the mandatory death sentence. She denied a stay of execution and had no regrets when he was executed.[59] Her courage and dedication to justice had prevailed in a very manly way over supposedly feminine foibles of timidity and leniency.

A more sensational case involved the issue of perjury. Perjury, or the practice of ignoring it, according to the editors of the Cleveland Foundation investigation, was one of the major problems of the court. "The giving of false testimony under oath seems to be rife," the report said, and "perjury committed in open court has existed without challenge."[60]

The case Allen was concerned with was that of William McGannon, Chief Justice of the Cleveland Municipal Court, who had become involved with criminals and was accused of a murder. McGannon was tried for murder and acquited, but it seemed obvious that some of the witnesses gave false testimony. Several individuals were indicted for taking bribes and bearing false witness, but when McGannon was tried again he was acquited for the second time. Many Clevelanders saw the case as a disgraceful travesty on justice.

In a third case, with Allen presiding, he was accused of perjury. In her courtroom he was found guilty and sentenced by her to the state penitentiary. It was only in her courtroom that he was found guilty of anything, and it was apparently Allen's clear instructions to the jury and her insistence that they could reach a verdict when the jury felt like giving up that brought a decision in the case. She charged the jury that they should consider only the facts in the case, that they were not concerned with the dispensation of mercy, and that they, as jurors, would be unfaithful to their trust if the facts demand conviction. Not only was McGannon sentenced to the penitentiary by Judge Allen but he was scolded for his behavior as she sentenced him. "Judges cannot think that they are above the law," she told him, "They must be subject to the law the same as private citizens. Judges ought to know the spirit of the law, which demands that all tell the truth in a court of justice . . . ."[61]

One of the reporters in the courtroom on the Saturday morning of the sentencing retained a vivid mental picture of the moment. Forty years later he could still see Judge Allen standing, not sitting, behind the bench, a slight glow on her cheeks, assuring McGannon in low and gentle tones that he had had a perfectly fair trial and deserved his sentence. In the reporter's mind the picture was one of unforgettable contrast between Allen's earnestness and composure and McGannon's pallor and hysteria.[62] The *New York Tribune* called the conviction and sentencing of McGannon "the most dramatic incident in the history of the Cuyahoga County courts."[63]

Most cases weren't sensational but reflected the problemic aspects of life, often problems remote from the personal experience of Judge Allen. She took careful and voluminous handwritten notes of testimony, making marginal comments on witnesses.

In one divorce case, for example, the plaintiff, a "red-faced" woman with "petulant lips," according to the marginal notes, who had married her husband in the old country and immigrated to Cleveland, testified that her husband beat her repeatedly, that he was often drunk, that they quarrelled violently, that he objected to the boarders she took in but collected the money while she did all the work. For the defendant, a "decent looking man" testified that he had often seen the plaintiff herself drunk and staggering under the influence of liquor and that he had seen ten or twelve men around the house for unknown reasons.[64]

Women jurors as well as women judges were new to the courts. The Ohio constitution made all enfranchised voters eligible for jury duty but most states did not and there was a long drawn-out battle over jury duty for nearly twenty years.[65] There was a great commotion about women jurors. Some said the facts of cases would be too much for women, there would be tears in the jury box or faintings, women would be too easy on criminals, and what if a jury of men and women had to be locked up together overnight? Judge Allen solved the problem of locking up juries by ordering separate rooms for men and women. She found women jurors as competent as men and emotional reactions more varied among individuals than between sexes; she said intelligent and educated individuals of either sex made the best jurors. She treated her juries with great respect and they returned the compliment. Members of her first panel of jurors wrote and signed a letter expressing appreciation for the honest, earnest and faithful manner in which she conducted cases and best wishes for success in the profession into which she was "so nobly" leading her sex.[66]

Sensational cases brought many letters of congratulation. The president of the Cleveland Federation of Women's Clubs, for example, after the McGannon case, wrote to say how proud they were of her and to offer the assistance of the Federation at any time and in any way.[67] During the Motto case, writers admired her courage and fearlessness as well as her conduct of the case.

In two years as a common pleas judge Florence Allen had demonstrated that a woman judge could serve with courage, wisdom and integrity, and contribute to the improvement of a court that was in need of reform. At the same time she urged other women to participate in court proceedings, especially as jurors, and told them they would lose none of the real elements of their womanhood, their idealism, or their power to sympathize. She believed women judges and jurors lent "a powerful moral backing" for administration of justice[68] and she was proof of her own words.

FOOTNOTES

[1] Diary, May 12, 1917.

[2] Emir Allen letter to Florence Allen, undated 1917, Allen papers, container 6, folder 1.

[3] Diary, December 23-31, 1917.

[4] It was said that Sherwin, who was known primarily for gratuitous social welfare activities, had the business acumen of her father, one of Cleveland's great industrialists. Sherwin papers, SL.

[5] Charles Thwing letter to Allen, April 17, 1917, WRHS, container 6, folder 1.

[6] Sarah Marcus, distinguished Cleveland physician, who tried to enter Western Reserve University medical school in 1916 wrote that the best they could come up with by way of refusal was that the school did not have any toilet facilities for women. Marcus promised that she would not need any, but still she wasn't admitted. She sought the help of Florence Allen and wrote that two years later Allen was successful in opening the medical school to women. From Kent L. Brown, Ed., *Medicine in Cleveland and Cuyahoga County: 1810-1976*, Cleveland: Academy of Medicine, 1977, p. 67.

[7] Diary, July 20 & August 8, 1918.

[8] Diary, September 23, 1918.

[9] Allen papers, WRHS, container 26, folder 3.

[10] Diary, December 20-25, 1918.

[11] *To Do Justly*, p. 40.

[12] *Life and Labor*, v. IX, January 1919, p. 14.

[13] According to Chafe, *The American Woman*, p. 52, 90% of the women had been working women before being hired by the railway company.

[14] Rose Moriarity was one of Ohio's first women politicians, according to Abbott, p. 47, who had run her home town of Elyria for several years from the city auditor's office. In the early twenties she was appointed to the Ohio State Industrial Commission, the first woman appointed to the Commission.

[15] Allen was involved as early as October 4, 1918 when she wrote a letter to Mayor Harry Davis asking for a meeting room for the women. Allen papers, WRHS, container 6, folder 1.

[16] *Life and Labor*, ibid.; J. Stanley Lemons, *The Woman Citizen: Social Feminism in the 1920s*, Urbana, 1975, pp. 22-24.

[17] Summarized from National War Labor Board Docket No., 491 in Allen papers, WRHS, container 6, folder 1.

[18] Alice Kessler-Harris, "Where Are the Organized Women Workers?" *Feminist Studies*, v. 3, No. 1/2, Fall 1975, p. 100.

[19] Diary, various entries 1911-1912.

[20] *History of NAWL*, p. 5.

[21] Allen papers, WRHS, container 24, v. 3.

[22] Sherwin papers, SL, scrapbooks, v. ?, microfilm reel 1.

[23] Ryan, p. 144. At the same time men in business were organizing such clubs as Kiwanis, Rotary, and chambers of commerce. Business women's clubs were female counterparts.

[24] Lemons, p. 44.

[25] In 1931 35.7% of the members were clerical, 14.4% were teachers, according to Breckinridge, p. 237.

[26] *Forty Years of Progress and Service, 1920-1960*, Columbus: Ohio Federation of Business and Professional Women's Clubs, 1960, p. 29. In Cleveland Business and Professional Women's Club papers, WRHS, container 2.

[27] Abbott, p. 75. The comment was attributed to Mary Grossman who later was elected judge of the Cleveland Municipal Court.

[28] Summarized from Lemons, p. 118.

[29] Allen papers, WRHS, container 26, folder 5.

[30] Correspondence in Allen papers, January 13, 1919, WRHS, container 6, folder 1.

[31] From newspaper clippings in Allen papers, WRHS, container 25, v. 4.

[32] Diary, April 1 and June 6, 1919.

[33] Letter from N. R. Howard to Allen, October 22, 1959, Allen papers, WRHS, container 8, folder 5.

[34] *To Do Justly*, p. 39.

[35] *Ibid.*, p. 40.

[36] Harper, v. 5, pp. 518-519.

[37] Diary entries, August, 1920.

[38] Letter of Allen to Homer Cummings, September 24, 1919, Allen papers, WRHS, container 6, folder 1; *Columbus State Journal*, Oct. 16, 1919, Allen papers, WRHS, container 25, v. 4; *Headquarters News Bulletin*, Ohio Woman Suffrage Headquarters, Warren, v. 4, No. 19, October 1, 1919 in NAWSA papers, LC, container 37, microfilm reel 25.

[39] *Cincinnati Enquirer*, September 28, 1919, Allen papers, WRHS, container 25, v. 4.

[40] Rose Moriarity, for example, who helped with the campaign was on the Republican National Committee, *To Do Justly*, p. 43.

[41] *To Do Justly*, pp. 41-42; Cleveland *Plain Dealer*, November 10, 1922, Allen papers, LC, container 6. Democratic friends Gongwer, Young and Pyke also encouraged her to run.

[42] On September 29, for example, according to her diary, Grand Jury duty was "heavy," but she made appearances at a group of church women, Grange, Sherwin Wms. Co., church supper, Catholic meeting Flynn's Hall.

[43] Abbott, p. 75; *Cleveland News*, September 22, 1920, Allen papers, WRHS, container 26, folder 4.

[44] *Cleveland Press*, October 29, 1920, p. 1.

[45] Dairy, September 8, 1920; *Cleveland Press*, Sept. 9, 1920, p. 11.

[46] Sandra Baxter and Marjorie Lansing, *Women and Politics: The Invisible Majority*, Ann Arbor: University of Michigan Press, 1980, p. 17.

[47] *Cleveland Press*, November 1, 1920, p. 1.

[48] Reginald Heber Smith and Herbert B. Ehrmann, *The Criminal Courts*, Part I of *Survey of Criminal Justice in Cleveland*, The Cleveland Foundation, 1921, p. 38.

[49] *To Do Justly*, p. 43; *Cleveland Press*, November 3, 1920, p.4.

[50] *Ohioana*, v. 2, No. 3, Fall 1959, pp. 106-108.

[51] *Cleveland Press*, September 9, 1920, p. 2.

[52] Allen's account of court problems in *To Do Justly*, pp. 45-54.

[53] Smith and Ehrmann, p. 70.

[54] The Cleveland Foundation, *Criminal Justice in Cleveland*, Cleveland, 1921.

[55] *To Do Justly*, p. 51.

[56] *Ibid.*, pp. 46-51.

[57] Smith and Ehrmann, p. 75; Allen's diary, April 8, 1921.

[58] As reported by Kate Carter in the *Cleveland Press,* November 2, 1922, p. 2. Allen's hand-written notes on testimony and witness are in the Allen papers, WRHS, container 11, v. 1.

[59] The case is described in *To Do Justly,* pp. 55-57. According to her diary August 9, 1921, she went home and took a 3-hour nap after denying the stay of execution.

[60] Smith and Ehrmann, p. 130.

[61] *To Do Justly,* p. 62. Her 14 pages of instructions to the jury are in Allen papers, WRHS, container 15, folder 1.

[62] Letter from N. R. Howard to Allen, February 9, 1962, Allen papers, WRHS, container 9, folder 3.

[63] The *New York Tribune,* June 26, 1921, container 30.

[64] From notes on cases in the Court of Common Pleas, Allen papers, WRHS, container 11, v. 1.

[65] Lemons, pp. 68-73.

[66] Letter from jurors, January 14, 1921, Allen papers, WRHS, container 6, folder 2.

[67] Letter from President of Cleveland Federation of Women's Clubs to Allen, May 16, 1921. This and other letters in Allen papers, WRHS, container 6, folder 2.

[68] *To Do Justly,* p. 48.

Chapter 5

A MODERN PORTIA

During the suffrage campaigns Allen had often thought she would like to run for Congress when women got the vote. In the summer of 1922 she considered running for the Senate. But her friends in the Democratic Party advised against it, feeling certain that the incumbent, Atlee Pomerene, would be elected. When there was a vacancy on the Ohio Supreme Court bench she decided to run for it. Young and Baker encouraged her to try it, and the movement to nominate her started in the Cleveland Business Women's Club.[1]

Again she ran on a non-partisan ticket and entered by petition and women did most of the work. When she announced her candidacy women from all over the state who had been in the suffrage campaign volunteered to help. So avidly did the sisterhood circulate petitions that more than double the required number were filed.

She was fortunate to find a very talented campaign manager, Susan M. Rebhan. Susan was about the same age as Allen, and had begun her career at the age of fourteen, managing the family farm in Illinois. By the age of nineteen she had completed teacher's college and was principal of a high school near Youngstown, Ohio. In 1922 she was a field secretary for the YWCA, the parent organization of the Business Women's Club, but she took a leave of absence from that position to become Allen's campaign manager.

Under Rebhan's direction, three young women divided up the state and went to every county to appoint a chairperson for the campaign, always a woman. The chairpersons named assistants in various districts, always women. The list of workers sounded like a roll call of the suffragist organization and all the allied women's clubs. As Rebhan later wrote, it was "always women, women, marching on the voters like an army,"[2] and bringing Allen's campaign platform to the voters.

The platform was concise and to the point and contained only 36 words. They were:

> I believe in law enforcement, justice for all, business methods applied to the courts, efficient work by public servants, respect for law, order and the courts. Politics should have no place in the administration of justice.

The platform was printed on three by five cards with Allen's name and picture and passed out by the thousands. Florence Allen clubs were formed in 66 counties to help with the work. Rebhan's instructions to organizational meetings for Florence Allen clubs said it was important to include women from both political parties, from a variety of churches, women's clubs and PTAs. If members could speak for the candidate that was very good, but at least they could pass out platform cards.[3]

The non-partisan posture was not always easy to maintain. A Norwalk commentator wrote that although Allen was running non-partisan she was a Democrat and if she were elected she would be a Democrat on the bench. The writer alleged that campaigner Myra Mills had "inveigled" many women in Huron county into signing petitions by this non-partisan "subterfuge" and that Miss Mills should look elsewhere for members of her Florence Allen clubs.[4]

Allen's friend from suffrage days and the street-car case, Rose Moriarity, who was a member of the executive board of the Cuyahoga County Republican Club, told her audience at the national convention of the League of Women Voters that she had been reprimanded by her party for supporting Allen, but that she had felt compelled to do so because the county had practically given up hope of ever cleaning out "the bad element" until Florence Allen became judge. Then, she said "we cleaned up the gang in Cleveland . . . her mere presence on the bench is what did it!" Moriarity predicted that Democrat and Republican women were going to elect Allen to the supreme court.[5] Vadae Meekison, Republican leader in Holmes County, stacked literature against Allen in her basement. Cleveland Republican Lucia McCurdy McBride came out for her.

Elizabeth Hauser joined the campaign, full of suggestions and good advice. Eva Epstein Shaw started a Florence Allen Club for men and women in Toledo. A special committee of interested men and women in Cleveland campaigned energetically. The Cleveland Ministerial Union, which ordinarily refrained from making political endorsements, made an exception in this case and endorsed Allen's candidacy. Every Sunday for two months before the election Allen spoke at the regular morning service of scheduled churches. She did not speak in campaign rhetorec, but on the topic " The Christian and Government." She included the idea that our forefathers founded this nation on Christian doctrine — the doctrine of human brotherhood and human rights — and that it is the duty of all citizens, and especially women, to feel responsible for preserving this doctrine and improving their community.[6]

Allen had arranged her court schedule so that she was on duty during the regular vacation time in August and had time off in October to campaign. During October she was booked for appearances like a vaudeville star, according to Rebhan.[7] There were meetings morning, noon and night, at clubs, homes and factories, in theater halls and in the open. The thirty six words became known all over Ohio.

Allen's physical appearance proved to be a special asset. No one could possibly, even subconsciously, think that here was a weak, frail woman who might waver in her decisions or be influenced by masculine counterparts. As a Lisbon, Ohio newspaper put it:

> Judge Allen is physically as well as mentally a big woman, hearty and wholesome looking . . . . her complexion is fresh and guiltless even of talcum powder . . . . with abundant light brown hair dressed in the style of fifteen years ago . . . white teeth that glistened when she smiled, but one noticed when the smile disappeared the mouth had an extremely firm line; a good face, a face to inspire confidence. She cares little for frills, her gown a simple one-piece black cloth relieved only by a little white lace collar . . . . The lady walks with a stride like a man and wears roomy, common sense shoes. Her voice has a masculine depth and lends itself easily to open air speaking. Judge Allen certainly has the courage of her convictions and scored dishonest and inefficient officials and dilatory . . . courts in a splendidly brave manner.[8]

Newspapers all over the state proclaimed her merits and her platform. Erie Hopwood, editor of the Cleveland *Plain Dealer,* had encouraged her to run and his paper was very supportive. The *Cleveland Press* again, as in 1920, displayed a sample ballot on its front page with instructions on how to mark it for Allen. Voters were encouraged to vote for her because she was a woman, because she was running on a non-partisan ticket, had the courage of her convictions and put human rights ahead of selfish ends.[9] In case any voters had doubts about a woman as a supreme court judge, they were reminded that even if she were elected there would still be six men on the bench.

The *Lima Times* sounded a sour note, considering her candidacy a "Polyanna" candidacy and a distraction. The editor could not find that she stood for anything and didn't think she would get many votes. Obviously he did not take a woman candidate seriously. Neither did the bar associations; their slate recommended other candidates.[10]

Neither party supported her. The Democratic Party often opposed her because it had two candidates who had entered the party primary. The Republicans asked their women not to support her, but many did anyway.[11]

Papa was in Cleveland, gave her his expert advice, and drew his friends into the campaign. John Barden, Papa's good friend from college days and catcher of his famous curved balls, was persuaded to chair a finance committee but his efforts were hardly needed. He wrote Emir after the campaign was over: "I have to laugh when I think that this campaign was put over by three or four women with a few men sitting at the table looking on and wondering where we would get the money to pay the bills."[12] Actually the women of Ohio contributed very generously to the campaign, and when expense accounts were filed Allen's campaign was by far the most expensive one among the judicial candidates, the money coming mostly from small contributions from individual women.[13]

There were six candidates for the two associate judgeships to be filled. Allen was the only non-partisan candidate in spite of the popular demand for non-partisan judges. In the election, Robert Day, a highly respected lawyer and judge, was the front runner and Allen came in second. The real contest was between Florence Allen and Benson W. Hough, a Republican candidate and popular World War I general. It was thought that Hough was sure to win and it was a surprising upset when Allen was elected by a plurality of 48,000 over Hough, carrying some 30 of the 88 counties,[14] and becoming the first woman judge in a state supreme court. Attorney Edward J. Dempsey, former mayor of Cincinnati, protested issuance of a certificate of election to Allen on grounds that the Nineteenth Amendment gave women the right to vote but not the right to hold office.[15] Several states did prohibit women from holding office,[16] but, although Dempsey's protest was widely publicized, no one joined forces with him and Allen was duly certified.

Allen was pleased that the *women* had won and rejoiced that a step had been taken toward the reform of removing the judiciary from politics. She predicted jubilantly that she was but the forerunner of what was bound to come in every state — women members of the supreme court. She had no comment about the five women who ran for the Ohio legislature, all of whom were defeated.[17]

Men elected to the Ohio Supreme Court receive little publicity, but the election of a woman was a new and remarkable event. Letters and telegrams of congratulation poured in from all over the country. Members of the press wired to ask why she thought she had won and what she thought a woman could accomplish on the bench. Some equated her to Shakespeare's woman lawyer Portia in "The Merchant of Venice," and Allen was hailed as "the Ohio Portia," "the Portia of the Midwest," or "Portia of the Prairies."[18] Allen was happy to be equated to the Shakespearean heroine for she said Portia set a poetically high standard for the woman advocate. In her own speeches, however, Allen more often referred to Deborah, the prophetess of ancient Israel, who sat under a palm tree and all the nations came to her for judgment. Portia is symbolic of mercy; Deborah is symbolic of wisdom. Judge Allen chose Deborah.

An appearance at the Cleveland City Club shortly after the election was a veritable love feast, with tumultuous applause, a standing ovation, and flowers from home-town admirers. The press heaped praises upon her. The *Dayton News* called it a "special triumph" because political experts forecast that she would be a negligible factor in the supreme court race. Several said that sex had played no part in the race and that Allen was elected on her merits. A less glowing commentator looked forward to her term without misgiving since the efficiency of males on the bench was not extraordinarily high.[19]

Allen gave full credit to the sisterhood for her victory and it was credit where credit was due. It seems most unlikely that she could have managed a state-wide campaign without party support and without women. Not only did the women plan appearances, raise money, pay her expenses, promote her locally and probably vote for her, but all the records show an incredible list of women who personally welcomed her, were so proud that she had come, saw that every need was taken care of, and took her into their homes as an honored guest. One correspondent wrote: "You are some pumpkins of a woman in every respect."[20] She was the women's woman. They capitalized on her reforming record, her utterly indefatigable energy, speaking talents, and open friendliness.

It would be a mistake to overrate the influence of the women's organizations in Allen's election. She was the beneficiary of the movement, but she was also exceptionally well-qualified. As the editor of the *Cleveland News* wrote:

> . . . if all women who may seek and attain public office were equal, or nearly equal, to Florence Allen in mental equipment for such service, and had her energy and industry, the most sanguine expectations of women who look for great results from equal suffrage might be realized. . .[21]

Even with exceptional qualifications it is possible and probable that she might never have had the chance to demonstrate them in a state which had been hostile to woman suffrage without the solid support of the women's organizations. In the history of women in politics, the election of Florence Allen to the Ohio Supreme Court in 1922 is one of the every rare examples of the power and possibilities of a united bloc of voting women. In this instance, women performed politically as advocates of suffrage had hoped and expected.

When the United States entered World War I women's organizations widened their purposes to include support of the war effort. After the war ended a new and very important cause emerged — that of maintaining the peace. The Allen family had idealistically supported the war and its goals as articulated by President Wilson. Both sons had volunteered for military service. One had given his life, the other was incurably wounded. What finer tribute could the family make to the sacrifice of its sons and brothers than to join the search for peace?

Allen actively supported the League of Nations until her non-partisan candidacy and position as judge forced her to be silent about such a political issue as the League and to seek new ways to participate in the cause of peace.[22] Ohioan John H. Clarke, Papa's classmate and a good friend of the Allen family, resigned as justice of the United States Supreme Court in 1922 to give active support to the League of Nations which it was impossible to do while on the bench, but Judge Allen could scarcely afford to give up her $8,500 salary to serve a public cause.

Very reluctantly she withdrew from the fight for the League and found a solution for her dilemma by joining a committee on the outlawry of war, of which Salmon O. Levison, a Chicago lawyer, was chairman, and Elizabeth Hauser was a member. The committee believed that the cause of outlawry transcended the League of Nations because it took the position that nowhere — including the League of Nations Covenant — was there a law or a treaty making war illegal. Allen popularized the idea of outlawry of war with the Cleveland League of Women Voters, and it was incorporated in the Cleveland Peace Plan which was presented by Hauser to the national convention of the League in 1922.[23]

Allen began working on a speech on outlawry that would become her most cherished and most frequently delivered speech. It was ready to present to very large audiences in 1923 at the National Convention of the League of Women Voters in Des Moines and the National Convention of the YWCA in Hot Springs, Arkansas. In Des Moines she shared the program with Herbert Hoover,[24] who at the time was enjoying much acclaim for his relief programs in Europe, and with Viscount Robert Cecil, a leader of the English peace movement.

In 1925 she gave the speech at the Conference on Causes and Cure of War, organized by Carrie Chapman Catt. Catt had been profoundly shocked when the United States did not join the League of Nations and set about organizing women for peace much as she had organized them for suffrage.[25] Eleven national women's organizations were invited to attend the conference. Basically Catt did not feel sympathetic toward the movement for outlawry, believing, quite correctly, that it weakened the strength of the movement to join the League of Nations. On the other hand she could not deny Allen's influence in the peace movement and her magnetic speaking talents.[26]

In many ways the peace movement was an extension of the woman's movement of the pre-war world. Many of the former suffrage leaders like Carrie Chapman Catt were in it; many of the social feminist reformers were in it: Jane Addams, Lillian Wald, Florence Kelley, Frances Kellor, and the rank and file of supporters were overwhelmingly women. Allen's speech included many of the ideas of the suffrage movement, clothed in new phrasing.

The speech opened with a reference to the rights specified in the Declaration of Independence:

> We find these truths to be self-evident — that all men are endowed by their Creator with certain inalienable rights, rights that cannot be given away — the right to *life*, liberty and the pursuit of happiness.[27]

The speech recognized women as different from men, more pure, more moral, more concerned with the family:

. . . woman's task is peculiar with regard to the abolition of war. We have to teach the human race that ethical standards can be set up and maintained between nations as well as between individuals. Women have to teach the coming generations that the rules of right and wrong can be applied to every group . . . . Women have to teach the coming race that this thing is not impossible; that law can be substituted for the use of armed force in the settlement of international difficulties.[28]

She called upon her listeners to search the latest books on international law and said "you will look in vain for any case which has held any nation guilty of the crime of making . . . war." Lasting peace will not prevail, she argued, unless nations can be held accountable for the crime of war. The law could be written by treaty, by international conference, or by the League of Nations. Private war between individuals had been outlawed, she said, and the next step in human history is the outlawry of war between nations.[29]

She stirred her audiences to action by saying that Americans must rephrase their slogan that the state can do no wrong to one that the state *shall* do no wrong.[30] She inspired women with the thought that they could do it alone, that they had succeeded in the past in implementing causes and they could do it again for this more important cause.

Accolades of praise for the speech poured in. Church publications picked up her ideas and elaborated upon them. Women's magazines requested publication permission and asked her to write other articles. Women's organizations requested speaking dates. The President of the Ohio State Bar Association wrote to President Coolidge that Allen had an excellent plan for advancing world peace.[31] In Cleveland she was selected as honorary chairmen of the Council for the Prevention of War which was formed by twenty-one women's organizations.

More invitations for speeches came in than one person could possibly fill, and radio helped to span the distances. A radio speech in 1924 from powerful Pittsburgh station KDKA brought great response from all over the midwest, New England, and the southeast. A listener from Eureka, Kansas wrote that "It seemed almost as if God was talking to us through you." Another from Cornwall on Hudson, New York thought the speech "was the best that I have ever heard" and that a woman of Allen's caliber should be president of the United States. Another from Orange, Georgia thought her speech should be heard in every home in the land.[32] People asked for reprints to give their friends or read to their clubs. High school debaters and their coaches, who in 1924 were debating the proposition "The United States should enter the League of Nations" wanted copies.

Allen tailored her speech to fit audiences. In Dayton, for example, she remembered with her listeners their suffrage days, and told them if they longed for the old thrill of working for women, greater days were ahead in the formation of "a permanent sisterhood of women fighting for mankind in a world poisoned by war."[33]

The peace movement was badly fragmented from within over goals and methods and attacked from without by patriotic societies. Antagonisms reached explosive proportions in May 1924 when the Fourth Annual Convention of the Women's International League for Peace and Freedom ended in a near riot. The speakers, including Allen, were sitting on the platform when a noisy altercation erupted on the floor between agitators from the Daughters of 1812 and the pacifists within the League over the so-called "Slacker's Oath," an oath which pledged men to refuse to be drafted or fight and women to refuse to give aid in any war effort. Allen was never a pacifist. As the uproar died down and Allen spoke she said that she did not advocate the abolition of defensive war nor the abolition of wars of liberation like the American Revolution. The complexion of the convention was radical, however, and went on record for the pacifist viewpoint of being opposed to all wars and all preparation for war. Allen spoke in opposition to these resolutions,[34] and was favorably commended by several Ohio newspapers for her moderate position.

Two weeks later Allen courageously led a peace parade in Cleveland sponsored by the Women's Council for the Prevention of War. The Chamber of Commerce and the American Legion claimed that it was inspired by socialist and communist agents and many organizations withdrew their support. As luck would have it, heavy thundershowers on the scheduled day discouraged many participants. Nevertheless, with Marie Wing as marshall on a "fine pancing horse," Allen led about 3,600 women through the streets of Cleveland in defiance of the opposition and the weather.[35] In 1925 the women's peace movement was further fragmented when the DAR and the American Legion Auxiliary organized the Women's Patriotic Conference.[36]

While the peace movement was beset by disunity, the majority of Americans were losing interest in the cause, believing that we had achieved isolation from Europe. The United States entered into very few treaties in the twenties, and denied both the League of Nations and the World Court. A few treaties among Europeans had been signed declaring wars of aggression a crime, and in 1928 leaders of the United States and France initiated the Kellogg-Briand Pact which renounced war as an instrument of national policy and 63 nations signed it. It was criticized as being unrealistic and spineless, but it appealed to idealistic Americans in the peace movement and passed the Senate almost unanimously.[37]

Allen made many speeches praising and promoting acceptance of the Kellogg-Briand Pact. She considered it the first declaration of the great nations that the state had no more right to kill, except in self defense, than the individual. She considered it a victory for democracy.

Many opportunities continued to come to her to speak or write for peace. War, she wrote, brutalizes the participants, results in social disintegration, and demoralizes the family. She often referred to a young man she knew (undoubtedly her brother Jack) who after his return from war, ill of the sickness from which he died, said to his mother, "All that you have taught me the world says is not so." Allen said that soldiers were praised for their courage, but that it was the courage of military discipline and fear, not the courage of self control. Society had been horrified, she said, by the crimes against property and fellow human beings committed by returning soldiers. Criminality among soldiers was to be expected, for "our armies, as all armies, establish an intensive culture of brutality." The brutality permeates society to the point where even children play at killing each other,. She thought it would take fifty years for the brutalizing effects of World War I to wear off.[38]

The Protestant ministry was not open to women, but Florence Allen spoke frequently from the pulpit to large church congregations on the responsibilities of Christians to keep the peace, imploring her listeners to trust their spiritual forces, to have the will to peace. She told them that we were spending eighty percent of our national budget on armaments because we are afraid, afraid of not being armed more than other nations. A man who spent eighty percent of his family budget on burglar alarms would be considered a weak specimen of humanity. We must dare to cease arming, we must dare to trust convenants of peace, for war does not end war but is only the prolific breeder of more war.[39]

In 1930 she made a series of radio addresses on the subject of disarmament. Wars, she said, are made by governments not by people, and

> When the fathers and mothers of this country demand that the revenues of the country be expended upon the school children, upon the roads, upon public health . . . then the great burden of taxpaying for useless [armaments] will be lifted, the black threat of war will be dissipated like the fog before the sun, and we shall begin to realize the perfectly feasible dream of the prophet that "nation shall not lift up sword against nation, neither shall they learn war any more."[40]

When an international disarmament convention was held in Geneva in 1932 women's organizations demanded that a woman be included in the U.S. delegation. The State Department announced that it would consider such an appointment if the organizations agreed upon a delegate. The officers of thirty national women's groups agreed upon Florence Allen, but the administration refused to appoint her because she was at the time participating in a political campaign as a Democrat.[41]

Allen's speaking and writing style had reached full maturity by the end of the twenties, forged in the cause of woman suffrage and refined in the cause of peace. Her messages were clearly and directly stated. She identified with her audiences through frequent use of personal pronouns,

71

intimating that "I" want to talk with "you" so that "we" may think together about something of concern to "us." Biblical quotations, exactly quoted with chapter and verse, lent a ministerial aura. In men's clothing Florence Allen might have been a magnificently inspiring minister of the word of God. Favorite quotations were from the Old Testament prophets, lamenting the decline of the Hebrew nation and beseeching its members to follow in the ways of the Lord. Examples from ancient history and the English and American past were woven skillfully into the fabric to increase the significance and interest of the topic being discussed. Small parables from daily life added relevance and liveliness.

Allen was at her best in an inspirational call to action, with the logical conviction that we should do it, the moral commitment that we must do it, and the optimism that we can do it. Many of her subjects were potentially very dull: keeping the peace, the fulfillment of the ideals of our forefathers, the ethics of law, the political responsibility of women. But in Allen's hands the topics became living subjects, personally important to every listener. A public address by Judge Allen was like a heart-to-heart talk, an uplifting, emotional experience. The sincerity of her message was beyond doubt. She loved public speaking and she did it superbly. She thought of it as her contribution to the advancement of worthy causes and the promotion of public good. Oratory was generally considered a masculine art, but few men equalled her in force and ability.

FOOTNOTES

[1] **Diary, May 18, 23, 1922 records talks with Young and Baker.** *Columbus Dispatch,* November 12, 1922, noted that the movement started with the Cleveland Business Women's Club, Allen papers, LC, container 6. *To Do Justly,* p. 64.

[2] The *Salt Lake Telegram,* January 7, 1923, second section, p. 1, from an account of the campaign written by Rebhan. Allen papers, WRHS, container 26, folder 7.

[3] From campaign material in Allen papers, WRHS, container 14, folder 5. Some of the Florence Allen clubs charged $1 to belong.

[4] *Norwalk Reflector Herald,* September 20 1922, Allen papers, WRHS, container 26, folder 6. It is interesting to note that in the election Allen came in first among the candidates in Huron County.

[5] Allen papers, WRHS, container 14, folder 5.

[6] Speeches from 1922 campaign in Allen papers, WRHS, container 15, folder 1.

[7] The *Salt Lake Telegram, op. cit.*

[8] From newspaper clipping in Allen papers, WRHS, container 26, folder 6.

[9] *Cleveland Press,* October 23, 1922, p. 2.

[10] *Lima Times,* October 29, 1922, from Allen papers, LC, container 6. The bar slate recommended Judge Matthews and Judge Day.

[11] According to Lemons, pp. 104-105, two prominent women on the state Republican Committee resigned rather than stop working for Allen.

[12] John Barden to Emir Allen, November 10, 1922, Allen papers, WRHS, container 6, folder 2.

[13] Noted in *Marion Tribune,* November 17, 1922, and many other newspapers. Allen papers, LC, container 6. The amount was $5,714.00. Other candidates spent from $1,000 to $1,500.

[14] Allen papers, WRHS, container 14, folder 5. She came in first in Ashland, Ashtabula, Geauga, Holmes, Huron, Lake, Lorain, Mahoning, Medina, Ottawa, Portage, Richland, Summit and Trumbull counties. In the same election Mary Grossman was elected judge of the scandal-ridden Cleveland Municipal Court and served for many years.

[15] *Marion Tribune, op. cit.*

[16] Iowa did not amend its constitution to permit women to hold office until 1926, and Oklahoma did not permit it until 1942. Lemons, p. 68-69.

[17] *Dayton News,* editorial, November 25, 1922, Allen papers, LC, container 6.

[18] *McCalls Magazine,* May, 1923, referred to her as "the Ohio Portia," Allen papers, WRHS, container 26, folder 7.

[19] From newspaper clippings, Allen papers, WRHS, container 6, folder 2.

[20] Letter from Minnie M. Serreys, Allen papers, WRHS, container 6, folder 2.

[21] *Cleveland News,* September 6, 1920, Allen papers, WRHS, container 26, folder 4.

[22] Letter of Allen to Professor Manley O. Hudson, June 6, 1923, explaining her refusal to make a statement about the League of Nations, Allen papers, WRHS, container 6, folder 2.

[23] Abbott, p. 87.

[24] There was such an overflow audience that they had to make their speeches twice. *To Do Justly,* p. 74.

[25] Mary Gray Peck, *Carrie Chapman Catt, A Biography,* New York: H. W. Wilson Co., 1944, p. 6.

[26] See *To Do Justly,* p. 76.

[27] The speech as given for the Conference on the Causes and Cure of War is reprinted in *To Do Justly*, pp. 153-162.

[28] *Ibid.*, pp 154-155.

[29] *Ibid.*, pp. 157-159.

[30] *Ibid.*, p. 161.

[31] Letters in Allen papers, WRHS, container 6, folder 2.

[32] *Ibid.*

[33] Paraphrased from Dayton speech reprinted in *The Herald of Gospel Liberty*, Allen papers, WRHS, container 6, folder 2.

[34] Account of the convention from the *Washington Post, May 4, 1924, Allen papers, WRHS, container 26, folder 8. Jane Addams was the leading pacifist.*

[35] *Abbott, p. 91.*

[36] *Lemons, p. 123; Breckinridge, p. 86.*

[37] *John A. Garraty, A Short History of the American Nation*, Third Edition, New York: Harper and Row, 1974, p. 452.

[38] Ideas from "Because Wars Unleash Demoralizing Instincts" by Florence E. Allen in Rose Young, Ed., *Why Wars Must Cease*, New York: Macmillan, 1935, pp. 99-199.

[39] Allen papers, WRHS, container 15, folder 1.

[40] *Ibid.*

[41] The women then proposed Dr. Mary Wooley, President of Mt. Holyoke, and she was included in the delegation.

Chapter 6

LURE OF POLITICS

Judge Allen took her judicial responsibilities seriously, as the guardian of the laws and ethics of American society. But she would have preferred to be a legislator and help to make laws instead of applying and interpreting them after they were made. She also thought she would be able to do more to advance the cause of peace as a legislator than as a judge.[1] She particularly liked the idea of being in the Senate because it dealt with international matters — matters in which women had had no voice. During 1925 she had "talked Senate" with Gongwer, Young, Clarke, and many others in the Democratic Party, with women friends, and, most of all, with Papa. They had not discouraged her.[2]

Atlee Pomerene had been the leading senatorial figure in the Democratic party for many years, but he had been defeated in 1922. Pomerene's defeat had been welcomed and promoted by suffragists for he had been a feisty opponent of woman suffrage, maintaining that the voters of Ohio had repeatedly voted against woman suffrage and it was his duty to reflect the will of his constituents.[3]

In February 1926 Pomerene announced that he would not be a candidate for the Senate. Allen immediately announced her intention to run in the primary elections and the Democratic party endorsed her. Newton D. Baker wrote the day following her announcement that he didn't know what her chance of success would be, but he thought she should resign from the Supreme Court before conducting a campaign.[4] She decided not to resign, probably feeling that she couldn't risk the gamble.

Besides her judicial duties at that time of year,[5] her schedule was loaded with peace talks, many of them requiring considerable travel. She added campaign speeches, sometimes staying up until the unheard of hour of four in the morning to read briefs and arriving at her office at seven. Fortunately she liked chicken and peas, and often noted in her diary the excellence of their preparation at dinners she attended.

When the Democrats gathered in Columbus in June it was obvious that party members hoped Pomerene would reconsider and run for the Senate. It was believed that if Pomerene were elected he would be a very promising presidential prospect in 1928. When he entered the dining room the applause for him was tumultuous. Allen and the other candidates were politely applauded, but it was evident that the party wanted Pomerene.[6]

75

Great pressure was put on Pomerene to run and before the meeting was over he had agreed. Clearly he was a more promising candidate than a woman, for no woman had succeeded in being elected to the Senate. Pomerene had been in politics since 1887, was Princeton educated, and had been receiving nationwide publicity as a special prosecutor in the Teapot Dome investigation. Democrats hoped that the other candidates would withdraw from the primary and that he would run uncontested. Two candidates did withdraw, but Allen did not. The *Plain Dealer* commented editorially that, "Even Miss Allen cannot fail to see that an uncontested nomination for Pomerene would be the best augary of a party victory in November. Were she to withdraw now she would put the party under an obligation which she cannot [otherwise] claim."[7]

The decision as to whether to continue her candidacy was a difficult one. Many advised her to withdraw, and the party withdrew its endorsement. Her women friends begged her to continue; they wanted her to beat Pomerene. She decided to continue.

Again the campaign was supported mainly by women, with Rebhan as manager. Rebhan enrolled 2,000 members in Florence Allen clubs. "Flying squadrons" of them circulated the state. In Columbus, Dayton, Cleveland, and other cities, women divided the cities into wards, precincts, and blocks and made house to house visitations. Women students of the Ohio State University Law School were among the most eager workers. A speaker's bureau was organized and called all sorts of organizations for permission to speak, at homecomings, picnics, anywhere. The week before election ten autos carrying two women each went to localities where Allen hadn't been able to speak and stayed for five or six days at their own expense.[8]

Most of Allen's campaign speeches emphasized the issue of peace. "Why should a woman be elected to the Senate?" she asked, answering that it was the branch of government that along with the president made treaties. There is much truth in the statement, she said, that old men make wars and young men fight them. Old men in foreign offices covet this or that colony, this or that oil field, this or that market, and the world race begins. The young men who fight wars cannot sit in the foreign office because they are too young, and so because of circumstances over which they have no control the young, the flower of the race, are sent to war. In war the heart of the mother is torn, she suffers all her son's suffering, she dies a double death in the death of her son. But now, she argued, there are women old enough, well trained and capable, who could and would represent the women and the boys in war questions better than some men and these women are needed in the Senate.[9]

Judging from audience questions, the public was more interested in prohibition than peace. Allen took a firm stand on prohibition; she believed in retaining the Volstead Act and enforcing it. The worth of prohibition, she believed, had not been tested because it had not been enforced.

Pomerene's stand on prohibition was equally clear. He opposed it on grounds that the people of Ohio had never voted for it and he wished to reflect the will of his constituents. There was ample proof that prohibition was not popular. A newspaper poll conducted in March 1926 showed that in the state of Ohio 15,761 respondents favored prohibition, 51,722 favored repeal, and 69,023 favored some modification.[10] Even rural communities, where Allen might have polled well, wanted to be rid of the Volstead Act because they disliked bootleggers.

One of the notable features of Allen's campaign was the strong support she received from the Railroad Brotherhoods, an organization which had been observing her liberal stand on labor cases in the supreme court. In the summer of 1926 the Brotherhoods published half a million copies of a special edition of their official organ, *Labor,* for distribution by Allen's campaign workers. "Labor is not supporting Judge Florence Allen for the Senate because she is a woman . . . ," it said. "Labor is supporting Judge Allen because she is comparably the best and biggest 'man' available for the job. In brains, character and experience, she towers head and shoulders above the field." Pomerene was characterized as "a bitter, vindictive enemy of the men and women who work."[11]

Allen also acquired some new male support. Probably atypical, but insightful, was the conversion of Professor C.B. Gohdes of Capital University, whose testimony appeared in Allen's campaign literature. Gohdes admitted that he had opposed the Nineteenth Amendment on the grounds that woman's contribution to society is as wife and mother and the interference with woman's functioning in the home sphere would spell social disaster. But then he heard Allen speak and was convinced that there are "exceptionally endowed, large-horizoned women" whose best contribution to society is in the field of political service. He found the "spiritual force" of her character so profound and her person so completely absorbed in the cause of peace that she had foregone the prerogative of wifehood and motherhood and instead chose to "mother in her ardent soul the war stricken, heart-broken, hungry millions of the world!"[12]

Pomerene did little campaigning, leaving it mostly to his friends. Instead he concentrated on his work in the Teapot Dome case which brought him much favorable publicity. Rebhan scheduled as many speeches as Florence could possibly make. It was essential to reach both men and women voters because it was necessary to declare one's party in the primary elections and a large non-partisan vote from women would not be expected. Allen was frequently "awfully tired."[13] When the votes came in Pomerene had won by a small margin. Allen thanked her campaign workers and took the train to New York to be with Bert.

In 1926 three women were elected to Congress, but no women were even nominated for the Senate. Women all over the country focused their attention on Allen's candidacy, according to her friend Sophonisba Breckinridge, who wrote that Judge Allen's defeat was more than the failure of an individual candidate and that "it was a reverse in a cause which to many women [she] embodied."[14]

Although Allen considered her decision to run for the Senate in 1926 "a grave political mistake,"[15] she might have been somewhat consoled by the opinions of friends that she had, all things considered, run very well against Pomerene.[16] Indeed, the Democratic Party had possibly made a mistake in transferring its support form Allen to Pomerene. Pomerene was defeated in the November elections by the Republican candidate. Allen's influence on the votes of women and labor might have been sufficient to bring the position back to the Democrats.

Part of the problem was that the emotional content had been washed out of the peace issue by eight years of peace and the feeling of security from European turmoil created by the policy of isolation. People had forgotten their bereavements, and perhaps did not want to be reminded. Florence Allen was a reminder. Not only did she recall the war of the past, but she also recalled the morality of the past. She was beginning to look like a figure of the past, for in the days of short hair and skirts and no bosoms Allen still wore long hair piled on top of her head, skirts well below the knees, and her figure was becoming rotund.[17]

When Allen took up her supreme court duties in January, 1923 she moved to Columbus and bought a big old house near the court house. Mamma and Papa came to live with her and the house became headquarters for the Allen family. Mamma continued her work with the Congress of Mothers and for many years was chairman of the Committee on Monogamous Marriage. Originally formed "to stem the advancing tide of sex degeneracy," it had evolved into a committee on sex education for parents. Mrs. Allen believed the responsibility rested squarely on parents to teach their children "to abhor premature sex experience in word, deed, and imagination." She praised the motives of the new birth control movement, but thought contraceptives reduced sex association to a physical basis and that it was better to appeal to men to exercise self control in the use of the power of procreation.[18] Her work for the committee ended as she became absorbed in the illness of her veteran son and more interested in the peace movement. Her loyalty to Smith College never abated. She marched proudly with her class in its fiftieth reunion. She made yearly contributions to Smith and wished she had much more to give because she felt it to be "a great stabilizing force in our tottering civilization."[19] Mamma and Papa celebrated their fiftieth wedding anniversary in 1927, and Florence kept their anniversary picture in a prominent place on her desk for years after.

Papa and Florence were very close. They often walked or talked or had lunch together and Papa's advice on politics was ubiquitous. He often accompanied her to her chambers, to court, or to speeches and took great pride in her achievements.

Brother Jack returned from the army hospital in Europe in 1919, but he was not well. He married Ruth Clark from Westerville, near Columbus, and they had a daughter, Corinne, whom Aunt Florence called Keenie. Home for Jack, Ruth and Keenie was the house in Columbus. Doctors advised from the beginning that Jack was seriously ill, but the causes were impossible to define. Whether it was the result of the trauma of his war experience, or, as his mother believed, a reverse reaction to simultaneous smallpox and measles vaccines administered in officers training camp which progressively damaged his brain tissues,[20] no one knew. He reviewed his law books but never took the bar exams. He moved about constantly, sometimes leaving no word of his whereabouts. Florence introduced him to friends who might give him a job, but nothing came of it. His finances were a problem, relieved by help from Florence and Papa. After five years of tribulation, the end for Jack came quickly in 1924 when he died of blood poisoning after a trifling injury. Florence sadly gathered his things and gave them to Ruth,[21] counting Jack as another war victim in her family.

Jack's death was indeed a sobering experience for the family. Emir's death in France in 1918 had been a great tragedy, but it was heroic, sacrificial and removed from daily living. Jack's death was painfully drawn out and disturbingly intimate. More than that, through cruel fate, the Allen family had lost its male leadership. There was no male of the quality of Jacob Tuckerman or Clarence Emir Allen — in fact no male at all — to carry the tradition of the family. Would a daughter take up the mantle of leadership?[22] Clearly Papa envisioned his daughter Florence in a leadership role in politics and public service, a role in keeping with the family tradition.

During Jack's illness Ruth and little Keenie had returned to Ruth's family home in Waterville. Florence visited Ruth frequently, lending her sympathetic interest and moral support. It was Keenie who captured Aunt Florence's heart. She took Keenie gifts and toys and played dolls and trains with her. She made it a point to go to school programs to hear Keenie speak her pieces. She took Keenie to visit Santa Claus and treated her often to ice cream and rides. On trips she sent her postcards and brought her souvenirs. Aunt Florence did all the things a doting aunt, or a father, might do. A picture of Keenie sitting with Aunt Florence while the latter read her a story was frequently used in the 1926 campaign.

Sister Esther, now a single parent, and her young son Emir came to live with Florence in 1927 when Esther took a position as Dean of Women at Ohio State. Esther and Florence built an enduring mutual support rela-

79

tionship. Helen and her husband Frank Shockey were in California and were having difficulty establishing themselves. Papa sent money for Frank to further his education and Florence subsidized Helen to do scholarly research for a book on the peace movement Florence planned to write. Helen plunged into research on the history of private warfare and its eradication and sent folios of her writings for Florence to use, but somehow the book never materialized.[23] Elizabeth (Weebie) and her husband Harry Sloane were permanently and comfortably settled in San Diego, but they were never far from the family's thoughts.

Susan Rebhan entered Ohio State University Law School when Florence moved to Columbus and lived with the Allens. She served as Judge Allen's secretary. Susan apparently found time to study in the big household, for in 1926 she passed the Ohio bar exams at the head of the group of 276 with a grade of 95.5%; the second in rank had a 92.5%.[24]

Frances Parkinson Keyes visited the Allen home in Columbus and described it for readers of *Better Homes and Gardens* in 1928. She found Judge Allen the personification of strength — strength of mind, strength of body, strength of character, strength of purpose, and her home utterly suitable for her character — a substantial dwelling, solid, square and brick. The furniture was carved, massive, and handsome, with paintings of mountain scenery on the walls. The living room was dominated by a fine piano. Dinner was served to the assembled family, including Keenie and Mrs. Keyes, with white-haired Mr. Allen presiding at the head of the table. After grace the food was rolled in on a tea wagon by a maid[25] and Mr. Allen served. The food, too, was substantial: roast lamb, mashed potatoes, brussel sprouts, and apple pie with cheese. Mrs. Keyes was barely aware of the food because the conversation was so fascinating, ranging from current events and politics to good literature and European travel. After dinner Mrs. Keyes and Florence adjourned to the bedroom to talk, where there was a huge carved bedstead and two comfortable chairs in front of the open fireplace.[26]

Friendship between Florence and Lois Tuckerman continued. Lois married DeLo Mook in 1923. DeLo was a graduate of Harvard Law School and member of a Cleveland law firm. He fitted in very well with the Tuckerman and Allen families. He was active in boy scouting and civic activities; several times he directed Cleveland's celebrations of Independence Day.[27] For Lois it was the beginning of a long and happy devotion to the cult of true womanhood.[28] She adored her husband and gave first priority to his comfort and his career. He was her hero; his companionship was her privilege. DeLo had three children, a ready-made family that Lois was happy to nurture as a wise and loving counsellor. Nevertheless, she was a person in her own right, interested and active in the world outside her family.[29] Lois was the kind of mother Judge Allen recommended.

During her 1922 campaign Allen bought a car to expedite her travels around the state and promptly personified it as Gypsy. Gypsy was a

Model T Ford and was a full-fledged member of the family. In its youth Gypsy was "going strong" and "leaped up hills." It had problems endemic to automobiles: it ran out of gas, had flat tires chronically, and the radiator froze in winter. Whether Florence ever remembered to fill the gas tank on schedule is unknown, but she did remember in due time to carry a tire iron and a key to the spare. Ohio mud was a seasonal threat to any car, but Gypsy always prevailed over it, getting her driver to state-wide speeches and meetings on time. In its old age it sometimes had to be rolled down hill to start, but it was never unloved, and Columbus neighbors knew Florence Allen coming or going by the chug-chugging of her Model T.

During her years in Columbus she continued to regard Cleveland as home and voted there. She often went to Cleveland for meetings or speaking engagements. She was a featured speaker, for example, at the big Cleveland Exposition in March, 1926. She often had lunch or dinner at the Hollenden Hotel, a favorite gathering place for Cleveland politicians. Her legal residence in Cleveland was an apartment which she and Susan maintained. They sometimes visited Mary Pierce, a distant cousin of Florence, who attended Columbia Teachers College and then came to Cleveland as a teacher and eventually director of Park School, a private school started by a group of mothers who wanted progressive education for their children. Mary lived in a house in Shaker Heights.

In her early days in Cleveland Allen became a confirmed hiker. She walked to her office every day, and on weekends, clad in full knickers and men's hiking shoes, she often took fifteen or twenty mile hikes to Cleveland's eastern suburbs and beyond. She was so fond of the country that as soon as she could afford it she bought sixteen acres of gullies and woods, including an abandoned shack, in Lake County. During the Columbus years she returned frequently to Cleveland; the visit always included a hike to the shack. Small improvements were made; the roof was repaired so the interior provided shelter. Florence kept the weeds down with a scythe and cleared the brush and wild grapevines from the trees.

Hiking was for pleasure and physical fitness, but perhaps she had a further motive, consciously or unconsciously, since she was a very purposeful woman. The question of physical endurance was a bug-a-boo in the advancement of women. In the nineteenth century it had been used as an excuse to exclude women from higher education on the assumption that the rigors of college life would be too much for their frail bodies. In the early twentieth century frailty was used as an excuse to prohibit them from equality in employment. Allen proved by her example that her physical stamina was not less than that of most men.

In spite of, or perhaps because of her exercise, Allen suffered from a great many aches and pains. Sore feet, aching muscles, and intermittent severe headaches tormented her and pills brought no relief. Finally she discovered osteopathy for her ailments, liked it and went for treatments often.

Drs. Helen and Mary Giddings, osteopathic physicians in Cleveland, not only treated her ailments successfully, but became friends and active political supporters. In Columbus she relied on Dr. Scott to keep her in shape. When she traveled to an unfamiliar town she sought an osteopath and judged the town poorly if she did not find one. She enthusiastically recommended osteopathy to her friends, and some took her advice, including Ruth Bryan Owen.[30]

Allen had a network of acquaintances with Ohio women as a result of her suffrage work and political campaigns. In the twenties the network expanded to include women from all states. She attended innumerable conventions of the NFBPWC, the League of Women Voters, the NAWL, the YWCA and other women's organizations, shuttling to Chicago, St. Louis, Kansas City, Minneapolis, Detroit, Boston, New York or Washington at a pace that would have undone an ordinary person. Her attendance was not passive, for she always served on committees and executive boards or as a speaker. Public speeches introduced her to an even wider audience, college women,[31] church groups and a variety of others. Thousands of women knew Florence Allen, as well as a fair number of men through the bar associations in which she was also active.

Honoria were not customary, but travel expenses were often paid for her trips. She often managed to extend the trips to visit relatives in California or friends in New York, Washington, or New England. Sight seeing was a fringe benefit of the traveling of which she never failed to take advantage. The court was in recess from mid-June to the end of September, freeing her schedule for traveling. When court was in session, judges were on their own after discussions and assignments to study briefs and write opinions. Allen spent so much time on trains that her berth doubled as a study where she could work without interruption.

Her horizons expanded to include western Europe. In 1923 she went to England as a delegate of the NFBPWC to the International Council of Women in London. Thereafter she spent some time in Geneva studying the functioning of the League of Nations. Between sessions she did some mountain climbing. The Alps, however, never replaced her affection for the mountains of her childhood.

A more memorable trip was one to England in 1924 with Papa and Susan to attend a joint convention of the American, Canadian, and British bar associations. The trip started auspiciously for there was a gym and a vibrator on the ship for exercise, and a piano in the ship's lounge where she played Schumann to the delight of passengers. In connection with the bar meetings there was a visit to Old Bailey to watch the revered English court in action. When Florence entered she was given the customary "posy," a custom which had arisen centuries before when the neighborhood was full of foul odors and the posy was needed to cover the stench.[32] The case was one of arson and Allen was surprised to note that there were no objections during the trial, which moved along with speed unheard of in America. Afterward she went to luncheon with the Lord Sheriff and evaluated the English food as "swell."[33] On another day she returned to Old Bailey to hear a murder case and was surprised that it took the jury only four minutes to arrive at its verdict.

She also had lunch and went to a garden party at Lady Nancy Astor's home and met and talked with several English politicians. Lady Astor was the first woman to be in the House of Commons, having inherited the seat in 1919 from her husband when he moved to the House of Lords. Allen spoke at the American Club and had lunch with the English women barristers. She discussed outlawry with people in the peace movement and went to hear Lord Cecil lecture in Toynbee Hall.

For Papa and Florence a special pleasure was going to the British Museum to see the Greek relics, the Elgin Marbles. Later they rented a car and visited many of England's places of historic interest, and after that to Holland for a peace meeting.

In an effort to reach a wider audience for the peace movement Allen explored the possibility of writing magazine articles. *McCalls, Good Housekeeping, New Republic, Atlantic Monthly*[34] and others were considered good possibilities. Bertha Miller acted as her editor and agent. Bert had remained in New York after graduating from NYU, but distance was no deterrent to the lifelong friendship between Florence and Bert. The publishing effort necessitated constant telephone calls and wires, sometimes every day, as they explored the vagaries of publishing. Occasionally Florence went to Westerly to work on articles where Bert would be close by. She carried the articles with her everywhere in case there would be spare moments to work on them. Editors seemed to be more interested in articles on the remarkable career of Florence Allen than in articles on peace.

Florence's weight problem distressed her greatly and when she bought new scales in 1925 she recorded that she weighed 223 1/2.[35] She had continued her exercises faithfully in addition to long walks and hikes. She bought a rowing machine and did Wallace exercises to victrola records. But the weight persisted. She began to diet, limiting herself for days at a time to nothing but fruit, apples or oranges. Gradually the weight went down but at great sacrifice to one who enjoyed food so much. Lunches which she might in former times have regarded as swell now seemed to be "too starchy."

She continued to play the piano and sometimes played duos with Esther. Papa listened attentively and said he got a good musical education from his daughters.[36] She was an inveterate reader of a broad range of literature. She found no book more worth reading than the Bible for beauty of phrasing and elevation of ideas. On an ordinary evening at home she could find pleasure in reading Blackstone and Keats; on a dull Sunday she might memorize as many as eight sonnets. And during her Columbus years she found a new joy in reading — detective stories.

Short hair became the vogue in the early twenties, but Florence didn't have her hair bobbed until 1929. The cutting caused her considerable anguish, for her classic hair style was to her a mark of dignified womanhood. The first cut she found quite unsatisfactory and unbecoming, but she soon found someone who could give her a modish cut, short and a little soft around her face and shingled in back as was the vogue of a "boyish bob." Everywhere she went her hair became a topic of animated conversation, and one of her fellow judges told her she looked like a football player.[37] Nevertheless, it was a practical style, properly fashionable and appropriate for her professional and personal appearance. The news services did not let the short hair go unnoticed. The *Franklin Chronicle* noted it as "live news in the drab existence on Ohio democracy," and surmised that she was going to run again for the Senate.[38] She thought about it, but she didn't do it.

Florence Allen firmly believed that the vote had liberated women and made them equal to men. All they had to do was seize the opportunity. Superficially in the nineteen twenties it appeared that women had been somewhat liberated. They put on more comfortable clothes, laid aside their corsets, bobbed their hair, talked about sex and other subjects formerly taboo, joined the men in saloons, now called speakeasies, and laughed at the Victorian morality of their mothers and grandmothers. Much of their conduct tarnished the image of women as morally superior to men. Role models were more likely to be found on the movie screen than on the public speaking platform. The idealism of prewar women was eroded by materialism as increasing consumer products and their advertising were designed to appeal especially to women.[39]

With the passage of the Nineteenth Amendment the women's movement had achieved the goal which for more than ten years it had focused on, and soon became fragmented. The NAWSA, which had had a membership of around two million [40] was replaced by the League of Women Voters which only a small percentage of NAWSA members joined. The Leagues' purpose was education, not political action. The National Woman's Party continued, but was small. In 1921 it introduced the Equal Rights Amendment in Congress, but the overwhelming majority of women and women's organizations did not want the ERA because they favored protective legislation for women.[41] Most women did not want a separate party, and, like Allen, affirmed that they wanted to work with the established parties. The parties offered small rewards; Harriet Taylor Upton, for example, was appointed to the Republican National Committee.

The multitude of women's organizations continued to flourish but their expectations and the goals of their members began to change. Aside from suffrage, most of them had never pushed for women's rights per se, but for reforms that were within women's traditional sphere such as better education, better care for mothers and children, pure food and drugs, reforms in morals and urban affairs.[42] The peace movement absorbed some of the most active and dedicated women.

A few of the reforms that women stood for in the teens and expected the liberation of suffrage to bring about succeeded, but many failed. The federal government did establish the Women's Bureau in the Department or Labor to monitor enforcement of protective legislation as a result of the efforts of women's organizations. The long struggle to bring minimum wage laws for women had succeeded in seventeen states by 1923, but they were declared unconstitutional by the U.S. Supreme Court.[43] Women's organizations worked very hard for the Sheppard-Towner Maternity and Infant Protection Act and finally achieved its passage but it was never implemented. A child labor amendment failed completely.[44] Legislators were indifferent or hostile to social reforms. Welfare measures that in the teens were thought to be motivated by womanly compassion were labelled Bolshevik or socialist in the conservative twenties. Some thought of Judge Allen as a "red."[45]

After the mid-twenties women's interests in social causes declined rapidly, and they turned to self-fulfillment and personal pleasures. Women's clubs which had attracted their members with educational speeches and inspired them to act for worthy causes now found them more interested in lunch or bridge or fashion shows. Clubs with clubhouses where members could swim, or simply enjoy themselves attracted younger women.[46] The mammoth General Federation of Women's Clubs which had supported many reforms began to return to purely literary programs.[47]

Women were not voting in large numbers or using the vote to their advantage; they weren't pressing for public office. Most women office holders were widows or daughter of deceased office holders. The women's vote was not a cohesive bloc in national politics. Overall woman suffrage did not bring the social and political reforms that were anticipated, and politics in the twenties were as sordid as any decade in history.

More women were working, but relatively fewer were entering the professions, except for the traditional ones of teaching and nursing. Careers had lost the fascination that they had for Allen's generation of college women,[48] and, as Florence Allen told women, "the world demands more of the business and professional woman that it does of a business or professional man."[49] Men's wages far exceeded women's and the gap was not narrowing. Sex was fashionable, marriage was in vogue.[50] The number of unmarried women was declining and the pressure to marry increased as social events were arranged more for couples than individuals.

By 1920 most law schools admitted women, several having done so during the war, Harvard and Columbia being the most important holdouts. Women were not entering in large numbers; men were entering in ever increasing numbers. A survey conducted in 1920 showed that less than one half of the women admitted to the bar were practicing law. The first reason given for not practicing was that the difficulties and discouragements met in entering the field were too great, that they met with considerable prejudice. Other reasons for not practicing were the low financial returns, timidity and lack of confidence, and marriage.[51]

How one woman felt about her profession was written in an article entitled "I Gave Up My Law Books for a Cook Book," in *American Magazine* in 1927. After ten successful years in private law practice, the author abandoned her career for the womanly sphere of homemaking. "He has his job and I have mine," she wrote. Her husband took over completely the earning of the daily bread and she gave him absolute freedom from the petty annoyances of the home. She found her reward in her husband's love, his good disposition, and his successful career.[52] The declining precentages of women in professional schools indicated that many preferred the private sphere of domesticity, although the figures are clouded by the fact that many schools placed quotas on the number of women admitted.

Florence Allen saw the home in a very idealistic light, not as a place where the wife sought self gratification or catered to the comfort and career of her husband, but as a place where mother and father worked together to raise children. "The purpose of the American home was and should be the building of American character," she wrote in 1928. Modern life in some ways threatens the home, and "it is the task of both parents to teach the old spiritual principles which were taught by our forefathers and our foremothers in the early American families if the American home is to survive in its integrity." The home itself is not safe unless the community is a fit place in which children may live. "The woman who sits in her own home," Allen warned, "and fails to vote and fails to do jury duty and fails to know for whom she is voting and what she is voting on, and fails to demand between elections that government do the thing it was created to do, helps to subvert the American home."[53] By and large, women of the twenties were not heeding Allen's advice. The idea of the educated and socially conscious mother to which Corinne and Florence Allen were so devoted was eroding and women were neither liberating themselves or reforming society.[54]

Allen's term as supreme court judge expired in 1928 and she ran for re-election. Most of the responsibility went to campaign manager Rebhan.

Support was easy to find for by this time Allen was well known and admired. Her campaign was non-partisan and avoided controversial political issues. She could berate both parties for supporting candidates for judicial offices that were supposed to be non-partisan. She continued to stand for reforms in the courts, but the main thrust of the campaign was that the candidate was an able judge and great citizen.[55]

She took special pains to speak at DAR meetings. The DAR had been critical of her "socialistic" leanings and her support of the Kellogg-Briand Pact, but the members seemed willing to forgive one of their own for her digressions and were pleased that she found more time for them than she had in previous campaigns. The Railway Labor Organizations supported her on the basis of her decisions favorable to labor in cases concerning safety regulations and strikes.[56]

The NAACP supported her, partly because she was the only candidate who was a member of their organization, and partly because of her judicial decisions, one stating that it was lawful for a board of education to prohibit showing "The Birth of a Nation" because of its racism and two others opposing segregation of schools.[57] Ministers and religious publications supported her on the grounds of her high morality and some because they thought "every gambler and bootlegger in the state is trying to defeat her."[58] To keep campaigners bubbling Rebhan supplied them with a series of mimeographed bulletins, "Talking Tips for Florence Allen." The literature recalled, among other things, that she was the granddaughter of Jacob Tuckerman, principal of New Lyme Institute, and the daughter of Clarence Emir Allen, a former teacher at Western Reserve College.

Allen spent all of July and August campaigning, traveling by slow stages in her own car. She always enjoyed campaigning and never thought of it as work. "It is vivifying," she said "to meet the people, to talk with them face to face, look them in the eye."[59] Sometimes, she said, it is more wonderful to make a campaign than to be elected.

She spoke at meetings of the WCTU, the Kiwanis, Eastern Stars and Rebekahs, church groups, and women's clubs. There was little pressure and she took time to renew old acquaintances, go on picnics, and visit points of interest. A pleasant event was a Labor Day speech at Geauga Lake Park, marred only by the fact that there were "a million cars" on the road.[60] She stood on her own record and won by a remarkable and gratifying plurality of 350,000, carrying 68 of the 88 counties, including for the first time such cities as Cleveland, Columbus, Youngstown and Akron.[61]

Congratulations were legion. Especially treasured was a letter from Papa telling her that it was "the most wonderful effort and success that I have ever known."[62] Lady Astor wrote a personal letter of congratulation and invited her to come to England for a visit.[63] Allen was unable to accept the invitation, but wrote that Maud Wood Park was coming to England.

Lady Astor and Mrs. Park found much in common and Astor wrote Allen thanking her for the introduction.

In 1928 Allen credited both men and women with her victory, saying that men and women of both parties and of every shade of opinion, coming from all sorts of varying groups had been converted to the idea that a woman can render real service as a judge. Victory for a non-partisan candidate was almost a miracle in any campaign; for a woman to be elected in a non-partisan campaign by such a huge plurality was a double miracle.

Allen's victory was even more remarkable because the election of 1928 was an overwhelming sweep for Republican candidates in Ohio. In partial recognition of the efforts of Ohio Republican women President Coolidge appointed Genevieve R. Cline, chairperson of the Ohio Republican women, to the bench of the United States Customs court in New York. Cline thus became the first woman appointed to the federal court system. It was, however, an appointment to a special court and not to one of general jurisdiction.

FOOTNOTES

1 *To Do Justly*, p. 77.

2 Diary, March 7, 1925, March 10, April 25, May 28, June 28, August 11, 28, and 30, September 6, and many other entries.

3 Information from Allen papers, container 14, folder 5. See also *To Do Justly*, p. 76.

4 Letter from Baker to Allen, February 9, 1926, Allen papers, WRHS, container 6, folder 3.

5 Her candidacy was announced on February 8, according to her diary.

6 Cleveland *Plain Dealer*, June 3, 1926, p. 1; June 8, 1926, p. 10.

7 Cleveland *Plain Dealer*, June 6, 1926, p. 8.

8 *To Do Justly*, p. 77. *The Woman Citizen*, October 1926, p. 40, Allen papers, SL, container A-6, folder 1.

9 Speeches from 1926 campaign, Allen papers, WRHS, container 15, folder 1.

10 *Cleveland Press*, March 20, 1926, p. 1.

11 Copy of *Labor* in Allen papers, WRHS, container 26, folder 10. Also reprinted in *Cleveland Press*, August 2, 1926, p. 16.

12 Mimeographed copies of Gohdes article "Why Florence E. Allen Impresses Me." in Allen papers, WRHS, container 14, folder 5.

13 Diary, various entries, June, July, 1926.

14 Breckinridge, pp. 303-304.

15 *To Do Justly*, p. 76.

16 Diary August 11 and 12, 1926. According to *The Woman Citizen, op. cit.*, she lost by 20,000 votes.

17 Judging from the many campaign pictures in the archives.

18 Corinne Allen papers, SL, container A-5, folder 2.

19 Letter of Corinne M. Allen to Florence Snow, August 19, 1929. SMITH 1879, box 80.

20 *Ibid.*

21 Diary October 2 and 3, 1924.

22 In the days when dynastic families ruled daughters sometimes escalated to power on the default of male leadership in their families. Queens Elizabeth I and Victoria of England, Maria Theresa of Austria and Catherine the Great of Russia are examples. In Florence Allen's day most women politicians were the successors of deceased husbands or fathers.

23 Helen was also to edit the book on outlawry. Helen A. Shockey letter to Allen, December 24 and 28, 1924, Allen papers, WRHS, container 6, folder 2. Research notes in container 14, folder 3.

24 Information from newspaper clippings in Allen papers, WRHS, container 26, folder 10.

25 The maid was very unpredictable. She was given to drinking and taking leave without asking, but she was retained.

26 Frances Parkinson Keyes, "Homes of Outstanding American Women, "*Better Homes and Gardens*, June 1928, pp. 12-13, 96-98, Allen papers, LC, container 1.

27 From *Plain Dealer* obituary,

28 As defined by women historians.

29 From personal interviews.

30 Letter from Ruth Bryan Owen, February 15, 1929, Allen papers, WRHS, container 6, folder 2.

31 She was a popular speaker at women's colleges: Vassar, Bryn Mawr, Smith, Wellesley. She gave a series of speeches at Vassar in 1923, according to her diary. She consulted occasionally with Elizabeth Hauser on "ideas and wording" of speeches, for example, Diary, March 23, 1923.

[32] Diary, July 15, 1924. *To Do Justly*, p. 96.

[33] Diary, July 15, 1924.

[34] Allen notes "finagling" for an article in *Atlantic Monthly*, Diary, November 21, 1924.

[35] Diary, March 2, 1925.

[36] *To Do Justly*, p. 71.

[37] Diary, October 1, 1929.

[38] *Franklin Chronicle*, December 12, 1929, Allen papers, WRHS, container 26, folder 12.

[39] See Ryan, pp. 153-158.

[40] Breckinridge, p. 68.

[41] Leading jurists opposed the ERA, finding it a benefit to only a small minority of women at the expense of the well being of millions. Felix Frankfurter and Roscoe Pound were among the leading jurists, according to Lemons, p. 186.

[42] Lemons, pp. 117-118. Mary Kinnear, *Daughters of Time: Women in Western Tradition*, Ann Arbor: University of Michigan Press, 1982, p. 176.

[43] In the case of *Adkins v. Children's Hospital*, 1923.

[44] Lemons, p. 143; Breckinridge, pp. 153-180; O'Neill, pp. 307-308.

[45] Peter Gabriel Filene, *Him: Her: Self: Sex Roles in Modern America*, New York: Harcourt, Brace Jovanovich, 1975, p. 75. Allen noted in her diary March 21, 1926 that she was called a "red" at a peace meeting in Grandview.

[46] Rothman, pp. 186-187; Breckinridge, p. 93.

[47] Lemons, p. 123.

[48] Chafe, *Women and Equality*, p. 29.

[49] *Pittsburgh Press,* June 12, 1926, Allen papers, container 26, folder 10.

[50] Ryan, pp. 152-153.

[51] Doerschuk, p. 58-59. The survey was conducted by the Bureau of Vocational Information under the auspices of a committee composed largely of college presidents, especially of women's colleges.

[52] Lucy R. Tunis, "I Gave Up My Law Books for a Cook Book," *American Magazine*, July 1927, pp. 34-35 and 172-177.

[53] "Significant Factors in Home Life as Revealed Through the Courts," address delivered at the annual meeting of the American Home Economics Association, Des Moines, June 1928 and published in the *Journal of Home Economics*, v. 20, No. 12, December 1928.

[54] According to Rothman, p. 178. Rothman writes that in the twenties "the proper role for the woman shifted from the nursery to the bedroom."

[55] Campaign material in Allen papers, WRHS, container 14, folder 5.

[56] Letter from Railway Labor Organization in Allen papers, WRHS, container 6, folder 2.

[57] *Ibid*.

[58] Ministerial letter in Allen papers, WRHS, container 6, folder 2.

[59] The *Chicago Sunday Tribune*, September 17, 1939, feature interview with Allen, in Allen papers, WRHS, container 27, folder 4.

[60] Diary, September 3, 1928.

[61] Allen papers, WRHS, container 14, folder 5. In the same election Ruth Bryan Owen was elected to Congress and served to 1933.

[62] Letter from Papa to Florence, undated, in Allen papers, WRHS, container 6, folder 2.

[63] *To Do Justly*, pp. 77-78.

Chapter 7

JUSTICE IN OHIO

The environment of the Ohio Supreme Court was in sharp contrast to that of the Cuyahoga County Court of Common Pleas. The Supreme Court was concerned with questions of law rather than questions of fact, the facts having been certified in the common pleas trial court or in hearings of state administrative boards. Witnesses did not appear before the Supreme Court, and the judges were removed from the emotionally charged atmosphere of the trial court with its parade of witnesses. No longer was it necessary for Judge Allen to take down in longhand the essentials of oral testimony or evaluate in the margins of her notebook the veracity and character of witnesses. Gone was the pressure of knowing that hundreds of cases were backlogged and that if extra minutes were taken on legal research someone down the line had to wait longer for his or her trial. The dockets of the Supreme Court were relatively clear, cases were heard promptly, and few cases were backlogged. The court was regarded as a tribunal for the determination of legal principles.[1] ╻

The Ohio Supreme Court did not rank highly among state supreme courts. A survey made in 1923 showed that the reported decisions of the Ohio court were cited by other states so infrequently that it ranked 24th among the states. Before 1912 only fifteen per cent of decided cases were reported with opinions, but the amended Constitution required that the court must state reasons for its decisions, and thereafter opinions were published with decisions. It was hoped that in the course of time the Ohio Supreme Court would have its proper position among the courts of the states.[2]

The work of the seven judges proceeded as a committee. They met together, decided on the cases to be heard, listened to arguments of the lawyers for both sides, studied the briefs and reached decisions. One judge was then assigned the task of writing an opinion. Although the opinion had to reflect the decision of the majority, it was one judge's opinion and was not subject to alteration by the other judges.

The judges became well acquainted as they worked together. At the beginning the presence of a woman on the bench caused some discomfort,[3] but it was Allen's intent not to emphasize sex differences or to confront men with charges of discrimination but to join them in equal duties. She was so conscious of her unusual position and so determined to fulfill her responsibilities that one newsman reported her as having a dual personality: "the austere jurist" and "the gracious homebody." So "brief and gruff" did he find her in the courtroom that she was "almost unrecognizable without her robes and judicial surroundings."[4] Judge Allen's ability and bearing soon earned the respect of her brethren and sex differences were forgotten.

The court's decisions were based on a strict application of the 1912 Constitution, the General Code of Laws and cases in precedent, and had the force of law. "Judicial opinions," Allen wrote, "must be a statement of the law applicable, and nothing else."[5] It would seem to be cut and dried work, but such an assumption overlooks the importance of the attitudes, viewpoints, and, indeed, the basic integrity of the judges on the bench.

Before Allen and Robert Day became judges in 1922 there had been criticism that some of the judges had "taken on age" and that the old timers had "emasculated every liberal tradition of the Constitution of 1912" and "overturned. . . . every liberal law that they had a chance at."[6] With the election of Allen and Day the liberals had a majority on the bench. The court in the twenties dealt with cases that concerned legislation adopted during the progressive era; its decisions clarified and entrenched that reforming legislation. The political climate of the twenties was conservative compared to the previous two decades. A judge whose viewpoint was that of the progressive era would be considered a liberal in the twenties and Allen and Day were so considered.

Progressive legislation was intended to blunt the abuses of industrialization and regulate the new industrial society. Regulatory commissions, such as the Industrial Commission, the Public Utilities Commission and others were empowered by the legislature, but their pronouncements were frequently challenged and had to be confirmed or denied by the Supreme Court. Municipalities were exploring their new rights of home rule, trying to organize orderly communities.

The first opinion Allen was asked to write was on the constitutionality of the Cleveland city manager plan, a system of city government devised by reformers and promoted by women's organizations during her years of residence in Cleveland. Cousin Dr. Jacob Tuckerman had been on the committee formed in 1916 to investigate the advisability of the plan and it had often been the subject of conversation at the Tuckermans. Under the auspices of women's organizations Allen had made many speeches explaining and promoting the plan by which a city manager was hired by a city council elected by proportional representation. The plan was presented to the electorate in 1921.

Political parties were not enthusiastic about a plan that would remove administration from politics. As a result the campaign for the city manager plan was conducted largely by women's organizations, especially the League of Women Voters. Most of the workers in the canvas for votes in

1921 were women[7] who idealistically believed that the plan would improve the efficiency of government. Concurrently the mayoral campaign of 1921 was a disillusioning spectacle of mediocre candidates quarreling among themselves and criticizing the administration at city hall. The crudities of the mayoral campaign boosted the prospects of the city manager plan, and it was accepted by the voters.[8]

In the cases of *Reutner v. City of Cleveland* and *Hile v. City of Cleveland* taxpayers' suits were brought against the city to test the constitutionality of the plan. The Supreme Court found it constitutional, and very appropriately selected Judge Allen to write the opinions confirming it.[9] In the first case the plaintiff contended that the magnitude of amendments to the old charter presented to the voters in fact a new charter and that the proper procedure for the adoption of a new charter had not been followed. In her opinion Allen wrote that the proposal made substantive changes in only 35 sections of the charter, made editorial changes in 105, retained verbatim 60 sections and was therefore not a new charter but an amended one. Another issue in the case was the validity of the system of proportional representation whereby the number of wards was reduced and voters were to vote for their first, second and third choice for councilmen. The plaintiff contended that the Ohio constitution entitled a voter to vote at all elections and that the new system permitted him to give first choice to only one candidate even though he was to elect five or more. Allen's opinion pointed out that the Ohio constitution gave cities unlimited powers of local self-government including the system of balloting.

In the second case the plaintiff charged that the city manager system denied a republican form of government and created a state within a state in violation of the United States Constitution. Allen affirmed the system as constitutional because it would act through representatives chosen by the people. She added that the system would operate under and enforce the laws of Ohio and the United States and thus was not creating a state within a state.

As soon as it was found to be constitutional the way was clear to implement the city manager plan. Allen's friend Marie Wing was an ardent supporter of the plan, ran for council as a non-partisan and was elected twice. After she completed her law degree, Susan Rebhan also ran non-partisan for council and was elected. William R. Hopkins, a classmate of Allen's father, was appointed city manager and served efficiently and enthusiastically from 1924 to 1929. The experiment was watched by cities across the nation and written about in school textbooks as a promising advancement in government.[10]

How did this reform which women had so eagerly supported turn out? Politicians continued to oppose it. More objective critics found that it was efficient but did not necessarily reflect the wishes of the voters. There was a continuing fight for repeal. In 1923 and 1925 the League of Women

Voters held open-air meetings in the parks and conducted a door to door campaign to save proportional representation and won. In 1927 and 1929 the League campaigned again, almost single-handedly, and won. In 1931 it was discovered that the first city manager had made a deal with the political parties to split patronage. Still, the League defended it, only to go down in defeat in 1931,[11] and a reform supported by women for efficient city government came to an end.

Other cities were testing their new authority under home-rule charters, with reform-minded councils trying to improve living conditions and regulate problems of growth. The Cincinnati city council decided to create a more orderly city by dividing its territory into zones and regulating types of buildings, height, set back, space around buildings, and so forth. An apartment builder who had violated the height and area prohibition sued the city, challenging zoning as being unconstitutional in taking private property without due process of law. Allen was proud of the opinion she wrote in the case of *Pritz v. Messer et al.* finding zoning within the city's power under the home-rule provision and within the police power to protect public morals, health and safety. She listed the benefits of zoning: relief of traffic congestion, reduction of fire hazard, prevention of slums, and protection of the home "from the rapid onslaught of urban life."[12]

There were many sewer cases and arguments over assessments were common. The voters of Cuyahoga Falls approved a sewer, sidewalk, and curbing project for a neighborhood to be assesed to property owners for not more than one-third of valuation. When completed the cost overran that figure and taxpayers sued to declare the project illegal and void. The lower courts decided for the taxpayers. In the case of the *City of Cuyahoga Falls v. Beck et al.* the Supreme Court reversed that decision with Judge Allen taking an opportunity to stress the responsibility for constant vigilance by citizens. She wrote that the taxpayers had not acted soon enough and that "by sitting through every step of the long proceedings, through the notice of the resolutions, through the estimated assessments of the freeholders, through the notice of assessment" the taxpayers had "deprived themselves of the right to question the action of council."[13]

Progressive reformers looked to the Public Utilities Commission of Ohio to regulate the rights of private truck and bus companies to use the highways and to grant use on the basis of public convenience and need. The PUCO decided on the benefits of proposed new or changed routes and granted or denied certificates. Challenge to the decisions of PUCO could be appealed to the Supreme Court. Most challenges came from the railroad companies and especially the interurbans that were hard pressed for riders by bus competition. The Cincinnati Traction Company, for example, challenged a certificate granted by the PUCO to the River Road Transportation Company for a bus line parallel to its route. The traction company claimed there was no need for another bus route, that railroad and bus service was available, and that the interurban was already losing money on the trip. In the case of *The Cincinnati Traction Co. v. Public Utilities Commission of Ohio* the Supreme Court found the evidence of the traction company justified and denied the PUCO grant, Allen writing the opinion.[14]

Some bus operators were clearly prospering at the expense of the interurbans. The Lake Shore Electric Railway Company sued a private bus operator between Lorain and Cleveland that had acquired permission to add new busses and change its schedule by ten minutes. The traction company provided evidence that the bus was stopping at the interurban station and soliciting customers. When the interurban schedule changed by ten minutes, so did the bus schedule. In her written opinion Allen reminded all concerned that certificates were granted for public convenience and need and not for private profit.[15]

Judge Allen considered herself a friend of labor and welcomed opportunities to write opinions on labor relations and the new Ohio workmen's compensation law. The question of the legality of picketing came up in Allen's first few weeks on the bench. The LaFrance Electrical Construction and Supply Company, in an effort to be rid of the union, had terminated the employment of all its workers and immediately rehired them, asking each employee to sign a contract agreeing to an open shop and to refrain from urging employees to quit or to join the union. Picketing by union members brought the case to court. Allen wrote the opinion in the case of *The LaFrance Electrical Construction and Supply Co. v. International Brotherhood of Electrical Workers* confirming the right of peaceful picketing, peaceful persuasion of employees to terminate contracts and peaceful persuasion of expectant employees not to accept work with the company.[16] Allen's labor supporters in Cleveland observed the vigor of her opinion with approval. The twenties were lean years for labor unions and labor legislation, and friends of labor were valued.

Knowledge of the issues involved in workmen's compensation had been part of Allen's intellectual baggage since her childhood days in Utah when Papa had pioneered labor legislation. In her years on the Supreme Court she helped to interpret and clarify the Ohio laws to the benefit of the workers. One such case was that of Hannah Fender, an employee of the Ohio Automatic Sprinkler Company, who had to have her thumb amputated as the result of an injury by a punch press. Workmen's compensation covered the injury, but Fender sued the company for failure to provide adequate safety devices. The company denied negligence and said the employee's negligence caused the accident. Earlier decisions of the Supreme Court had found that workmen's compensation protected employers from such lawsuits. Allen was pleased to have written the opinion in the Fender case, which reversed earlier decisions and found the employers could be sued for failing to provide safety devices.[17] Allen wrote that the legislature never intended the workmen's compensation law to prevent the employee from being able to sue his employer in case of violation of the law.[18] The Fender case by no means settled the issue, but it did indicate a new direction of the courts in favor of the worker.

What constituted a compensable accident was a very difficult question. Mr. Polcen, for example, worked for a chemical company. He claimed that one day at work a violent coughing fit occasioned by sulphuric fumes caused a reopening of the rupture he had had for ten years and that this was an accidental injury and therefore compensable. The Industrial Commission claimed it was not an accidental injury. Witnesses testified that there was nothing unusual about the day it happened, that everybody coughed all the time in the chemical works from sulphuric fumes. The Supreme Court did not agree with the decision of the Industrial Commission and found Polcen's rupture a compensable accident, Allen providing the reasoning in her opinion.[19]

Among the many so-called progressive labor laws were those regulating work for women. In 1919 the Ohio legislature passed legislation prohibiting women in sixteen or more occupations, including jobs as bell hops, taxi drivers, meter readers and many others. Women were prohibited from working at night or lifting weights over 25 pounds. The conception that home and motherhood was woman's role and that the health of future mothers should be protected was so entrenched that there was no pressure of cases in the courts to modify the legislation. Only the prohibition against taxi driving was removed in the twenties, and then only during daytime hours.[20] Women generally and women's organizations, along with union workers who felt threatened by female competition, and state legislators joined in regulating women's hours, occupations, and working conditions.[21] Only the National Woman's Party objected that the legislation limited women's options and that it should apply to men as well as women. On the contrary, the U.S. Women's Bureau investigated the effects of protective legislation in 1928 and concluded that it was not a handicap to women but had raised standards for thousands of women.[22]

Women's organizations also favored minimum wage legislation for women, but that reform was thwarted by the United States Supreme Court in 1923 in the case of *Adkins v. Children's Hospital.* In his decision Justice George Sutherland argued that women had achieved equality through the Nineteenth Amendment and that such legislation was obsolete.[23] A way around the Adkins decision was found, however, and states continued to pass minimum wage laws for women. Ohio adopted one in 1933, with the support of women's organizations.[24]

Judge Allen favored protective legislation and was firmly committed to the idea that women functioned in a separate sphere. Her attitudes toward her own career were in direct contradiction, for she insisted upon the same assignments and responsibilities as her brethren. Other professional women had the same experience. The National Women's Medical

Association was one of the first to oppose protective legislation and to endorse the ERA.[25] The NAWL opposed such legislation by 1927 and moved toward support of the ERA.[26] The NFBPWC decided to remain neutral on protective legislation in 1921, dropped it from its legislative program in 1922, and finally endorsed the ERA in 1937.[27] It was only business and professional women, however, who opposed protective legislation. The League of Women Voters stoutly defended it into the sixties. Protective legislation was one of "the ideological rocks" that fragmented the woman's movement.[28]

Women were not supposed to know very much about or be interested in mechanical things. Judge Allen, not wanting to be spared such assignments, welcomed opportunities to write opinions on cases involving mechanical things. The case of *The Fisher Bros. Co. v. Brown, Secty. of State* involved the question of horsepower.

Trucks were taxed to compensate for the damage they did to the roads, and the question arose as to how the damage could be assessed, with the legislature deciding that horsepower was the best measure. The cost of licenses was graduated according to horsepower. This criterion was soon challenged by the The Fisher Bros. Co., a larger grocery company in Cleveland, that owned a fleet of 24 Pierce Arrow delivery trucks. The Pierce Arrows had 30 horsepower motors and each license cost $186.40. Lawyers for the company claimed horsepower was not the determining factor in damage done to roads, claiming that White trucks, for example, with horsepower of slightly under 30 could carry equal weight, travel at the same speed, did just as much damage, and the license cost only $66. The common pleas court found that the horsepower formula did lead to discrimination and was therefore unconstitutional; the court of appeals reversed that decision, and the Supreme Court agreed that horsepower was a fair and equitable standard of measure. Allen wrote the opinion including a sophisticated technical defense of horsepower as the criterion,[29] demonstrating her expertise in what was assumed to be of interest only to men.

Allen was glad that as a judge she had the opportunity to strengthen the public school system, for she believed that "next to the home" the public school system is the basis of American life.[30] She wrote the opinion finding it constitutional for the legislature to apply tax funds from one district to other districts, arguing that good education benefitted the entire state and not merely the district where the taxes were paid.[31] Other decisions affirmed the right of all students to education no matter how far they lived from school, and upheld the legality of the state retirement fund for teachers.

Some cases demonstrated unresolved problems in our society and were indicative of future issues. One such issue revolved around the rights of the accused and convicted. In Camden, for example, a man was arrested for possession of intoxicating liquor. The mayor promptly locked him in the local jail, declaring "I don't want to hear anything out of you" in response to the arrestee's noisy protest. The lower courts supported the mayor, but the Supreme Court reversed the decision. The refusal of the mayor to hear argument indicated bias and prejudice, Allen wrote, and deprived the defendant of his fundamental right to counsel.[32]

In another case the accused was convicted of deliberate and premeditated murder and sentenced to death by electrocution. The accused had no money to hire counsel or pay a doctor for a psychiatric examination, and the court-appointed attorney had not entered a plea of insanity. In a split decision of the Supreme Court, with five concurring and two dissenting, Allen wrote that the accused had not had due process of law, that a psychiatric examination was "a matter of right," and that the case must be returned to the trial court.[33]

In another case a lawyer was prevented by the warden from seeing a prisoner in the Ohio penitentiary. The lawyer wanted to see the prisoner about possible error proceedings in his case, but the warden claimed it was his absolute right to reject or to allow visitation. Allen wrote for the Supreme Court that "a convict incarcerated in the Ohio penitentiary is not civilly dead and has right to consult with his attorney with regard to error proceedings as with regard to the case itself."[34]

Violations of prohibition laws were greatly expanding the work of the federal courts during these years but came to the state courts only in cases of incidental complications. Sometimes public officials themselves were parasites on the illegal liquor industry, a situation doubly disgusting to Judge Allen. In the case of *Scott v. The State of Ohio* the safety director of Youngstown was charged with accepting jewelry, furniture, building materials and money for protection of bootleggers and speakeasies. The defendant claimed the lower court had heard prejudicial and incompetent evidence in reaching its decision against him. A young woman testified that he had made improper proposals to her and promised to overlook her family's sale of liquor if she would go riding with him and "show him a good time." The defendant claimed this evidence was not sufficient to prove a solicitation of "any valuable or beneficial thing." Judge Allen and her brethren agreed that the defendant was asking the young woman to betray her virtue and that therein he was asking for something of value. Allen believed there were no greater sinners than government officials who violated a public trust, and she took the opportunity to expound this idea in her opinion.[35]

One of the most significant cases for Allen's future concerned the problem of racial discrimination. She did not write an opinion but concurred in the decision. A young black woman, Doris Weaver, was a student in home economics at Ohio State University. As a part of their senior year, majors were expected to live in a cooperative house, each with a roommate, and to apply their knowledge working and eating together. Weaver had no roommate and was assigned a room with the instructor in an adjoining house. Aside from the rooming arrangement, her educational experience was the same as that of the other women. Weaver sued the university for discrimination. The court decided against Weaver, finding that "purely social relationships cannot be regulated by law and that no constitutional right had been violated."[36] The case would assume personal importance for Allen when she was being considered for a federal judgeship.

The Ohio Supreme Court bench was not known for its integrity, and Judge Allen found some of her brethren not very "high-minded." Some of them, she thought, regarded their offices as private property for exploitation. She found that to be true in the case of *State ex rel Bowman v. Board of Commissioners of Allen County* involving sewer construction, where the county commissioners had issued bonds to build a sewer system that benefitted only a small area and had let the contract for construction to a private company. The Supreme Court in 1929 found the bonds invalid "because of the gross abuse of discretion of the county commissioners." Those interested in profiting from the construction refused to give up and within two years had convinced four of the judges to change their minds, rehear the case, and render a decision favorable to building the sewer. There were some "fiery sessions" among the judges over the case, and in a dissenting opinion, Allen stoutly maintained her original view that the taxpayers were being unfairly burdened by public officials serving private enterprise for profit.[37]

In another case Allen angered Chief Judge Carrington T. Marshall by writing an opinion requiring the rehearing of a case involving the mishandling of school funds where it was obvious that Marshall had close social and business connections with the defendants.[38] Allen openly criticized Marshall, as did the other judges, for setting himself up on a pedestal and assigning cases for opinions that would reflect his views. By 1932 considerable bitterness prevailed in the court,[39] and Allen was among the first to divulge her criticisms to the public.

Allen's image as a woman reformer continued to shine brightly as a result of her judicial opinions, public speeches and articles. She had the courage to confront the law profession on its own grounds — in the bar associations — and to reprimand its members for their selfish attitudes and practices which were in contrast to her ideals for the profession. In a speech in 1928 to the Judicial Section of the Ohio Bar Association she said that the ancient Athenians talked about the law as if it were exciting, even getting up before dawn to discuss it, but in America too many people saw the law not so much as a way to establish justice among human beings and to affirm human rights as to serve their own individual purposes. "Can we say that in fact in this country we have made human rights supreme?" she asked. Lawyers can make the law a living power, she told them, if they abolish technicalities, elevate the jury system, do away with perjury, and set up a standard of public service in the conduct of criminal cases.

She faulted law schools for dwelling on education in the affairs of private property and private enterprise and neglecting matters that dealt with public property and public enterprise. She faulted lawyers for allowing the merits of controversies to become enmeshed and overshadowed by technicalities. She called on lawyers to mold public opinion to think of jury duty as a privilege and an opportunity and to help secure more intelligent persons and elevate the character of the service given. She warned of the increase in perjury, increasing because people thought lightly of it. It was up to the lawyers, she said, to strike at that "dastardly distortion of justice." She said justice must be the purpose in criminal cases instead of a game between lawyers of both sides trying to hang acquitals and convictions on their belts the way Indians hung scalps. Lawyers and judges must cooperate on these great ends, she concluded, and as long as they do the sun of America will never set, but will always rise.[40]

At mid-life, as her second term in the Ohio Supreme Court drew to a close, Judge Allen could reflect that she had served her constituency well in improving the quality of life in the cities, extending the public school system, and advancing the benefits of labor in a growing industrial society. For women she had demonstrated that a woman judge could serve on a court of last resort with efficiency and influence and earn the respect of the legal profession. She might also reflect that she was dealing with the law after the fact, in a court that was not highly regarded among courts, and with colleagues less idealistic than she.

News of Judge Allen's good work spread beyond Ohio. As early as 1930 *The Christian Science Monitor* suggested the appointment of a woman to the federal court system and specifically suggested Allen. President Hoover wrote his Attorney General William Mitchell about it, and Mitchell responded that he would like very much to appoint a distinguished woman if he could find one.[41] Allen did not receive the call, possibly because she was a Democrat and the administration was staunchly Republican.

FOOTNOTES

[1] According to Carrington T. Marshall, *A History of the Courts and Lawyers of Ohio,* New York: The American Historical Society 1934, v. I, pp. 224-227.

[2] *Ibid.,* p. 227.

[3] *To Do Justly,* p. 79.

[4] *The Boston Traveler,* March 24, 1923, NAWSA papers, LC, container 37, microfilm reel 25. The article described Allen's appearance as that of a woman who could handle a team of horses or embroider a pillow case.

[5] *Columbus Citizen,* June 2, 1934, Allen papers, WRHS, container 26, folder 7.

[6] *Akron Beacon Journal,* September 19, 1922, Allen papers, WRHS, container 14, folder 5.

[7] Lemons, p. 125.

[8] For a description of the mayoral campaign see Rose, pp. 788-780.

[9] *Reutner v. City of Cleveland,* 107 OS 117 (1923) and *Hile v. City of Cleveland,* 107 OS 145 (1923). *To Do Justly,* p. 81-82.

[10] See *National Municipal Review,* Supplement XVIII, March 1929, pp. 203-220, "Five Years of City Manager Plan in Cleveland."

[11] Lemons, p. 125-126; "The League in the Cities, No. 10, Cleveland," *Woman Citizen,* v. XI, June 1926, p. 30.

[12] *Pritz v. Messer et al.,* 112 OS 628 (1925). *To Do Justly, p. 83.*

[13] *City of Cuyahoga Falls v. Beck et al.,* 110 OS 82 (1924).

[14] *The Cincinnati Traction Co. v. Public Utilities Commission of Ohio,* 112 OS 699 (1925).

[15] *The Lake Shore Electric Ry Co. v. Public Utilities Commission of Ohio,* 118 OS 173 (1928).

[16] *The LaFrance Electrical Construction and Supply Co. v. International Brotherhood of Electrical Workers, Local No. 8 et al.,* 108 OS 61 (1923). *To Do Justly,* p. 84.

[17] *To Do Justly,* p. 85.

[18] *The Ohio Automatic Sprinkler Co., v. Fender,* 108 OS 149 (1923).

[19] *Industrial Commission of Ohio v. Polcen,* 121 OS 377 (1929).

[20] 06 Ohio Abstracts 186, *State v. McCune;* Lemons p. 106.

[21] Alice Kessler-Harris, "Where Are the Organized Women Workers?" *Feminist Studies,* v. 3, No. 1/2, Fall 1945, p. 101; Aileen S. Kraditor, Ed., *Up From the Pedestal: Selected Writings in the History of Feminism,* New York: Quadrangle, 1968, p. 295.

[22] Lemons, p. 195.

[23] Chambers, pp. 68-69.

[24] Abbott, p. 97.

[25] Lemons, p. 252.

[26] *Women Lawyers' Journal,* v. XV, July 1927, p. 4; Lemons, p. 253.

[27] Lemons, p. 45.

[28] Susan Becker, "International Feminism between the Wars: The National Woman's Party versus the League of Women Voters," in Lois Scharf and Joan M. Jensen, *Decades of Discontent: The Woman's Movement, 1920-1940,* Westport: Greenwood press, 1983, p. 223.

[29] *The Fisher Bros. Co. v. Brown, Secty of State,* 111 OS 602 (1924). *To Do Justly,* p. 84.

[30] *To Do Justly,* p. 83.

[31] *Board of Education of Silver Lake Village School District v. Korns, Auditor, et al.,* 107 OS (1923).

[32] *Decker v. The State of Ohio,* 113 OS 512 (1925).

[33] *Evans v. The State of Ohio,* 123 OS 132 (1930).

[34] *Thomas, Warden v. Mills,* 117 OS 114 (1927).

[35] *Scott v. The State of Ohio.* 108 OS 475 (1923).

[36] *To Do Justly,* pp. 91-92.

[37] *State ex rel Bowman v. Board of Commissioners of Allen County*, 124 OS 174 (1931). *To Do Justly*, pp. 90-91. *Cincinnati Times Star*, March 15, 1932, Allen papers, WRHS, container 26, folder 14.

[38] *State ex rel Turner v. Marshall*, 123 OS 586 (1930). *To Do Justly*, pp. 88-90.

[39] *Cincinnati Times Star*, March 15, 1932.

[40] Florence E. Allen, "The Living Power of the Law," Allen papers, WRHS, container 14, folder 2.

[41] Information from John R. Schmidhauser, *Judges and Justices: The Federal Appellate Judiciary*, New York: Little Brown and Company, 1979, p. 59.

Chapter 8

A FEDERAL APPOINTMENT

Allen's senatorial campaign and defeat in the primaries in 1926 was an exhausting and disappointing experience, but it had not quieted her ambition to be in the law-making sector of the government. She had lost to a man of great political stature, one of Ohio's favorite sons, and it could hardly be considered an embarrassing defeat. Her election to the Supreme Court in 1928 by a very flattering margin in a heavily Republican year erased any doubts about her ability to attract votes.

Papa and Florence often talked about her political future, Papa's ambitions for his daughter enlivening his later years. They talked about another try for the Senate or as governor of Ohio, but took no action.[1] Her father was no longer with her when she decided to run for the U.S. House of Representatives in 1932, but he surely would have approved since his own political experience was as a congressman from Utah. Perhaps most important in making her decision was that she was "sick of the intolerable situation" in the Ohio Supreme Court and wanted a better platform for her views on matters of public importance.[2]

Nineteen thirty-two promised to be a good year for the Democrats. The 1928 elections had been a landslide for the Republicans but their popularity had been eroded by the lingering depression and the voters were ready for a change. Allen did not make her decision hastily. She talked it over with her family, especially Esther, with her long-time advisors Rebhan, Hauser, and Kellor, with many people in the party, and decided to run for Congress from the twenty-second district,[3] which included part of Cleveland and many of its suburbs. Allen knew the area well and had many connections and supporters there. In 1928 she had had a large plurality in the district in her non-partisan campaign for the Supreme Court,[4] and in 1932 she easily became the candidate for the Democratic party.

Serious disadvantages confronted her. One was that the voters were heavily Republican, and a popular Republican incumbent, Chester A. Bolton, opposed her. Another problem was that the candidates were not free to define their own issues because burning issues of the day demanded attention and were not to be put aside. The burning issues were prohibition, economic revival, and the veteran's bonus, none of them easy issues for Florence Allen.

It seemed apparent that the end was near for prohibition and vote-conscious candidates who had long favored it were changing, supporting either outright repeal or a referendum on the Volstead Act. Practical people, wet and dry, lamented that large quantities of alcoholic beverages were being consumed illegally, and that a tax on legal beverages would relieve bankrupt public treasuries. Allen modified her former firm stand for prohibition by declaring that she also favored democracy and that the voters should have the right to choose through a referendum. As for herself, she maintained that she believed in prohibition as firmly as ever. Her campaign literature avoided a definite stand on the issue and claimed that the prohibition question was being used as a smoke screen to cloud other issues, especially the depression and the sad state of the economy.[5]

The WCTU had previously supported her whole-heartedly and this new stand caused confusion. After correspondence between Allen and WCTU representatives, the organization again supported her candidacy,[6] but speeches for their group were not numerous. An advocate of prohibition could easily reason that a referendum would only delay repeal and was therefore not worth a vote. Bolton's stand on prohibition was forthright; he favored repeal.

The question of economic revival focused on the Hawley-Smoot tariff act which provided high protective tariffs and was defended by the Republicans. Allen and Bolton debated the issue at the invitation of the Lakewood League of Women Voters before a large audience. Bolton argued that the Hawley-Smoot tariff protected the American working man and American industry. Allen took the Democratic party stand that high tariff stifled world trade, produced enormous unemployment, lowered purchasing power, contributed to industrial profits, and caused world resentment.[7] Allen wrote in her diary that she and Bolton were "most polite" to each other and she was pleased with the good newspaper coverage of the debate.[8]

Allen's criticism of Republican foreign trade policy became more militant as the campaign progressed. "I shall vote for a drastic retrenchment in the Department of Commerce, which has tripled its expansion in the last seven years," she was quoted as saying by the *Cleveland Press*.[9] Readers might find that an agreeable statement, for the Commerce Department had grown rapidly since the war and taken on some of the prerogatives usually associated with the State Department.

No one had very positive ideas for the revival of the economy. World wheat prices dropped to an all-time low a week before election. News of bankruptcies, mortgage foreclosures, and unemployment boded ill for the future. Aside from a change in foreign trade policies, Allen could only suggest immediate reduction of government expense, abolition of useless departments and elimination of extravagance. She hedged on the bonus question, opposing an immediate cash bonus for all veterans, but recognizing the bonus as an obligation of the government and advocating immediate payment to persons disabled in service and to dependents of those killed. Bolton called for immediate payment of the bonus.

She also campaigned for disarmament as a way to insure peace. In 1932 that was not a critical issue, although the *Christian Century* noted that Allen's election would increase the peace delegation in Congress.[10]

She spoke at churches, women's clubs, civic clubs, and veterans' groups. Women supporters had teas, suppers, receptions and barbecues for her. For the first time speeches to black and ethnic groups were numerous, including Italian, Armenian, Jewish, and Bohemian groups. Most audiences she rated in her diary as "good" or "swell," but a new experience was an "unfriendly" audience and a meeting that was "a flop."[11]

The Women's Division of the party was in the formative stages, ably led by Mary Dewson, whom Allen had known since suffrage days.[12] Democratic women participated in the 1932 campaign in unprecedented numbers and added a national dimension to Allen's campaign. Four women speakers were selected by the Women's Division and financed by the party to campaign nationally.[13] One of them, her good friend Ruth Bryan Owen, spoke for Allen's campaign at a rally at the Statler Hotel in Cleveland.

Four speeches on national radio hook-ups were also arranged by the Women's Division. Carefully choosing "just the right woman speaker for the right place," Judge Florence Allen was selected to speak on the international trade and tariff issue.[14] Bitterly assailing the Hawley-Smoot tariff, she declared that "through our suicidal policy of economic isolation we have done everything to halt the wheels of progress" and have "ruined our foreign trade."[15]

In previous campaigns the two major Cleveland newspapers had been very supportive of Allen. She counted Louis Seltzer, editor of the *Cleveland Press*, and Erie Hopwood of the *Plain Dealer* as old friends.[16] In 1932 neither paper supported her. Editorially the *Cleveland Press* took the stand that Bolton never left his views in doubt and made his stand very clear, but that Allen had not been "as forthright in the statement of her position on a number of questions as we should wish a candidate for Congress" Bolton, the editor continued, was sincerely committed to work for repeal of the eighteenth amendment and Allen would go only so far in reversing her former dry position as to promise a vote to submit the question of repeal to the people. "She would not be in Washington a positive force, working in and out of season to bring the prohibition era to an end," the editorial concluded. The *Press* was pushing for legal beer immediately and the tax it would provide. The paper also emphasized that Bolton had been "an extremely effective agent in Washington for his constituents and in communicating the needs of the community,"[17] and criticized Allen for neglecting her supreme court duties and taking her salary during the campaign.[18] Allen defended herself by saying there was no law prohibiting judges from campaigning and that her resignation would upset the smooth operation of the court.

The Cleveland *Plain Dealer* expressed a different viewpoint but one equally damaging to Allen's candidacy. The editor believed that she erred in judgment when she decided to step down from the bench. She was, the editorial continued, "the ideal fruit of a non-partisan judicial plan" and would be as sure of an unlimited tenure on the bench as anything in the field of elective office can be. The editor thought that if Allen were elected in 1932 in the anticipated Democratic wave her reelection two years later would be very doubtful. The twenty-second district would have to start over again training a representative and the Supreme Court would lose a valuable member. "We admire her liberal political attitude on most public questions," the article continued, "but we think her stand on prohibition is unsound and not in keeping with the national platform of her own party."[19]

Republican Bolton won the election by a modest majority. Allen congratulated him and he praised her for the high type of campaign she had conducted. In the national election the Democrats won a sweeping victory, but in Ohio, where the Democratic party had been badly fragmented for several years, Roosevelt won the presidential race by only a slim margin.[20]

Perhaps Allen did not expect to win this election. No sign of disappointment appears in her diary or papers. She wrote Mary Dewson that to her it was "a thrilling victory" and that most thrilling was the part women played in securing it.[21] Compared to her 1926 campaign against Pomerene she had not worked very hard; she was not "tired stiff." She took time to visit relatives and tour in the east with Susan and Mary. She did not rearrange her judicial schedule to allow time for campaigning. Nevertheless, win or lose, she had piled up some political chips by running for the Democratic party and her reward was soon forthcoming.

A few days after the election she went to New York to discuss appointments with Frances Kellor[22] and Mary Drier, who was an intimate friend of Eleanor Roosevelt. When she returned a personal letter was waiting for her from James A. Farley, Democratic campaign chairman, thanking her for her contribution to the party and expressing regret that she was not elected.[23]

Allen replied that even though she didn't win the campaign she made a better showing than any Democrat had ever made in a presidential year in that particular Republican district. She added that she was glad she had a chance to lift her voice for Governor Roosevelt in a national broadcast, and that "from the scores of letters that have come in I know that the broadcast did have some effect."[24]

Scores of letters had indeed been received after the network talk, praising her speaking ability and her ideas. "You have made the best political speech in this campaign," wrote a listener from Allentown,

Pennsylvania, "you have stated facts even clearer than governor Roosevelt, and he is a mighty fine speaker." A listener in San Diego, California, who identified himself as an old man who had been listening to political talks since the Grant-Greeley campaign and therefore qualified as an expert, wrote that "the best political address of this campaign was delivered by a woman. It was not a feminine appeal to the throbbing heart of women, it was directed to the intelligence which a voter is supposed to have . . . ."[25]

Political parties had not accepted women into their decision-making circles since passage of the suffrage amendment, but had encouraged women's divisions, auxiliaries for getting out the vote, and had rewarded them with the patronage of a few political appointments as Genevieve R. Cline, who had worked very hard for the Republican women's division in 1928, was rewarded with an appointment as judge of the United States Customs Court in New York. Cline's appointment was enthusiastically supported by the NAWL but opposed by men lawyers on account of her sex.[26]

The size and effectiveness of the Democratic Women's Division in 1932 was unprecedented. After Roosevelt's victory the women expected appointments, and the party was prepared to reward their services.[27] The highest aspiration was for a woman in the cabinet. Using her Women's Division connections, Dewson conducted a massive campaign of endorsement of Frances Perkins as secretary of labor.[28]

During the campaign for Perkins, Ohio national committee-woman Mary Boardman wrote Farley that since Roosevelt was considering the appointment of a woman to his cabinet she had a suggestion for ending "the deplorable chaos in the party in Ohio." She suggested that Judge Florence Allen be considered for appointment to the cabinet to promote party unity in Ohio and the reelection of President Roosevelt.[29]

Roosevelt appointed Frances Perkins as Secretary of Labor, the first cabinet post ever assigned to a woman. Perkins had a settlement house background and a long record of investigative and administrative positions concerned with the welfare of industrial labor, male and female, and was industrial commissioner of New York state while Roosevelt was governor. Eleanor Roosevelt said that the post had been given to her not only because there was a demand on the part of women that a woman should be given a place in the cabinet but because Perkins was better qualified than anyone else, man or woman, for the job.[30] Allen wrote the president to tell him that "everyone here in Ohio" was delighted with Perkins' appointment and that "women everywhere are proud of you for having had the courage to place a woman in this outstanding position . . . ."[31] She wrote a similar letter to Mrs. Roosevelt, who responded that she would very much like to meet her.[32] Their busy schedules made meeting difficult, although several attempts were made.

Allen's term of office as judge in the Ohio Supreme Court was to expire in 1934. She was fed up with the arbitrary justice meted out by the court[33] and was apprehensive about another campaign after her 1932 failure. When a vacancy occurred in the United States Court of Appeals for the Sixth Circuit late in 1933 she decided that she would be interested in that appointment. The sixth circuit included Michigan, Ohio, Kentucky, and Tennessee and the next appointment was to go to an Ohio lawyer on the recommendation of Senator Robert J. Bulkley. That Allen had given the appointment some previous thought seems evident from the fact that Judge Hickenlooper died two days before Christmas, 1933 and Carrie Chapman Catt wrote to Mary Dewson the day after Christmas that Judge Allen would be interested in an appointment to the vacancy.[34]

Allen had excellent connections in Washington. Homer Cummings was Attorney General and reviewed judicial candidates and was well acquainted with Allen and her family. Another family friend, Harold M. Stephens, was Assistant Attorney General and worked with Cummings. Stephens was, in fact, another of Florence's cousins. Their families had been good friends in Salt Lake City, and Florence and Harold had grown up together in the Congregational Sunday School.

Mary Dewson's endorsement was critical. Allen had two conferences with her,[35] and later wrote Dewson that "you helped me over the biggest hurdle,"[36] the hurdle presumably being that of the appointment of a woman to the federal judiciary. In Ohio Susan Rebhan proceeded immediately to organize a movement to promote Allen's appointment, first presenting her name to W.A. Julian, United States Treasurer and Democratic national committeeman from Ohio. Rebhan and Judge Will P. Stephenson of the Ohio Supreme Court asked Bulkley to recommend Allen.[37] And Florence hastened to collect a dossier for Cummings' approval.

Rebhan called for public support for Allen's appointment, and, with her prodding, Cummings, Bulkley, and Roosevelt were soon bombarded with letters recommending her. Chief Judge Carl V. Weygandt of the Ohio Supreme Court wrote Cummings that after several years acquaintance he regarded her "as a lawyer and judge of unquestionable integrity, industry, ability, and judicial temperament."[38] Stephen Young wired that Allen's promotion, like that of Ruth Bryan Owen, who had been appointed minister to Denmark, would be pleasing to women everywhere. Retired Justice John H. Clarke, whose voting record in the Supreme Court had been remarkably liberal, wrote to Bulkley and Cummings commending her. "As the daughter of my college classmate," he wrote, "I have been interested in her career and think her opinions equal if not superior to any others coming from the Ohio Supreme Court in recent years."[39] Many supporting letters were sent by Ohio judges, lawyers, and bar associations.

Carrie Chapman Catt, Maud Wood Park, Mary Drier, Sophonisba Breckinridge, Frances Perkins, and many other feminists and club women wrote in favor of her appointment. The Ohio Federation of Business and Professional Women's Clubs equated Allen and Frances Perkins as women who held beacon lights for thousands of women to press onward. Mary Boardman wrote for the Federated Democratic Women of Ohio that Allen was the ideal of representative womanhood and that her appointment would be considered a recognition of the women of Ohio. The Women's Republican Club of Toledo and Lucas County wrote that Democratic and Republican women alike would approve her appointment.[40] Allen's friend from the old Ohio suffrage days, lawyer Eva Epstein Shaw from Toledo, wrote that "None of the applicants who were being considered up to the time of the nomination compares with Judge Allen in the matter of education, experience, ability, and standing."[41]

The Grand Lodge Brotherhood of Railroad Trainmen gave unqualified support and its representative wrote Roosevelt that "labor in general has genuine confidence in Judge Allen."[42]

Rebhan filled Allen's calendar with speaking engagements around the state, and again the audiences were "wonderful," "nice," and "swell." Elizabeth Hauser pitched in to help with correspondence and publicity. Altogether 238 individuals, three labor organizations, 81 social and political organizations and 32 lawyers wrote endorsements for her appointment.[43] Undoubtedly a very high percentage were from women and women's organizations.

The most strident opposing voice was that of Clayborne George who wrote for the Legal Defense Committee of the Cleveland NAACP that it was unanimously opposed to Allen's appointment because of her agreement in the decision against Ohio State University student Doris Weaver. The dissent was aimed at the entire Supreme Court bench, however, as George wrote: "We believe that by this opinion, an opinion reeking and pregnant with racial discrimination, Judge Allen and her associates disbarred themselves from any further judicial consideration."[44] The committee asked Bulkley to use his influence against such appointment. The Cincinnati chapter of NAACP sent a similar letter.

Newton D. Baker wrote Allen that he was not endorsing her and had made no endorsements to the Roosevelt administration for reasons too complicated to bother her with.[45] Baker's firm sent an attorney to Washington to oppose her appointment.[46] In response Judge Stephenson went to Washington to support it.[47]

There was criticism that Allen's opinions on workmen's compensation had not been universally sympathetic to labor and that she had been lenient about enforcement of closed shop contracts. Allen attributed the criticism to former Chief Judge Marshall whom she had attacked so vigorously for his conduct in the Ohio Supreme Court. Lawyer friends were persuaded to write to President William Green of the American Federation of Labor that Allen was more liberal and more favorable to labor than any other judge in Ohio. Most distressing to Allen was a query from Frances Kellor about the closed-shop case. She hastened to explain her reasoning, and convinced Kellor to support her.[48]

To Rebhan and Allen, Bulkley seemed slow about making up his mind and making his recommendation. At the end of January, 1934, Dewson wrote to Mrs. Roosevelt: "Heavens, How I hope he [the President] will appoint Florence Allen, particularly since there has been no federal recognition of the women in Ohio . . . ." Mrs. Roosevelt responded promptly with a memo to her husband asking about Judge Allen's chances.[49] Meantime, Pontius had written Rebhan that the problem was that Allen was a woman.[50]

By mid-February there were signs that the appointment was being considered, for a representative of Homer Cummings came to Cleveland to talk with common pleas judges about Allen.[51] At the end of February the Attorney General sent his recommendation finding Allen "preeminently qualified" along with the endorsement of Bulkley, Ohio congressmen and other key figures to the President.[52] Roosevelt sent Allen's nomination to the Senate early in March.

In the Senate it was reviewed by a special subcommittee of the Judiciary Committee and reported favorably but "without enthusiasm."[53] The Senate confirmed the nomination unanimously. President Roosevelt signed the appointment and it became official on March 23, 1934, Allen's fiftieth birthday, perhaps at the very moment when the judges of the Ohio Supreme Court had put aside their differences for a surprise birthday party for her, complete with a cake decorated with fifty birthday candles.[54]

Congratulations poured in from all over the world. There were dinners and banquets in her honor. In Cincinnati the Business and Professional Women's Club sponsored a great banquet honoring the new judge at the Netherlands Plaza Hotel. Two hundred organizations joined in the festivities, and laudatory speeches abounded. In Cleveland the Bar Association and women's organizations honored her with a large banquet; in Washington the women lawyers had an elegant luncheon. There were many letters of congratulation, including those from Frances Perkins and Ruth Bryan Owen, who invited her to visit Denmark. There was even a letter from Mrs. Upton, who was living in retirement in California on meager financial resources.[55]

Newspapers proclaimed the news with far more fanfare than the lukewarm approval of the Senate Judiciary Committee merited. The *Cincinnati Post* called the appointment "a happy choice," breaking precedent by introducing a woman into the nation's second highest tribunal, outranked only by the United States Supreme Court.[56]

The appointment did break precedent but it did not start a trend. It was a single incident, the result of a fortuitous combination of circumstances: an unusually effective women's division in the party, the presence

110

of a feminist first lady, and a well-qualified woman judge with helpful political connections and the support of a nation-wide network of women's organizations. Public statements emphasized that she had been appointed because she was a well qualified judge not because she was a woman. Stephenson and Cummings said that their most arduous task in securing the appointment was to see that she was not rejected because she was a woman.[57] Privately Allen thought that Roosevelt had appointed her for "shock effect" and that he wasn't really serious about appointing women to high court positions.[58]

From 1934 to her retirement in 1959, and for many years thereafter, Judge Allen was the highest ranking woman jurist in the land and there were no other contenders for the honor. She alone faced the challenge of proving that a woman could survive and prove herself in the higher echelons of the federal courts.

FOOTNOTES

[1] According to her diary Papa and Florence were seriously considering another run for the Senate as late as January 27, 1930. June 1, 1930 she noted that her father hoped she would run for governor.

[2] *Cincinnati Times Star*, March 15,1932, Allen papers, LC, container 7.

[3] Her diary records talks with Bulkley and Young in Washington on January 25, 1932; on January 28 she talked with Mrs. Pyke and they decided the 22nd district "seems good." February 5, 1932 she went to Warren and "talked Congress" with Hauser.

[4] According to a memo at the end of her diary for 1931.

[5] From campaign materials, Allen papers, WRHS, container 14, folder 5.

[6] Letter from WCTU April 7, 1932, Allen papers, WRHS, container 6, folder 4.

[7] Debate reported in Cleveland *Plain Dealer*, October 1, 1932, p. 1.

[8] Diary, September 30, 1932.

[9] Cleveland *Press*, October 12, 1932, p. 4.

[10] From campaign materials, Allen papers, WRHS, container 14, folder 5.

[11] The audience at a PTA meeting was "unfriendly," diary September 30,1932; October 22, 1932 a workers' meeting was "a flop."

[12] According to Susan Ware, *Beyond Suffrage: Women in the New Deal*, Cambridge: Harvard University Press, 1981, p. 31, Dewson and Allen met in 1914 at the NAWSA convention. Dewson was active in the suffrage campaign in Maine and at one time was president of the Consumer's League.

[13] They were Ruth Bryan Owen, ex-representative from Florida, Nellie Taylor Ross, former governor of Wyoming, Emily Newell Blair, director of Women's Democratic Clubs, and Frances Perkins, Industrial Commissioner of New York. From "Report on 1932 Campaign: Women's Division," p. 5. Dewson papers, RL, container 14.

[14] Other network women speakers were journalist Fannie Hurst, Anna Dickie Olesen of Minnesota, and Hattie Caraway, candidate for the Senate from Arkansas. *Ibid.*

[15] *Cleveland Press*, November 1, 1932, p. 9.

[16] She had known Seltzer since early suffrage days; Hopwood was a friend of the family. Hopwood died in 1928 but the editorial policy of the *Plain Dealer* did not change greatly. Allen conferred with Seltzer about her campaign according to her diary on February 20 and September 17, 1932, at which time the talk was "not satisfactory."

[17] *Cleveland Press*, October 26, 1932, Allen papers, WRHS, container 26, folder 14.

[18] Editorial *Cleveland Press*, December 1, 1932, Allen papers, WRHS, container 6, folder 4. The Cuyahoga Bar Association demanded that she resign from the supreme court if she were a candidate for Congress, but Allen replied that the Ohio constitution did not require her to do so. *Dayton Journal*, March 27, 1932, Allen papers, LC, container 8.

[19] Cleveland *Plain Dealer*, October 11, 1932, p. 8.

[20] Ohio came in 41st of the states for Roosevelt and was marked as a "danger" state in Dewson's papers, RL, container 14. According to the *Cincinnati Enquirer*, April 1, 1934, Allen came within 19,000 votes of defeating Bolton, Allen papers, WRHS, container 26, folder 17.

[21] Note on Christmas card to Dewson, 1932, in Dewson papers, RL, container 1.

[22] Diary, November 20, 1932: "To see Kellor and much talk of appointments." She visited Frances Kellor and Mary Drier about twice a year for most of her life, but this trip seems to have been for a special purpose.

[23] Letter from Farley to Allen, November 18, 1932, Allen papers, WRHS, container 6, folder 4.

[24] Letter from Allen to Farley, November 30, 1932. *Ibid.*

[25] Letters in Allen papers, *Ibid.*

[26] *History of NAWL*, p. 19; *Women Lawyers' Journal*, XVI, July 1928, p. 2.

[27] See for example letter from James A. Farley to Mary Dewson, February 20, 1933 asking for suggestions as to what should be done for the various women throughout the country who had done such a remarkable piece of work. Dewson papers, RL, container 14.

[28] Records in Dewson papers, *Ibid.*

[29] Letter of Boardman to Farley, January 7, 1933. Allen papers, WRHS, container 6, folder 4.

[30] Joseph P. Lash, *Eleanor and Franklin*, New York: Signet, 1971, pp. 515-516, from a speech, March 24, 1933. It is interesting to note that although Perkins was unmercifully ridiculed and criticized in office she survived during Roosevelt's entire presidency and brought about many new benefits for working people that social feminists had been calling for for many years.

[31] Letter from Allen to Roosevelt, November 2, 1933. Roosevelt papers, RL, OF #15 Department of Labor, box 4, miscellaneous 1933-1935.

[32] Letter of Allen to Eleanor Roosevelt, May 1, 1933 and Eleanor Roosevelt to Allen, May 5, 1933. Eleanor Roosevelt papers, RL, ER correspondence, 1933.

[33] Her diary notes "fighting" with the Chief over the assignment of cases December 10, 1932.

[34] Note in diary December 23, 1933, "Hickenlooper dies." Letter of Carrie Chapman Catt to Mary Dewson, December 26, 1933. Allen papers, WRHS, container 6, folder 4.

[35] According to her diary, one on November 23, 1933 and another on February 8, 1934.

[36] Letter of Allen to Dewson, March 4, 1934, thanking Dewson for "coming to the front for me as you did." ". . . you helped me over the biggest hurdle." Dewson papers, RL, container 1.

[37] Letters in Allen papers, WRHS, container 6, folder 5.

[38] Letter from Weygandt to Cummings, December 27, 1933. Allen papers, WRHS, container 6, folder 5.

[39] Letter from Clarke to Bulkley, January 8, 1934, Allen papers, WRHS, container 6, folder 5. *To Do Justly*, p. 94.

[40] Letter of Frances Perkins to Roosevelt, January 15, 1934. Roosevelt papers, RL, OF 209f, 6th Circuit, 1934-1938. Other letters are in Allen papers, WRHS, container 6, folder 5.

[41] Shaw's letter in National Archives and Records Service, Legislative and Diplomatic Branch, U.S. Senate, Committee on the Judiciary, with Docket No. 144.

[42] Letters in Allen papers, WRHS, container 6, folder 4.

[43] Figures from Allen papers, LC, container 7. Also WRHS, container 18, folder 1.

[44] Letter from Clayborne George in Allen papers, WRHS, container 6, folder 5.

[45] Letter from Baker to Allen, January 24, 1934, Allen papers, WRHS, container 6, folder 5. Baker had wanted the presidential nomination in 1932 and was "dismayed" at Roosevelt's victory and refused to support him, according to Arthur M. Schlesinger Jr., *The Age of Roosevelt*, v. I, *The Crises of the Old Order*, Houghton Mifflin, Boston, 1956, pp. 311-312.

[46] *To Do Justly*, p. 94.

[47] According to a hand-written note in Allen's handwriting in Allen papers, WRHS, container 1, folder 4.

[48] All correspondence in Allen papers, WRHS, container 6, folder 5.

[49] Letter of Dewson to Eleanor Roosevelt, January 24, 1934; ER letter to FDR, January 29, 1934. Roosevelt papers, RL, OF 209f, Sixth Circuit, 1934-1938.

[50] Letter of H.C. Pontius to Rebhan, February 5, 1934, Allen papers, WRHS, container 6, folder 5.

[51] Cleveland *Plain Dealer*, January 19, 1934, p. 8.

[52] Attorney General's letter of transmittal to President Roosevelt dated February 28, 1934. Roosevelt papers, RL, OF 209f, Sixth Circuit, 1934-1938.

[53] The words are those of Senator King (Democrat, Utah) who was chairman of the subcommittee that reviewed Allen's nomination, quoted from *Washington Post*, March 14, 1934, Allen papers, LC, container 7. According to the records in the National Archives of the U.S. Senate, Committee on the Judiciary, Docket No. 144, one member of the committee "protested."

[54] *Youngstown Vindicator*, March 24, 1934, Allen papers, LC, container 8.

[55] All letters in Allen papers, WRHS, container 6, folder 5.

[56] *Cincinnati Post*, March 24, 1934, Allen papers, WRHS, container 30.

[57] *Columbus State Journal*, February 26, 1934, and several other sources, Allen papers, WRHS, container 25, folder 16. *To Do Justly*, p. 95.

[58] From personal interview.

Chapter 9

AMONG THE BRETHREN

The media generally and women's organizations in particular as well as many lawyers and personal acquaintances had greeted Allen's appointment to the Federal Court of Appeals with enthusiasm and approval. There was no outburst of applause, however, from the brethren of the federal court establishment. None of the judges of the Sixth Circuit favored her appointment and one of them was reported to be so upset he took to his bed for two days.[1] Judge Allen was not apprehensive for she had learned from experience that judges who at first had opposed a woman peer came to accept her when they found that she did her work conscientiously and effectively.[2] It was her goal to perform so that the male judges would find a woman judge acceptable.

The court house itself was built with the needs of the brethren in mind. The new woman judge had to make a long trek to the public areas of the building to use the rest room, and it was weeks before permission could be acquired from Washington to appropriate one of them and equip it with a lock and key to give her some privacy. Commodious spittoons were standard installed equipment beside all judges' chairs, and were constant reminders of the gender of the individuals who were expected to occupy those chairs.

These unimportant matters did not bother Judge Allen and were regarded with good humor, but criticism of her work was a different matter. There were four judges, one from each state in the circuit, and three sat for each case. During their two weeks in Cincinnati they heard cases, conferred together, came to decisions and then returned to their homes to write the decisions assigned to them by the presiding judge.

The written decisions of the Court of Appeals were expressions of the reasoning of the concurring judges and had the force of law. This was in contrast to the Ohio Supreme Court where the law was stated in separate syllabi and the opinion was the reasoning of one judge and was not subject to alteration by others. In the circuit court the decision was drafted by one judge, then sent to the concurring judges for criticism or approval, finally altered and rewritten as the pronouncement of the court. Discussion and correspondence was extensive. Federal appellate judges were close to the top in the hierarchy of courts. The vast majority of cases would never go to a higher court, and appellate judges were conscious of their important position. They wanted decisions that would reflect well on the court and render maximum justice.

The work method was new to Judge Allen. She was not accustomed to "help" from other judges and took criticism personally. She felt she was being criticized for trivialities and trumped-up criticisms that would not be made of other judges, which indicated to her that a woman judge was not being treated equally.[3] Her diary was dotted with notations of "mean" letters, particularly from Judge Charles C. Simons,[4] who was indeed a stickler for well-written opinions, but who in the long run became one of Judge Allen's advocates. In later years letters from Simons commending her excellent opinions accumulated among her papers.

In the beginning, when she felt she was being discriminated against, law clerk Luke Lyman was a meticulous assistant and masterly moderator. Recently graduated from law school, newly married and considering himself lucky to find a good job in the depths of the depression, he approached his work with vigor and devotion. He carefully checked every word and statement in her writing, verifying all lower court records and lawyers' briefs and searching for additional supportive cases. He knew that any decision written by a woman judge would be picked apart and must be good to survive, and he took a very positive view of the criticisms of the other judges. In his view criticisms would have come to any new judge, regardless of sex, and should be taken for their constructive value.[5]

Gradually the criticism subsided. Allen became accustomed to the give-and-take system and the brethren grew accustomed to her presence, acquired respect for her ability and regarded her as a good judge in a congenial atmosphere of equality. The fellowship never extended to lunch, however, for the men betook themselves to the University Club or elsewhere where woman were not admitted, while Judge Allen hiked "to get rid of the stuffiness" or lunched with women friends.

The most important case of Judge Allen's career was that of the *Tennessee Electric Power Company v. The Tennessee Valley Authority*[6] in 1937. The problems of the Tennessee river and its valley had been in the public spotlight for a generation. American frontiersmen had found the river an avenue of westward passage before 1800 and the valley began to be populated. Easy passage and boat traffic were obstructed by a sharp drop in the river's course at Muscle Shoals, Alabama. No one had been able to master the shoals and rapids. During World War I the federal government started to build munitions plants and a dam at Muscle Shoals to provide electric power for the munitions plants.

The project was not completed before the war ended and for the next fifteen years there was great political controversy about Muscle

Shoals. The problem was augmented by the fact that the Tennessee valley was deforested and eroded and the population lived in poverty. Floods added to the desolation and caused great property damage.

Senator George Norris promoted a plan whereby the government would complete the dams and produce fertilizer and generate electricity. Controversy centered around whether the government should own and operate the facility or whether it should be transferred to private enterprise.

The National League of Women Voters studied the project and as early as 1921 called upon Congress to complete the dams in line with the Norris Plan. In the middle twenties the NLWV conducted an intensive survey of power development and regulation, with every chapter in the country conducting a local investigation and education program, and in 1925 the NLWV adopted a platform that Muscle Shoals be treated as a public asset. Farm and labor organizations favored the plan, but, according to one historian, the NLWV was the only citizen's organization to support and campaign for the project.[7]

As time passed the emphasis of the Norris Plan changed from fertilizer to power production and private power interests became alarmed at the prospect of competition. In 1928 and in 1931 the Norris Plan passed Congress and the NLWV supported it with a massive educational campaign, but presidents Coolidge and Hoover vetoed it.[8]

When Roosevelt became president he favored the Plan as a model of social and economic regeneration of a poverty area. Most of the legislation of the first hundred days of his administration was an effort to keep the system from falling apart, but, in the view of historian Arthur Schlesinger, the enactment of the Tennessee Valley Authority Act "stood out as an earnest of the better America which dedicated men might create."[9] The Act empowered the TVA to control the flooding of the river, to develop its navigation, and produce and market electric power as consistent with such purposes. Eleven dams were to be built and the project was allotted up to half a billion dollars. Municipalities in the depressed area anticipated buying power from the TVA and building distribution plants with funds from still another government agency, the Works Progress Administration.

The constitutionality of the TVA was soon challenged by eighteen private power companies, charging that the real purpose of the TVA was to sell electric power and that this was unfair competition. The question came to the federal courts when the first dam was completed in 1936. An Alabama court found the building and the scope of the dam within the constitutional authority of the TVA,[10] but at the request of private power companies District Court Judge John J. Gore of Tennessee granted a preliminary injunction prohibiting further TVA development until a case covering all the dams could be heard. It seemed likely the case would end up in the U.S. Supreme Court.[11]

For several months the case was in limbo, with the TVA and the composition of the Supreme Court bench major issues in the 1936 presidential campaign. The Supreme Court had been the chief roadblock in the implementation of Roosevelt's policies. During his first term it had overruled and voided twelve acts of Congress which he thought critical to his reform program,[12] the major point of contention being the extent to which the federal government could regulate the economy. The inclination of the court was conservative, several of the justices having been appointed in the twenties. President Harding had appointed four justices during his three-year term; Roosevelt had not had a chance to appoint *any* during his entire first term.

With the aid of Homer Cummings and others, Roosevelt put together a package of judicial reforms including the right of the president to appoint one co-justice per year up to the number of justices who had passed the age of seventy. Several had passed that age. The proposal created a furor with the overwhelming majority of judges, lawyers, women's organizations and other articulate sectors of citizenry opposing it.

President Roosevelt won a resounding victory in the 1936 election, and interpreted it as a mandate from the people to continue his policies. He pushed his plans for judicial reforms. The plan to change the Supreme Court failed, but by August 1937 Congress had passed other sections of the package, including pensions for retiring justices and a section providing that no injunction could be implemented setting aside an act of Congress except on hearing before three federal judges, one circuit judge and two district judges. The TVA case fitted the specifications exactly.

Judge Gore and Judge John D. Martin of Tennessee were the district judges; Judge Allen was the presiding circuit judge. Allen became the presiding judge by default of the other three circuit judges, two of whom were unacceptable because of conflict of interests, and the third because of illness.[13] Allen was uniquely qualified for the case. As a Clevelander she was thoroughly acquainted with the issues surrounding the building of the Cleveland municipal power facility, which to a degree had served as a model for the Norris Plan. One of the proponents of the TVA wrote Allen that it was the effectiveness of the Cleveland municipal light plant which gave Norris and the rest of them the idea from 1921 on that it would be worth while to fight for Muscle Shoals.[14] In the Ohio Supreme Court she had heard many cases involving municipalities and power.

The Sixth Circuit judges had considered the case in the spring of 1937 at the request of TVA lawyers, but had returned it to the district court where the case was filed. During the summer in Colorado Allen had spent her time reading her law books and Supreme Court decisions. She was confined to quarters most of the summer after fracturing an ankle, so there was plenty of time for study.

While she was studying the country was witness to the pros and cons of the case. A congressman called for the impeachment of Judge Gore for defying the will of Congress, declaring that his injunction was "doing more to promote communism than all the soapbox orators in America."[15] The TVA commissioners themselves could come to no agreement as to their purpose vis-à-vis the private companies and aired their differences publicly. The Supreme Court refused to consider the case, saying it must first be heard in Tennessee. Spokesmen for the private utilities said the companies would be destroyed by tax-subsidized competition. No compromise could be found; a showdown was inevitable.

Normally Florence Allen led an extraordinarily active life; when news came of her participation in the TVA case her energy reached new heights. There followed immediately a quick trip from Colorado, one day at home, on to New York and Westerly over roads that seemed worse than usual and complications with tires that had already gone too far, one day at home in Cleveland to go to the office and the shack, pack for Columbus for a day with Esther and Dr. Scott, and on to Nashville in early September for conferences with Judges Gore and Martin.[16]

The hearing began in Chattanooga late in November. Florence and Mary Pierce, who was on leave of absence from Park School, rented a cottage on Lookout Mountain in an area called Fairyland where the judge could walk with her dogs every day. Mary went about making the cottage comfortable and managing the household. Judges Gore and Martin, the Lymans and others were invited for Thanksgiving dinner prepared by Mary, complete with turkey and all the trimmings. Allen did not have time for much socialization and was careful to maintain judicial isolation, but she did become well acquainted with Judge Martin and his family and it was a lasting connection. Some time later Allen successfully supported Martin for appointment as an appellate judge; Martin supported Allen for appointment as a Supreme Court justice.

The TVA case was heralded by the *New York Times* as one of the most important and far reaching cases in American history, testing the extent to which the New Deal could carry forward the "collectivist tendencies" of its whole nationwide power program as opposed to the individualism of existing power companies.[17] On the opening day Newton D. Baker, Allen's former political friend, was there as chief counsel for the plaintiffs. His presentation for the stalwarts of private enterprise was superb.[18] Unfortunately Baker died at his home in Cleveland during the course of the trial, but his law firm represented the plaintiffs without interruption. Wendell L. Willkie was there on the opening day as President of the Commonwealth and Southern System with which several of the companies were affiliated. James Lawrence Fly headed the TVA attorneys as chief counsel.

Counsel for the plaintiffs declared that the stated purpose of the TVA for flood control and navigation was a sham to cover up the real purpose which was power production. Counsel declared that the TVA had used unconstitutional methods of selling and distributing the power, and had also violated the states rights to regulate utility rates by setting up federal yardsticks on price, rates that were subsidized by taxpayers' money. Counsel for the TVA maintained that navigation and flood control were the true purpose of the project, that power production was incidental, and that a great plan for the conservation of natural resources would be destroyed if the TVA were eliminated.[19]

Predictions were that the trial would be a long one, but several decisions of the judges served to consolidate evidence and save time, decisions very much in the style of Judge Allen. The judges denied a motion for a deposition from Secretary of the Interior Ickes on the role of the WPA in financing the building of transmission lines and distribution stations for municipalities. The judges ruled that they would not admit as evidence a mass of newspaper reports and public speeches by TVA personnel but would only admit official statements made in congressional committees and the like. The judges ruled they would not hear cumulative evidence of competition from all the separate utility companies but only typical evidence from representatives of two groups, the big companies and the small companies.[20] The judges were surely aware that the Roosevelt administration was very interested in this case as a possible turning point in court attitudes toward the New Deal programs and that delay did not serve the purpose of the government.

Judge Allen's court began promptly at 9:30 in the morning and ended promptly at 4:00 in the afternoon. On one day a witness was ready for cross-examination at 3:58. The soliciter asked Judge Allen if she wanted to suspend court at this point. "Court will suspend in two minutes," she replied, "Proceed."[21] Court reporters worked in fifteen-minute shifts, leaving immediately to have their notes transcribed. Within a few minutes after the court closed the record was ready so the judges could take it home for study. In the midst of the case Judge Allen was invited to the White House for dinner with the Roosevelts, but she replied that she was too busy to accept.[22] Given a choice between meeting and socializing with top political people or staying on the job and adhering to duty created no dilemma for her; she chose duty.

An array of witnesses were examined and cross-examined in the small, high-ceilinged, brown-paneled courtroom. This was a case in equity and the decision rested on physical evidence rather than cases in precedent. Engineers testified as to whether or not the reservoirs of the dams had been built to provide a water level suitable for flood control or power production. Navy men testified as to whether or not the money appropriated for waterways was too much for simple navigation or if something more was in mind. Experts for the private power companies testified that there was adequate power in the region before TVA and that in most rural areas there was no demand for power because there were only "low-rental houses, shacks and Negro cabins, where neither the landlords nor the tenants are willing to install electricity."[23] Other experts testified that the TVA did not advertise its power but upon request made it available to county cooperatives and municipalities, none of them former customers of the private companies.

On January 15 attorneys for the power companies and the TVA summarized their cases in a crowded courtroom, and Judge Allen promised a decision the following week. She spent many sleepless nights while she worked on it, sometimes getting up to work from three to six in the morning. Day after day she wrote in her diary that she was "dog tired." She offered her work to Judges Martin and Gore for revision as a panel decision, but they graciously conceded that it was her work.[24] When the time came, she read aloud the entire decision in the courtroom, all 8,000 words of it. *Time* magazine reported that a hush fell over the courtroom when she came out to read the decision, but that seventy minutes and several gulps of water later it was clear that the TVA had scored a monumental victory.[25] The *New York Times*, which often finds nothing important enough for a front-page headline, proclaimed in headline "Whole TVA Is Ruled Valid"[26]

The decision found that the TVA did not conspire to destroy private utilities, that municipalities were not coerced to buy its power, that the private companies would not be forced to lower rates, and, most importantly, that the function of the TVA was flood control and navigation and that power production was incidental:

> Under the statute, therefore, the generation of electric energy is specifically required to be incidental to the exercise of constitutional powers under the interstate commerce clause, and the operation complies with this requirement. The record shows that the dams are adapted by their construction to combined use for flood control and improved navigation, and to generate electricity. All experts agree that the pondage at each of the dams on the main river and also at the storage dams on the tributaries can be drawn down, and that space thereby made available is capable of being used to store flood waters in the rainy season. It appears from the uncontroverted testimony that the erection of the main-river dams will create a nine-foot navigable channel. We find from the weight of evidence that Norris has been used for the purpose of controlling floods. These facts are not controverted, except by opinion evidence.
>
> Certain expert witnesses, in answer to hypothetical questions, stated that the dams might be operated for the primary purpose of power. Thousands of pages of testimony and numerous exhibits were introduced to show that Congress might have adopted a better plan than the TVA unified system. Experts equally qualified testified to the contrary.
>
> The court is of opinion that the relative value of these various plans is immaterial, since it has been established that the TVA project is reasonably adapted to use for combined flood control, navigation, power and national defense, and that in actual operation the

creation of energy is subordinated to the needs of navigation and flood control.[27]

The utility companies immediately appealed the decision to the U.S. Supreme Court; it affirmed Allen's opinion.[28]

The case was judged strictly on the basis that the federal government has control over navigable waters, but it stands in history as one of the first cases in a new orientation of the courts toward more responsiveness to social needs. It helped to establish the liberal tradition of government action on behalf of the disadvantaged and underprivileged.

The practical results of the case were to end the legal objection to the TVA. The legal results were to limit the rights protected by nonexclusive franchises,[29] as in this case the franchises of the private power companies had not protected them from competition from other agencies. In the long run, however, the private companies survived side by side with the TVA and the Tennessee valley was rehabilitated. Within twenty years, before the building of the dams was completed, it was no longer thought of by liberals as a great step forward. The question of private versus public enterprise dropped out of the discussion and the new liberals thought of the TVA as a mindless extension of the bureaucracy, growing needlessly at the expense of the environment.

With her appointment as a federal judge, Florence Allen's future was surely in the judiciary branch of government and not in the legislature. Three unusually successful campaigns for judgeships and a presidential appointment, balanced against two failures in campaigns for legislative office, was convincing evidence that the public was willing to accept a woman as the keeper of the laws if not as the maker of the laws. An appointment to the United States Supreme Court would be the crown of a judicial career.

When she was appointed to the Federal Court of Appeals several people recalled that it had been a stepping stone to the Supreme Court. There were a number of women in the Democratic Party who continued pressure for appointment of women, with Eleanor Roosevelt leading the list. Mrs. Roosevelt's friend Mary Drier and Frances Kellor, who had become an important figure in labor reform and international arbitration, were avid promoters of Allen's career.[30] After the TVA case was finished Allen went to New York for a visit with Drier and Kellor.[31] Allen always felt that she had a close link with Mrs. Roosevelt and felt that the latter went out of her way to be nice to her. Eleanor was often in Florence's mind, perhaps more than reality merited. Allen met Mrs. Roosevelt only after she became first lady and they were not in the category of personal friends, although they clearly admired each other. In her newspaper column, "My Day," Roosevelt complimented Allen as a "remarkable speaker" and one who was able to inspire her audiences.[32]

For nearly five years Roosevelt had no opportunity to appoint a Supreme Court justice. He was eager to do so and to change the complexion of the court to one more congenial with his liberal viewpoints. Beginning in 1937 and during the following two years he had a chance to appoint four justices in rapid succession. The president and the public regarded these appointments as extremely important and interest ran high. Allen's name was proposed for every vacancy.

Support for Allen reached full tide during the TVA case, first when Roosevelt was searching for a successor for Justice Sutherland. The *Washington Daily News*, for example, announced on January 12, 1938 that Roosevelt was "toying with the idea of naming a woman to the high bench." Why not appoint Judge Florence Ellinwood Allen, the editor asked, adding that she was handling the TVA case to the satisfaction of both sides, that she was a woman of rare courage and scholarly mind, and would take her place beside the illustrous liberals on the court.[33] *Life* magazine published a full-page color portrait of her in her judicial robes. The caption noted that "wiseacres would not be surprised if the precedent breaking President were to choose her" for the Supreme Court.[34]

The five Scripps-Howard newspapers in Ohio conducted a spirited editorial campaign. The editor of the *Cleveland Press* praised her for her sincerity and fidelity, her pioneering spirit, her Spartan sense of duty. The editor complimented her for thinking "as a man" and for lacking "the hard-boiled attitude so often accompanying women successful in competition with men."[35] Other Cleveland newspapers supported her, including foreign language newspapers. Hungarian *Szabadsag*, for example, recommended her editorially as "one of the most talented of judges."[36] On a streetcorner in downtown Cleveland an admirer gave away free stamps to women who would promise to write to the president urging her appointment.

Senator Vic Donahey of Ohio was her constant supporter and proposed her name to the president and attorney general; Senator Bulkley approved. Old friends Judges Stephenson and Weygandt of the Ohio Supreme Court gave their enthusiastic support. Judge Martin of Tennessee, one of the judges in the TVA case, was an ardent activist for her cause. Senators Borah and Norris favored her. Democratic War Veterans, 6,500 strong, supported Allen, so their president wrote to Roosevelt.[37]

Women, as usual, rallied their influence. To the party women were added a number of academicians. Dean Sophonisba Breckinridge, a brilliant and recognized scholar whom Allen had known at Hull House, wrote to the attorney general and the president asking them to focus on Allen. Harriet Elliott, Dean of the Women's College of the University of North Caroline, marshalled support. Women's organizations, especially the NFBPWC, the NAWL, and the AAUW, officially supported her, sent resolutions to Washington, and encouraged their members to write personal letters.[38]

Tragically missing was Susan Rebhan's consummate skill as a campaign coordinator. Rebhan, unfortunately, died in 1935. Also missing was the activity of the network for women's promotions surrounding Mary Dewson. Its activities had diminished rapidly after 1936.[39]

On January 14, 1938 Allen's name was eliminated as a possible successor for Justice Sutherland,[40] but the campaign continued for Justice Benjamin Cordoza was ill and expected to retire. Ohio Democrats in Congress rallied to Allen's support. Harold G. Mosier wrote to the president recommending her, noting especially that she possessed "extremely liberal views." John McSweeney circulated a petition among the Ohio delegation for her support. Anthony A. Fleger "heartily endorsed" her and wrote Roosevelt that she "would meet with the approval of the majority of the practicing lawyers of the country."[41]

In March, 1939 the prospects brightened again. Roosevelt announced that he had a "surprise" when asked whom he would appoint to follow retiring Justice Brandeis. Washington was soon filled with reports that Allen was the surprise.[42] Mary Pierce tried to step into Rebhan's place as organizer, and wrote Judge Martin for advice. He replied that he heartily supported Judge Allen, identifying her as a person with "a warm heart and a cool brain." He urged immediate action because Roosevelt presumably had only one more year in office, and if Roosevelt didn't appoint her she probably wouldn't get it. "Now is the time to strike," he wrote Pierce, with advice to "let the women be turned loose now, with insistent demand for her appointment for the next vacancy." Pierce replied that she had "taken the bull by the horns, so to speak" and would do everything she could.[43] But Mary's talents were not in this particular arena. When the announcement came it was the appointment of William O. Douglas that was Roosevelt's surprise.

Some adverse criticisms were made of Allen, as was to be expected. In December 1938 the syndicated column National Whirligig, News Behind the News included an item about a federal circuit judge who was suing the internal revenue collector for attempted tax collection because the Constitution says a federal judge's salary cannot be diminished. Judge Florence Allen was said to be egging the judge on. Anyone who knew Allen would recognize this as patently false, but she was upset about it. She wanted to deny the charge publicly, but her friends advised her to do nothing in response. Her only response was to write to Eleanor Roosevelt that she always paid her income tax and was not among the judges opposing it.[44]

More alarming was an item in Drew Pearson's column, Washington Merry-Go-Round, in March 1939 stating that Florence Allen had not been appointed because her reversal record was so bad, perhaps worse than that of any other prominent federal judge, and that Attorney General

Frank Murphy had been shown a list of cases in which her decisions had been reversed. Allen immediately asked Luke Lyman and others to check the records for reversed decisions. They found that in the Ohio Supreme Court only one of her opinions and one of her *per curiam* decisions had been reversed. Her opinion which had been reversed concerned the duration of a contract between a municipality and a private power company when no duration date existed on the contract. Allen's opinion found the contract holding as long as mutually agreeable to both parties and ruled that the municipality, which wished to terminate it, could do so, a rather predictable decision for Judge Allen. The U.S. Supreme Court reversed the decision in favor of the private power company, a rather predictable reversal at that time. In the Federal Court of Appeals, twenty-eight decisions had been appealed, and only one had been reversed. Allen sent the information to the attorney general, who replied that he had never seen the list to which Pearson referred, but that he was glad to have the information anyway.[45]

The appointment never came, much as Allen hoped for it.[46] She was ambitious for herself and for the image of the Allen family, whose presence was always with her. The Supreme Court was the epitome of her career line. She was also genuinely ambitious for women, ambitious to prove that the expectations of the suffrage movement were coming to pass.

Why wasn't Judge Allen appointed to the Supreme Court in the late thirties? In her autobiography she wrote that she regretted the matter came up specifically during the TVA case.[47] And for the success of her appointment it was regrettable. There had been too much talk that any judge defending the TVA could count on being a friend of the president. Roosevelt's appointment of Allen in proximity to the TVA decision would have appeared to be crudely political, and Roosevelt was, above all, a masterly politician. Even in her home town it was observed that her appointment during the climax of the TVA case would have been regarded as a political move. There was probably "a collective sigh of relief" from the top row of government officials, the Cleveland *Plain Dealer* reported when Roosevelt had not picked Allen — "a good woman jurist appointed for political reasons" would have been deplorable.[48]

Was sex a barrier? Roosevelt said that sex was no barrier and that he knew of no reason why a woman couldn't be appointed.[49] Eleanor Roosevelt said that sex was no barrier, but added that the appointment should be made on the basis of the fitness of the individual and not the sex.[50] Sex was a very great obstacle in acquiring the qualifications of fitness.

The four men who were appointed — Hugo L. Black, Stanley Reed, Felix Frankfurter, and William O. Douglas — had qualifications that far surpassed those of Allen or any other woman. One of the new judges was a graduate of Yale and another was a law professor at Yale. Women of that generation weren't at Yale. Florence Allen's brothers went to Yale! Two of the new judges were graduates of Columbia Law School. Allen very much wanted to go to Columbia, but it admitted women only in the summer session when classes were not filled by men. The fourth of the new judges was a graduate of Harvard Law School and a professor there.[51] Women weren't at Harvard.

All four of the new judges had a wide range of experiences that would be impossible for a woman to acquire. Hugo Black had been elected U.S. Senator for ten years before his appointment. Voters had not been willing to elect women senators. Stanley Reed had had years of experience as a trial lawyer, as counselor for federal bureaus, and finally as soliciter general. Felix Frankfurter had spent several years in government service, was a close advisor of the president and had an intimate connection with Justice Brandeis. William O. Douglas had a wide range of experience, and was chairman of the Securities and Exchange Commission when appointed. No woman in America had had the opportunity to match these qualifications. It would be more than forty years before women's handicaps were taken into account in making appointments. Allen's best qualification was her judicial experience; Roosevelt did not make appointments on the basis of judicial experience.

All of the new judges were confirmed liberals, supporters of liberal causes and the New Deal. On these grounds Allen could qualify. It was rumored in 1939, before the appointment of Douglas, that the inner presidential circle was looking for "a pronounced liberal,"[52] and that qualification she did not fully meet. She identified herself as a "liberal-conservative," and *Time* magazine in 1934 evaluated her as "middle-of-the-roadish."[53] Allen was liberal in the sense of sympathy toward all humankind and a love of freedom as specified in the Constitution and the laws of the land. She believed that justice under law is achievable, as the classical Greek philosophers had believed justice was achievable. She believed it the responsibility of the state to relieve the suffering and exploitation of all its citizens, a view kindred to New Deal philosophy. On the other hand, her most important liberal causes, women and peace, were dormant if not passé in the late thirties, and people no longer cared very much about "the idealistic values of yesteryears" to which she clung.

Roosevelt might have considered that had Allen been appointed she would not have been able to shed the albatross of womanhood. His own wife was criticized for her violations of the traditional image of womanhood, and Frances Perkins was vigorously criticized, partly because she was a woman in a man's office. Roosevelt had had enough trouble with the Supreme Court without adding the hazard of appointing a woman, an appointment which the public, furthermore, did not want. In January, 1938 in a public opinion poll on the question would you like to see the next appointment to the U.S. Supreme Court go to a man or a woman, 74 per cent had responded that they would like to see a man appointed and only 16 per cent wanted a woman.[54] The time was not ripe for a woman justice.

FOOTNOTES

[1] *To Do Justly*, p. 95.

[2] *Ibid.*, p. 96.

[3] From end papers in diary, 1936.

[4] Diary 1934-1937.

[5] From personal interviews.

[6] *Tennessee Electric Power Company v. The Tennessee Valley Authority*, 21 F Supp. 947.

[7] The historian is Lemons, pp. 131-132. Preston J. Hubbard, *Origins of the TVA: The Muscle Shoals Controversy, 1920-1932*, Nashville: Vanderbilt University Press, 1961, p. 20 also includes an account of the NLWV's work for the Norris Plan.

[8] Lemons, p. 133; Hubbard, p. 234.

[9] Arthur M. Schlesinger, Jr., *The Age of Democracy*, v. 2, *The Coming of the New Deal*, Boston: Houghton Mifflin, 1958, p. 319.

[10] *Ashwander v. Tennessee Valley Authority*, 297 U.S. 288. (1936)

[11] *New York Times*, November 16, 1937, p. 1.

[12] Leonard Baker, *Back to Back: The Duel Between FDR and the Supreme Court*, New York: Macmillan, 1967, p. 111.

[13] *To Do Justly*, p. 107.

[14] Letter of Judson King to Allen, January 31, 1938, Allen papers, WRHS, container 6, folder 6.

[15] *New York Times*, January 15, 1937, p. 10.

[16] Diary, September 10-27, 1937.

[17] *New York Times*, November 16, 1937, p. 1.

[18] From personal interviews.

[19] *New York Times*, November 16, 1937, p. 1.

[20] *Ibid. To Do Justly*, pp. 108-109.

[21] *The Chattanooga Times*, November 18, 1937, p. 1, Allen papers, WRHS, container 27, folder 2.

[22] *To Do Justly*, p. 110.

[23] *New York Times*, November 25, 1937, p. 27.

[24] *To Do Justly*, p. 111.

[25] *Time*, January 31, 1938, p. 12.

[26] *New York Times*, January 22, 1938, p. 1. The transcript of the testimony numbered 8,380 pages and more than two million words. The decision is reprinted in *To Do Justly*, pp. 178-201.

[27] *To Do Justly*, pp. 197-198.

[28] *Tenessee Electric Power Co. v. Tennessee Valley Authority*, 306 U.S. 118 (1939).

[29] Summarized from notations about the case in the *University of Pennsylvania Law Review*, v. 86, April 1938, pp. 667-669, and the *Michigan Law Review*, v. 37, May 1939, pp. 1134-1138.

[30] See letter of Frances Kellor to Allen, January 18, 1938, Allen papers, LC, container 1.

[31] Letter from Allen to Mary Drier, March 6, 1938, thanking her for "friendship and hospitality shown me last week." Mary Elizabeth Drier papers, SL, box 6, folder 90.

[32] June 27, 1938.

[33] *The Washington Daily News*, January 12 and 15, 1938, Allen papers, WRHS, container 27, folder 3.

[34] *Life*, January 17, 1938.

[35] *Cleveland Press*, January 15, 1938, Allen papers, WRHS, container 27, folder 3.

[36] *Szabadsag* (Cleveland), January 12, 1938, p. 1.

[37] Letter from Frederick W. Fray to Roosevelt, January 18, 1938, Allen papers, LC, container 1.

[38] Correspondence in Allen papers, WRHS, container 6, folder 6. Report of NAWL support, *New York Times,* July 25, 1938, p. 17.

[39] According to Susan Ware, *op.cit.,* the women's division couldn't do much for Florence Allen in 1938 because it was "a generation on the wane." pp. 116-131.

[40] Cleveland *Plain Dealer,* January 14, 1938, p. 13.

[41] All information from Cleveland *Plain Dealer,* January 15, 1938, p. 3.

[42] *Washington Times-Herald,* March 14, 1939, Allen papers, SMITH, box 5, folder 5.

[43] Letter from Martin to Pierce, January 16, 1939; letter from Pierce to Martin, January 18, 1939, Allen Papers, WRHS, container 6, folder 6.

[44] Letter from Allen to Roosevelt, December 7, 1938, Allen papers, WRHS, container 6, folder 6; Eleanor Roosevelt papers, RL, ER correspondence, 1938.

[45] All information in Allen papers, WRHS, container 12, folder 4. *To Do Justly,* pp. 112-113.

[46] According to personal interviews, she hoped for it but didn't expect it. Her conferences with people in the political network were not committed to paper.

[47] *To Do Justly,* p. 110.

[48] Cleveland *Plain Dealer,* January 18, 1938, p. 4.

[49] *New York Times,* January 14, 1938, p. 14.

[50] *To Do Justly,* p. 110, and Lash, p. 516.

[51] Information about justices from *Who's Who.*

[52] *New York Herald Tribune,* March 14, 1939, Allen papers, WRHS, container 27, folder 4.

[53] *Dayton Journal,* February 24, 1934, and *Time,* March 19, 1934, both in Allen papers, LC, container 8.

[54] 10% had no opinion. Hadley Cantril, Editor, *Public Opinion, 1935-1946,* Princeton: Princeton University Press, 1951, p. 389.

Chapter 10

THE TUMULTUOUS THIRTIES

The thirties were tumultuous years for Florence Allen, marked by times of sadness and joy, personal problems and personal success. Both of her parents died in the early thirties. As their health declined, caring for them in the Columbus home became difficult and it was decided that they should go to San Diego to be with Weebie and Harry who were better able to care for them. Esther took them out on the train. Florence was very involved with their financial affairs as medical bills mounted. The great depression took its toll on the family assets as she sold stocks at low prices and borrowed money to cover the bills.[1]

Corinne Tuckerman Allen died in August, 1931, one of the last of the Smith first class of 1879. Her youthful dedication to motherhood, moral purity, and social reform had inspired her for a lifetime, but greatly saddened her later years as she lost both of her sons to war and interpreted social change as moral degeneration. Her example of motherhood remained a model for her daughter Florence.[2]

Clarence Emir Allen died in July, 1932. He had been the most influential individual in his daughter's life. Although he perceived women in general in the special sphere of motherhood and morality, when it came to his own daughter, and especially after his sons died, he perceived her as a professional woman in the rough, competitive and masculine fields of law and politics. He had been extremely generous with his fatherly guidance and her success had brought him great satisfaction.

Among the unclouded joys of the early thirties was the Mexican connection. Always an internationalist, Allen had been interested in Mexico since her lecturing days with the YWCA when official American attitudes toward Mexico had been hostile. By the late twenties relations had softened somewhat, and tourism had revived.

In 1930 Allen was invited to go to Mexico for lectures and seminars arranged by the Committee on Cultural Relations of the World Council of Churches. It was an ideal arrangement for Allen and the committee. The committee's goal was to educate American tourists to understand Mexico and travel there as goodwill ambassadors in a spirit of Christian brotherhood. Judge Allen was both knowledgeable about Mexico and an eloquent advocate of Christian brotherhood. For Florence travel for pleasure alone was almost sinful and prohibitively expensive. Subsidized travel for a good

129

cause was pure joy. Her heart and mind were open to understanding the Mexicans and she felt that theirs were open to an understanding of America.[3]

During the summer of 1930 she visited Mexico City, San Louis Potosi and Querataro. At Cuernovaca, which she thought "heavenly" but where she had the inevitable bout with indigestion, she participated in seminars with Mexican scholars on inter-American relations, the Monroe Doctrine, immigration and deportation problems and problems of communism. Bertha Miller went with her to share the touring. The following winter she read everything possible about the country, studied Spanish, and gave lectures on Mexico. The following summer the lectures and touring and enthusiasm expanded. Mary Pierce went with her and a college friend from the class of '04 and her husband joined them. Back home speeches on Mexico to women's clubs, Exchange and Kiwanis clubs, and civic and church groups proliferated.

The campaign of 1932 and family problems precluded a visit that summer, but the expedition in the summer of 1933 was of the extensive proportions dear to Allen's heart. In July she went to Chicago for the International Women's Conference and made a major address at a large meeting of the NFBPWC. From there she went to Mexico where she conducted several seminars, participated in innumerable conferences, and had dinner at the ambassador's house. Her sisters Weebie and Esther and nephew Emir joined her for sight-seeing tours to learn more about the country. After her commitments were fulfilled, she took a flying trip to San Francisco to see her sister Helen and her husband Frank and a sentimental journey to Salt Lake City to make family cemetery arrangements and have a memorial service for her parents. Susan Rebhan and Mary Pierce joined her for fishing and mountain climbing in Colorado, and on the way home they stopped in Chicago to see the women's exhibit at the World's Fair[4] which memorialized Allen as one of eighteen outstanding women of the last hundred years.

Allen was very happy with the Mexican connection, feeling privileged to have had a part in easing tensions with a neighboring country. From the outset it was her intention to enjoy Mexico while learning about it and to persuade others to enjoy and learn. Where else, she asked can we so easily combine a pleasure tour and a peace pilgrimage so effectively?[5]

When Allen became a federal judge her living pattern became more complicated than ever before with regular commuting from Cincinnati where the court met, to Columbus, to Cleveland, to the shack in Lake County on week-ends and Colorado during the summer.

Cleveland was home. Florence and Susan and Mary shared a house in Shaker Heights. The three of them shared life's joys and sorrows in a comfortable family setting without benefit of men. Their commitments to each other were deep and enduring, although each led a separate life and

130

had an outstanding career. Each was a very remarkable woman in her own way.

Susan was a busy and successful practicing lawyer. She was in partnership with another woman lawyer, Dorothy Hyde, and they had an office in downtown Cleveland. Susan maintained an apartment in the city and ran for the city council in the declining years of the city manager system. She won easily, but after one term resigned saying that political jockeying of municipal affairs had become distasteful. She gave up the apartment and became a full-fledged resident of Shaker Heights. For twelve years she managed Allen's campaigns and they were masterpieces of organization! Susan and Florence worked together in many other ways, particularly in financial matters, and they enjoyed traveling together.

Susan's life was an extraordinarily active one. She was at one time or another vice president of the Cleveland Bar Association, vice president of the YWCA, secretary of the Ohio Mutual Mortgage Company, a director of Women's Hospital and of the Business and Professional Women's Club, and president of the Ohio League of Women Voters. She was a loyal Episcopalian, an Eastern Star, a member of the American Association of University Women, of the National Association of Women Lawyers, of the Women's Benefit Association and several other organizations.[6] Susan and Florence were truly a remarkable pair.

Mary continued as director of Park School and her responsibilities along with the social obligations involved kept her fully occupied. The depression put fearful obstacles in the way of the school's continuance. In one of his many unsung charitable gestures, John D. Rockefeller had donated land for use of the school, but enrollment was a problem as the tuition became a burden to some parents, and the school's finances caused Director Pierce considerable grief. In early 1935 tuition was cut in half to encourage enrollment, and in the following September it did increase, but Mary had been "very upset" about the situation for many months. In the spring of 1936 the school's problems were again "discouraging," and again the following year.[7] In the spring of 1937 Director Pierce was granted a year's leave of absence. The public announcement noted that Miss Pierce had been seriously ill during the preceeding winter and that the sabbatical was for her recovery.

Mary did have a small operation in the fall, but most of the time during her leave she was busy being Florence Allen's "cousin," a relationship that developed into a full-time role as companion and hostess. When her leave was over Park School announced Miss Pierce's replacement by a male director and considerable changes in the faculty and curriculum of the school, a new sports program being most newsworthy.[8] Mary's experience was typical of that of many women in positions of authority in the thirties who found themselves replaced by men. Mary's career change was more graceful and inconspicuous than most because she had a cousin to lean on.

Other single and unemployed women in the depression did not fare as well.

Florence maintained an office in downtown Cleveland and did most of her work there. Mrs. Ellis McClure was her secretary for many years, and was one of the few people she never called by first name, nickname or abbreviated name. Very few people gave Judge Allen orders, but Mrs. McClure did! Luke Lyman was her law clerk and Luke and his wife Helen socialized frequently with the judge. Lois and DeLo were also frequent visitors. Florence liked to entertain informally in the house in Shaker Heights, providing her guests left early enough to accommodate her early retiring hour so that she could get up at her usual five in the morning.[9]

Womanly domesticity had no appeal for her. She frequently told reporters that she did not have the time or energy for cooking or sewing or hanging drapes or picking out furniture any more than the men judges did.[10] She spent very little time shopping, a pastime ordinary women found fascinating as consumerism engulfed America. She had most of her clothes made by a favorite dressmaker, but fashion did not interest her. She asked friends to pick out hats for her and then jammed them on her head without benefit of mirror.

Her beloved niece Keenie came to Cleveland in the fall of 1930 to enroll at Park School. At first Ruth came to Cleveland to be with Keenie, but Ruth was never really divorced from her family in Westerville and in 1934 she went back. Keenie remained in Cleveland for a final year at Park School, staying with a family who were friends of Aunt Florence. Florence took a very active role as surrogate mother, at first "talking" with Keenie about staying out nights and buying things and missing school and smoking, and later "laying down the law" on such activities.[11] Aunt Florence went to everything Keenie participated in and enjoyed being with her.

The following year Keenie went to Westtown Quaker school in Pennsylvania. Aunt Florence paid the tuition, but it was not easy, and she had to request permission to pay it in installments because of other "very heavy financial burdens" which made it "a real effort for me to keep Corinne in school."[12] Although they could ill afford it, Florence and Ruth were making plans for college for Keenie.

In her walks Florence was likely to be seen with one or two or even three dogs, usually cocker spaniels. She lavished them with affection and in the thirties Keepsie, in particular, was a real charmer. Keepsie arrived a few days before Christmas, 1934. At first the little dog was kept in the kitchen and howled about it. But soon she was behaving quite well, especially at night, and went walking with the judge every day, morning and night. Keep developed quickly into "an angel," and "a perfect lady," and her mistress believed "everyone falls for Keep," in spite of the fact that she liked to dig in other people's lawns. The judge went to the shack "with Keep to see the dogwood" or "with Keep to cut grapevines." Keep barked at babies and cats, but was afraid of anything bigger. A big white-faced dog in Lake County scared her badly, and during the summer in Colorado three deer chased her out of their domain. Deer-fly bites and burrs brought special attention from her mistress.

It was a very sad day in the life of the judge when Keep was hit by a car, just before Thanksgiving, 1935 and died two days later. "I can't get Keep off my mind," wrote the judge as the little dog hung between life and death. Mary soon found another Keepsie, perhaps a brother or sister of the original. The new Keepsie was "very thin and scared" but ready to join the family. By the next Christmas the judge was moved to write on her Christmas cards:

> Keepsie and Dusty are lively and lusty,
> Their little tails wag day and night.
> They send you this greeting,
> We wish we were meeting
> With you when the Xmas dawn's bright.[13]

Visitors found Keepsie luxuriating in a big comfortable basket by the fireplace. She loved candy and was permitted to indulge. Perhaps with her own weight problem in mind, the judge was known to nibble on chocolates and pass the rest to Keepsie.

There were trips to the shack almost every week end, with strenuous exercise hiking, taking care of the trees that she loved, gathering baskets of apples, pears, and grapes, cooking steaks outdoors for lunches with friends. The beauties of nature never passed unnoticed, in the spring the blood-root, dogwoods and wild geraniums, the heavenly white violets near the waterfall, the apple blossoms, and especially the trilliums. In the fall the grapes were a delight along with hickory nuts and bittersweet, and in the winter red twigs in the snow. Pheasant, quail and flickers found food and refuge in the bushes.

During the court term Judge Allen spent two weeks of the month in Cincinnati hearing cases. On the way to Cincinnati she usually stopped in Columbus to visit Esther, who continued to live in the big old house there. She and Esther walked along Walnut Creek or in Conkle's Valley and shared personal confidences. There was always a visit to Dr. Scott for osteopathic treatment. Esther's son Emir went to Yale, graduated from medical school and took an internship in Cincinnati. Aunt Florence saw him often until he married and moved to New England.

She lived in a hotel in Cincinnati, rose early, took her usual half hour of exercises, walked to the court house, walked two or three miles at lunchtime to get rid of the stuffiness, and walked back to the hotel. In the early years the court was not very busy. There were often days without court work and she felt frustrated at being away from home. Work or not, she went to the movies almost every night. Newspeople welcomed her and identified her as a member of an old Cincinnati family, the granddaughter of Jacob Tuckerman, at one time president of Farmer's College. Judge Allen's family was always a family of teachers, Cincinnati readers were told, for her father had been a professor of Greek and Latin, her mother a founder of the PTA, her sister a dean of women, and the judge herself began her career as a teacher before shifting to law and still read Greek for pleasure.[14]

Summers usually meant several weeks near Loveland, Colorado. It was quite an entourage that made the trek out and back, with Florence, Mary and Susan, the dogs and a trailer. They stayed in cabins or pitched a tent in parks or near gas stations or occasionally in a farmer's field. Accommodations were often rated according to how convenient they were for the dogs.[15]

The place in Colorado was located on a beautiful glacial moraine, with a continuous slope going up in a series of tiers which invited climbing. Florence arose at five o'clock almost every morning, long before anyone else except the deer, elk and beavers were about, and walked briskly with her dogs in the fresh mountain air. By the time the rest of the household was up she had done a day's work and had a fine appetite for the mountain trout and pancakes, the specialty of the house, served on the screened porch.[16] She found it exhilarating to climb the moraine, but she also spent hours reading and playing the piano. She felt that music was the reality of her inner life. Her favorite music had changed from the romantic fantasies of Schumann to the mature sonorities of Brahms.

The summer place was a mecca for relatives and friends, reminiscent of earlier days in Salt Lake City. Mary was an expert fisherman, hauling in trout by the sixes and eights. Neophytes joined her with great expectations, sometimes fulfilled. There was entertainment for everyone: horseback riding and hiking and camping, a great variety of wildlife to be observed, and sightseeing nearby.

After their vacation together in 1935 Susan returned to Cleveland ill with intestinal influenza. Two days later she was in the hospital and very uncomfortable. Florence and Mary did everything they could in the way of caring for her, but by the middle of September Susan was dead, at the age of 49. Mary arranged for the funeral service at Trinity Cathedral, Marie Wing organized a committee for a fitting memorial,[17] and Florence took care of her estate.

With Susan gone and Mary retired, Florence became the breadwinner of the household. To make matters worse, Florence had fallen heir to an awesome debt. She had served as accommodation signer on notes for two friends who had invested in the Alcazar Hotel. With the death of both friends and the hotel's financial collapse in the depression, Florence was left to pay off the notes and to be very involved in the affairs of the hotel.[18]

The Alcazar had been built in the golden days of the twenties when real estate experts had said that Cleveland needed two apartment hotels. In spite of that modest prognostication, seven had been built. The Alcazar was a handsome building in Spanish style, tastefully appointed with tiles and other imports from Spain. Bondholders had liens of nearly a half million dollars against it and there was, in addition, a second mortgage.[19] With the depression and the surplus of apartment hotels, the Alcazar could not pay its debts. The mortgage was foreclosed and Allen was called on to make good the notes.[20] She could have avoided the burden by declaring bankruptcy, but her sense of loyalty and integrity compelled her to make the payments.[21] It took her ten years to pay off the debt which had befallen her as co-signer of the notes.[22] Mary and Florence were very hard up and sometimes literally counted their pennies and waited anxiously for Florence's paycheck.

Allen's health was relatively good in the thirties. The wretched headaches disappeared and many of her aches and pains were what might be expected by anyone who exercised so vigorously. In Cincinnati she fell down some steps in the old court house building, breaking two teeth and bruising her face. She earned the admiration of her fellow judges by insisting on continuing her duties in spite of the pain of her injuries and the embarrassment of a bandaged face.[23] She always worried about her health, however, and suffered from many symptoms, most of which passed away. In the fall of 1939 she was bothered by a little arthritis, but it didn't stop her from getting a new saw for sawing wood.

She continued to be very concerned about her weight, recording it in her diary frequently, sometimes three times a day. She took up swimming and had a 45-minute swim at lunchtime in the YWCA pool in Cleveland or Cincinnati or elsewhere almost every day. The rowing machine and the victrola records fell into disuse as weight controls, but simple abstainence was constant. Suppers of bananas and milk and ginger-ale snacks replaced the pastries and fudge so beloved in her youth. She did not go so far as to give up oysters in Philadelphia, lobster in Boston, lunch at Schraft's in New York, or grape pie at the shack, but these were only occasional dispensations. Fortunately she did not lose her sense of humor about it. When a reporter asked her what she liked to do most, she replied that if she could she would climb a mountain daily — "one not too high for a fat woman." An observer in 1935 reported that she ate only about one-third of what an average person ate but seemed to have incredible amounts of energy anyway.[24] The following summer she could record that she weighed 168,[25] but at the slightest relaxation of vigilance that figure bounded over 200.

Tradition required federal judges to refrain from making public statements on controversial questions, and at first Judge Allen was very conscientious about observing that tradition. One frustrated correspondent gave up in despair, reporting that the only pronouncement he could get from her was recitation of Shakespearean sonnets.[26] Reporters continued to hover around her, however, for even her personal appearance was good news copy, and soon she found there were things she could talk about. One was women.

"Women are just as intelligent, broad-minded and ethical professionally as men," she told a Memphis reporter, adding that the line of demarcation between the sexes is non-existent. She declared that since women had received suffrage their progress in business and the professions had been remarkable and only the centuries would tell the extent of this advance. "Given the proper training, possessing the determination to withstand the hard knocks to be met in a career, and imbued with a desire for success, a woman has an even chance with men" she continued.[27]

Allen's recipe for a successful woman lawyer was a strange mixture of housewifery and the Protestant ethic: "Take one generous dose of persistency. Add one large measure of industry, the kind that takes no thought for dances, evening parties or prolonged vacations. Mix thoroughly and season with a goodly portion of sense of humor and several ounces of tact" When speaking to an audience of women she added, "—and don't be emotional. It's what the men expect us to be."[28] As far as her own success in being appointed federal judge was concerned she credited it to "the great woman movement. The place didn't come to me — you gave it to me."[29]

By far her most widely published comment had to do with the unmarried woman. The comment was made before an audience of 2,000 at the NFBPWC convention in Chicago in 1933 and was broadcast nationally. The thought was that the depression had immortalized unmarried women:

> During this entire period of financial stress the unmarried woman earning her living has stood out like a shining star. I do not know what many a family would have done if it had not been for that refuge from their problems, the "old maid" in the family. When married women were being turned out of their jobs because they were married, and when fathers and breadwinners lost their employment and had nowhere to turn, it was the salary of the "old maid" in thousands of homes that kept them going. . . .[30]

Allen had made the comment casually and was embarrassed and disappointed that it was picked up by newspapers while the essence of her speech on the need for funds for education and efficiency in government was ignored. Editorial comment on the old maid idea was widespread and favorable, ranging from a Toledo editor who wrote that it was high time a little praise went to the old maid for her staunch attitudes to one in Houston who regretted that he didn't have an old maid in his home.[31]

136

Allen's embarrassment stemmed from the fact that competition for jobs during the depression had fostered hostility between married and single women. Working wives had encountered widespread discrimination which women's organizations deplored, especially the NFBPWC,[32] to whose members Allen was speaking. Thereafter Judge Allen took care to avoid distinctions between married and unmarried women and spoke only of the courageous role women were playing in difficult times.

Scores of newspapers and magazines publicized Allen's judicial appointment. One of the most analytical articles were was by Bertha Miller for the *New York Evening Post* and concluded with the idea that "the suffragists of old hoped to make available specially gifted women for public service. In Florence Allen we have such a women."[33] Willie Snow Ethridge of the *Washington Post* was unable to get "an answer to anything" out of the judge and settled for a description of the woman, who looked to him just as he thought a woman judge should look: Junoesque in stature, dressed simply in black with a rather severe hat on her big head, friendly in her manner, with a low delightful chuckle and a face often wreathed in smiles — "as natural as a tree and just as comforting to be around."[34]

Several writers took Allen's appointment as an opportunity to remind readers again that Roosevelt had appointed an unusual number of women, and that it was a step forward for women. An article in the *Chicago Sunday Tribune*, featuring an interview with Judge Allen, piqued the reader's interest by proclaiming that "The triumph of the woman movement is the greatest extension of freedom witnessed in our time. Allen is the outstanding example of what that freedom can mean."[35]

A view in opposition was expressed by Jean Lyon of the *New York Sun* who wrote that all the more honor was due Florence Allen for forging ahead in a decade that had been disastrous for women, the most honored one up to that time being Mother Dionne who had produced quintuplets. Lyon reminded her readers that women in Italy had been pushed out of their jobs by a dictator, women in Germany had been sent back to their washboards, and right here "in the land of the free," even with a woman in the cabinet, there were five fewer women in state legislatures in 1934 than in 1933. Her conclusion was that some individuals were forging ahead but that the cause of feminism was weakening.[36]

Historians, aided by the advantage of hindsight, agree with Jean Lyon. Suffrage had not liberated women, for the position of women is part of the social fabric of society. The suffragists of Allen's time had not wanted to change the social structure. If they had they would have joined the Socialist Party, which was eager to have them and promised a new society based on equality. Or they would have joined the National Woman's Party which had the potential of creating a united bloc of women's votes for women's issues.

The suffragists had anticipated participating in traditional politics, but by 1934, even Allen recognized that they were not forging ahead. "The fight for women's rights is not yet won," she wrote. "There has indeed been a setback against women in office. This is felt very strongly by all women, who like myself have been compelled to face the electorate and answer the unspoken question why any woman should be earning anything any way."[37]

During Roosevelt's administration a few women were appointed to high government positions, to positions not previously held by women: Frances Perkins in the cabinet, Ruth Bryan Owen in the diplomatic corps, Florence Allen in the judiciary. They were all exceptionally well qualified. Even so they probably would not have been appointed without pressure from women's organizations, especially the women's division of the party. They were tokens of gratitude for party participation.

At a lower level, a number of women social reformers were included in the new welfare bureaus of the government.[38] These women were hired not because they were women but because they were exceptionally well qualified in social service work. Many of them had started as social feminists, donating their talents to the poor and underprivileged.

Prospects for increasing numbers of women entering government service through experience or women's demands for reform were not bright. Women's organizations continued to be less interested in reform through political action and more interested in self-fulfillment for their members. The membership of the NLWV declined during the thirties.[39] The climate for reform was much healthier in the thirties than it had been in the twenties, but women were not taking up the cudgel.

As far as the judicial process was concerned, Judge Allen believed that women's chief contribution to justice was on juries, but the states were very slow about including women on juries. She spoke and wrote often in defense of the jury system and women jurors in particular. "I know of no one thing that will do so much toward the establishment of justice . . . as the passage of legislation making women eligible for duty," she told a Connecticut audience when that state was considering a proposal to make women eligible.[40] "An immeasurable service has been done the courts in the 21 states where women can serve on jury." she wrote for the *Yale Daily News*. "Their intelligence and conscientiousness has raised the standard of jury service."[41]

Allen was typical of the suffragists who had expected too much from the vote. What Allen referred to as women's "progress in business and the professions" had not been remarkable in fact. During the depression of the thirties the proportion of women in the professions declined.[42] College-educated women no longer felt the pioneering thrill of forging the way in a new profession.[43] Professional women clustered in the traditional professions of teaching and nursing; 53 per cent in teaching and 19 per cent in nursing in the 1930 census. Men in the professions were much more evenly distributed.[44] Women in professions were paid less money than men and were rarely picked for top positions.

In the law profession, Allen noted the need for unusual industry and tact in order to succeed. She wrote in 1930 that there were "roughly speaking, 69 times as many men practicing law as women." Her figures reflected a decline in the proportion of women lawyers since 1920. True, there were twice as many women lawyers in 1930 as there were in 1920, but the number of men lawyers had also doubled.[45] Allen admitted that women lawyers had far to go before they actually made an impress on the practice of law. She thought the reason was because women were "new in the field, and to some extent as yet handicapped."[46]

During the depression it was notable that women were not faring well in their usual refuge, the public sector. More than half the states passed laws prohibiting the hiring of married women in the public sphere, and in their traditional profession of teaching even single women found that hiring boards preferred men.[47] Married women continued to work in the private sector where employers looked favorably upon their willingness to accept low wages;[48] the number of married women available for domestic service far exceeded the demand. The number of women working remained nearly constant during the thirties, but the numbers of women in professional work declined while the numbers in less rewarding work increased.

In industry, in addition to working for lower wages, women's opportunities continued to be limited by protective legislation. Eleven states, however, had found ways to legislate minimum wages for women.[49] Although Judge Allen was publicly noncommital on these issues, she had helped to write the court's decision upholding Ohio's minimum wage laws for women and children.[50] Working people generally approved the special legislation for women. When the state of New York wrote a new constitution in 1938 it was proposed that an equal rights clause be added to include the idea that laws regulating employment should be based on the nature of the work and not on the sex of the worker. The proposal was shouted down by advocates of special legislation for women.[51]

As time passed the gulf widened between those who favored protective legislation and those who opposed it. The ERA had become respectable by the end of the thirties and its supporters more enthusiastic. The NFBWPC endorsed it at their annual convention in Atlantic City in 1937, after several years of debate. It went on record as "opposed to any legislation designed to protect women only, asserting its belief that sound legislation should be based on the nature of the work and not on sex." So jubilant were the proponents at finally having achieved action that "a victory procession on the boardwalk was staged immediately. . . ."[52] Judge Allen refrained from expressing her opinion on the ERA, claiming judicial isolation since it was becoming a controversial issue.

139

In the case of non-professional working women, Breckinridge in 1933 found it an "extremely interesting development" that women were proving their physical capabilities in physical education and athletic achievement. She noted that the information Judge Brandeis had used in 1908 in the case of *Mueller v. Oregon* "contained a great volume of testimony rather than evidence" on the fraility of women. Although she did not oppose protective legislation, she noted that real evidence was proving the expectation that normal physical exercise need not be a handicap to women in industry.[53]

The idea that woman's role in society is that of homemaker and mother intensified during the depression. In a public opinion poll conducted in 1938 respondents were asked whether they approved of a married woman earning money in business or industry if she had a husband capable of supporting her. Only 22 per cent approved and 78 per cent disapproved.[54] Women's magazines, advertising and the media reinforced the image of the woman in the home. Young women were more apathetic about careers than they had been in Allen's generation and increasingly they chose marriage rather than a career, or gave up a career for marriage. It was thought that girls who were too smart or too educated didn't catch husbands; it was better to be beautiful than smart.[55]

The popular conception was that women worked for pin money, in spite of constant evidence that women worked because of economic need. An investigation of the U.S. Bureau of Labor before 1910 brought out the fact that great numbers of families were dependent on the wage-paid labor of women and girls and should have destroyed the pin-money myth.[56]

The science of psychology reinforced the model of the married woman as homemaker. American psychologists had accepted the ideas of German psychologist Sigmund Freud with the enthusiasm of new converts. His essays on femininity, published in 1933, emphasized the importance of sexuality and Freudians argued that the happy, well-adjusted woman married and satisfied her instinctive sexuality and sense of motherhood.[57] Any deviation in the form of acting like a man, such as seeking a career outside the home, could result in complexes and neuroses. The single woman was sexually frustrated. Thirty years earlier, studying music in Berlin, Florence Allen had observed with distaste the German emphasis on the physical relationship in marriage and the relegation of women to kitchen and nursery, now conceptualized in America by Freudian psychologists.

Whatever the fate of women in the thirties, as their progress toward equality was impeded by economic exigencies and social prohibitions, the way had been legally clear since 1920 for women to achieve success in politics and the professions. Only a small number of women had done so, but their success was hailed as symbolic of a promising future.

Florence Allen was riding the tide of success in the middle thirties and women were proud of her. Women's clubs planned study programs on the career of Florence Allen. Publicists recalled that the Federal Court of Appeals of the Sixth Circuit had in the past been a stepping stone to higher positions, having supplied four judges for the U.S. Supreme Court and one president. By the beginning of 1935 a League for a Woman President and Vice President had been founded and opened headquarters in Brooklyn. The NFBPWC nominated for president Florence E. Allen and for vice president Josephine Roche, then Assistant Secretary of the Treasury. People laughed at the idea, much as they had laughed at the beginning of the women's rights movement a century earlier. A snide commentator asked if women were to steer the ship of state who would rock the cradle, but concluded that women might be better at guiding the state than men at rocking the cradle. The founder of the League, once an active Roosevelt campaigner, was serious, however, and announced plans for promoting state organizations.[58]

The nomination by the League was not congenial to Allen's thinking and she had not sought the nomination. Her papers indicate no conferences or correspondence with the founder of the League. She believed women and men should join forces in the traditional political parties. She was a great admirer of President Roosevelt, who was the heir of earlier progressives and who had implemented many of the liberal social policies women's organizations had advocated for decades. She hastened to write to Eleanor Roosevelt that she had no intention of running for president and included a copy of her public statement that "No woman during my lifetime, however qualified, will be nominated, much less elected, President of the United States."[59]

FOOTNOTES

[1] From various diary entries 1931 and 1932.

[2] It is interesting to note that Allen did not visibly share her mother's concern about moral degeneracy.

[3] *To Do Justly*, pp. 114-120.

[4] Diary entries July 12 and September 2, 1933.

[5] Florence E. Allen, *An Adventure in Understanding*, pamphlet published by the Committee on Cultural Relations with Latin America, New York, 1930.

[6] Information from Cleveland *Plain Dealer*, September 14, 1935, Allen papers, WRHS, container 26, folder 18.

[7] From various diary entries.

[8] Information about Park School from Cleveland *Plain Dealer*, January 17, 1935, p. 5; September 17, 1935, p. 11; June 10, 1937, p. 10 and July 21, 1928, p. 21. Within a few years Park School was absorbed in Park Synagogue.

[9] From article by Grace Goulder Izant in Cleveland *Plain Dealer*, October 6, 1935, Allen papers, WRHS, container 1, folder 1.

[10] *Ibid.*

[11] Diary October 19, 27, November 24, December 15, 1934, January 20, 1935 and elsewhere.

[12] Letter from Allen to Westtown Quaker School, June 15, 1936. Allen papers, WRHS, container 6, folder 6.

[13] All quotations from diary entries, 1934, 1935, 1936, 1937.

[14] *Cincinnati Post*, May 5, 1934, Allen papers, WRHS, container 26, folder 17.

[15] Various diary entries.

[16] Description from Harold Stephen's speech at NYU banquet in 1948, Allen papers, WRHS, container 18, folder 1.

[17] Cleveland *Plain Dealer*, obituary, September 14, 1935.

[18] Diary entries about conferences on Alcazar are frequent from 1931 to 1936.

[19] Cleveland *Plain Dealer*, July 7, 1936, p. 2.

[20] Diary, April 30, 1935.

[21] From personal interview.

[22] *To Do Justly*, p. 78.

[23] *Ibid.*, pp. 97-98.

[24] *Cincinnati Post*, February 24, 1934, Allen papers, LC, container 8, and Izant, *op cit.*

[25] Diary, August 31, 1936.

[26] *New York Sun*, December 28, 1934, Allen papers, WRHS, container 26, folder 17.

[27] *The Commercial Appeal* (Memphis), December 28, 1937, Allen papers, WRHS, container 27, folder 1.

[28] *Columbus State Journal*, February 24, 1934, Allen papers, WRHS, container 26, folder 16. *Independent Woman*, December 1939, p. 385, Allen papers, SL, container A-6, folder 1.

[29] *Toledo News-Bee*, undated 1934, Allen papers, WRHS, container 26, folder 17.

[30] *Chicago Daily Tribune*, July 13, 1933, Allen papers, WRHS, container 26, folder 15.

[31] *Toledo Times*, July 16, 1933 and *Houston Post*, August 3, 1933, Allen papers, WRHS, container 26, folder 15. White middle-class women in professional careers remained overwhelmingly single up to 1940, according to Ryan, p. 188.

[32] Lois Scharf, *To Work and To Wed: Female Employment, Feminism, and the Great Depression*, Westport: Greenwood Press, 1980, p. 35.

[33] *New York Evening Post*, March 7, 1934, Allen papers, WRHS, container 26. folder 17.

[34] *Washington Post*, April 28, 1934, Allen papers, WRHS, container 26, folder 17.

[35] *Chicago Sunday Tribune*, September 17, 1939, Allen papers, WRHS, container 27, folder 4.

[36] *New York Sun*, December 28, 1934, Allen papers, WRHS, container 26, folder 17.

[37] Letter from Allen to Frieda Kirchway, editor, *The Nation*, March 21, 1934, Allen papers, WRHS, container 6, folder 5.

[38] Chambers, p. 255. Marie Wing of Cleveland was appointed to the Social Security Board. Marion Harron, another friend of Allen, was a presidential appointment to the Board of Tax Appeals. Harron was unique in that she had no political background.

[39] So Breckinridge estimated, p. 68. Accurate membership figures are not available.

[40] *New Haven Sunday Register*, March 13, 1927, Allen papers, SMITH, box 1, folder 3.

[41] *Yale Daily News*, On National Affairs, v. 1, No. 3, November 12, 1927, Allen papers, SMITH, box 1, folder 5.

[42] William Henry Chafe, *The American Woman: Her Changing Social, Economic, and Political Roles, 1920-1970*, New York: Oxford University Press, 1972, p. 59.

[43] Chafe, *Women and Equality*, p. 29.

[44] Breckinridge, p. 189.

[45] Membership in the American Bar Association grew from 1,718 in 1902 to 29,008 in 1936, according to Edson R. Sunderland, *History of the American Bar Association and Its Work*, ABA, 1953, p. 14.

[46] Florence E. Allen, "Women in the Law," in Earl G. Lockhart, *My Vocation, by Eminent Americans*, New York: H.W. Wilson, 1938, pp. 190-192. Breckinridge, p. 188, from 1930 census figures says: In 1920 there were 1,738 women lawyers; in 1930 there were 3,385.

[47] Scharf, pp. 84-85.

[48] Ryan, p. 188.

[49] Chambers, p. 63.

[50] NAWSA papers, LC, container 37, microfilm reel 25.

[51] Information from *Boston Traveler*, July 11, 1938, Allen papers, LC, container 7.

[52] *A History of the National Federation of Business and Professional Women's Clubs*, New York: NFBPWC, 1944, p. 74.

[53] Breckinridge, pp. 191-194. She included many specific examples of women having accomplished remarkable physical feats, concluding with Amelia Earhart and her solo flight across the Atlantic.

[54] *The Gallup Poll: Public Opinion 1935-1971*, v. 1, *1935-1948*, New York: Random House, 1972, p. 131. 19% of men approved and 81% disapproved; 25% of women approved and 75% disapproved.

[55] Mirra Komarovsky, *Women in the Modern World*, Boston: Little Brown and Company, 1953, pp. 77 and 82.

[56] According to Breckinridge, p. 100.

[57] The notion is elucidated in Helene Deutsch, *The Psychology of Women: A Psychoanalytic Interpretation*, v. II, *Motherhood*, London: Research Books, 1947.

[58] *New York Evening Journal*, February 15, 1935, Allen papers, WRHS, container 26, folder 18.

[59] Letter of Allen to Roosevelt, February 12, 1935, Allen papers, WRHS, container 6, folder 6. Copy of public statement attached to letter in Eleanor Roosevelt papers, RL, ER correspondence, 1935.

Chapter 11

THIS CONSTITUTION OF OURS

During the wave of publicity about the TVA case and the possible appointment to the Supreme Court, Allen was asked by G.P. Putnam Sons if she would be interested in writing an autobiography or compiling a book of speeches for them. The publishers offered to provide the assistance of a collaborator to ease the task of production, and indicated that they were particularly interested in an autobiography, for many people were genuinely interested in what kind of a person Florence Allen was and how she had managed to accomplish so much in this man's world. After some months of negotiation and conferences with the collaborator it was agreed that two books would be published, one on the United States Constitution and an autobiography.[1]

Exactly whose idea the book on the Constitution was would later become a matter of contention. Allen maintained that it was her idea and there seems little doubt but that it was, for the Constitution was an intimate part of her life. As a child she had memorized parts of it at her father's knee, as a graduate student and law student she had studied constitutional law, and as a judge she had dealt with the Constitution for nearly twenty years. Promotion of understanding of and respect for the Constitution was a worthy cause, and, perhaps more important, the thought must have crossed her mind that an interpretation of the Constitution might improve her chances for appointment to the Supreme Court, perhaps serve as a substitute for the scholarly treatises on the law which she had never written.

The Constitution was not politically controversial and thus was within the parameters of a federal judge's freedom to write and speak. On the other hand, it was not a dead issue, for a contemporary historian, Charles Beard, had identified the founding fathers as upper-class men more interested in the preservation of private property than the establishment of an egalitarian democracy. Beard's idea was repugnant to Florence Allen, but it had provoked popular discussion.[2]

Besides feeling that she was well qualified to write on the Constitution, Allen was prepared to put a book together. A few months after the TVA case she had taken a leave of absence from the court to give a series of lectures on the Constitution at Bryn Mawr College. "I thought a judge could lecture with impunity on the Constitution and that's why I accepted,"[3] she told a reporter. Bryn Mawr was distinguished among women's colleges. Its ardent feminist President M. Carey Thomas had passed on, but her spirit loomed over the campus. She exhorted women "to live up to their brains," and saw to it that Bryn Mawr students had the same preparation and training as men at Harvard and Yale.[4] Judge Allen laid aside her judicial robes and relaxed in the midst of intelligent and educated young women, the kind of young women with whom she could identify easily, in an atmosphere of mutual admiration. There were pleasant, informal conversations between the judge and the students on such subjects as careers for women, how to play Chopin and care for cocker spaniels. Aside from the pleasures, there was a body of lecture material suitable for a book.[5]

Bertha Miller was very excited about the book project as it began to take form. She set about transforming Allen's words which were intended to be spoken to good readable style. Letters from Bert to Taffy, as Florence was called affectionately by Bert, flew back and forth every day or two, with phone calls in between. As the work progressed Bert waxed more and more enthusiastic. "It's a peach," she wrote, "truly a grand little book — [I] get crazier about it all the time."[6] Her conscience got her up at all hours of the night to go over some particular sentence to see that the meaning was right. When Florence's responses didn't come as soon as Bert hoped, Mary stepped in to assist and explain.

Meanwhile, the publisher's collaborator, Janet Mabie, hovered nervously on the periphery of activity. She felt that the book was originally her idea, but admitted that her participation in the finished manuscript was "practically invisible." She sought conferences with Allen on the autobiography anytime, anywhere, entirely at the judge's convenience. A few agreeable conferences resulted but most of the time Allen was too ill or too busy to confer and didn't find time to read and return the copy Mabie drafted on her childhood years.[7]

When the manuscript on the Constitution was completed it was sent to William Allen White who reviewed it favorably and found it "a splendid piece of work, illuminating, scholarly, at times eloquent and always interesting." The times were crying, he said, for just the kind of interpretation of our Constitution that Allen had written and it should be required reading in every high school and college.[8]

Allen was very unhappy when she found that the publisher had set a price of two dollars on the book. She hoped that it would sell for one dollar and in multitudes of copies. "It is not my notion to try to make money," she wrote the publisher, adding "It is really not just publishing a book that appeals to me, but having my ideas for whatever they may be worth, go out in usable form."[9]

Putnam's representative replied that "the merchandising of books is the publisher's main *raison d'être* and the whole question of the effect of prices on sales is a province where his judgment and experience should prevail."[10] He assured her that the company would send many examination

146

copies and that if there proved to be sufficient demand it would be brought out in a cheaper textbook edition. And Janet Mabie, who had very gracefully conceded that she would get no royalties from the book which had been her idea, wrote in response to Allen's inquiry that they would try to serialize the Constitution book, perhaps in *Cosmopolitan* or *Atlantic*. She volunteered the additional information that they had always intended to serialize the autobiography.[11]

This Constitution of Ours was published in 1940, without previous serialization, at a price of two dollars. The main theme of the book was that the Constitution is more than a framework of government; it is an instrument of freedom. The Constitution launched our country, Allen maintained, into a hitherto uncharted experience in government by the will of the people. The book was dedicated to her father, Clarence Emir Allen, and surely he would have been proud of her interpretation. Her thought that "history does not reveal elsewhere a like phenomenon, an amazing and unprecedented spectacle, a union of multitudinous wills into one general will,"[12] would have fitted very well into one of Papa's Fourth of July speeches.

She refuted the theses of Charles Beard by writing that the men who wrote our Constitution were well fitted by intellect and training to create a free and efficient government, and that no unbiased student would believe that the goal of the Constitution was economic or that it was formed to secure the power of the moneyed class. The men who wrote the Constitution were direct descendants of men and women who came in search of freedom and they drafted the instrument while a powerful love of liberty was still fresh. To say that financial motives were the paramount motive in framing the Constitution ignores the primary fact that many of these men had risked everything to attain independence from England.[13]

The threat of war was very real and much in Allen's mind as she wrote. She found it a revolutionary advancement that for the first time in the history of any great nation the power of declaring war and making treaties had been placed in legislative hands by the Constitution rather than executive hands, an advancement which had given us many decades of peace. She used the issue of joining the League of Nations as an example of people power. The United States would have joined the League at the close of World War I if the decision had been that of the president to make, but congress and the voters opposed joining and the decision was theirs. She contended that if there were no other benefit from the American system than the 150 years of peace which it had brought us, the document would be justified. As a result of our system ". . . we violate no nation's honor, we attack no nation's freedom."[14]

Over time the executive branch had become more powerful than the founding fathers anticipated, and Allen explained that intervention in the affairs of other countries, especially in Latin America, had come about by executive decision. The Monroe Doctrine, for example, is an executive doctrine, never declared by Congress. Intervention in Latin America has been by presidential order and is a violation of the spirit of the Constitution. She felt optimistic about changes in that respect, arguing that recent changes in attitudes toward Mexico were the result of the pressure of public opinion.

She paid great respect to our freedoms of religion, press and speech, even though at least one of her own speeches had been subject to censorship. In 1939 when she was asked to give the major address for a huge memorial service for Jane Addams in Chicago's lakefront park, she had been required to submit her speech to park authorities for examination for unAmerican content, as was required of all speakers in the park.[15]

Allen wrote that the preamble of the Constitution introduced a new principle in government: promotion of the general welfare. The principle had resulted in unparalleled access to education, libraries, roads, public health services, and parks. Our great wealth had not accrued to a ruling class but to all without distinction of nationality. The psychological effect of the Constitution underlines our lives, she wrote, and

> What it means to be an American cannot be defined on the basis of birth, language, place, or condition. A man might be born here and yet not be an American, because to be an American is a faith, a belief, an intuition, and a conviction about freedom. His birthright springs not merely from the soil, but from the ideas of freedom upon which the country was founded. My own earliest realization of the fact that I am an American came, I think, with my first remembered Fourth of July — a home celebration, my father reading the Declaration of Independence to his young children.[16]

Allen's conclusion elevated the Constitution to articles of faith:

> Liberty cannot be written ready made into a character. It must be written into our hearts, and thus sent on by us as a living force to the next generation. Here in America we do have great and living traditions. But only by graving them as articles of faith on the hearts of the people can they be realized.[17]

Reviews of the book were generally good, although individual readers had qualifications. A lawyer friend in Cleveland wrote to Allen pointing out that although she spoke of the blessings of liberty and freedom throughout the book she never mentioned the obstructions to liberty and freedom which existed in New Deal policies. He thought that the Roosevelt administration's labor legislation, child labor laws, and regulation of interstate commerce were utterly irreconcilable with the principles of the Constitution. "A few strong words from you," he concluded, "would have been of great value."[18]

Critics of this sort would have found no consolation in Allen's thinking. She believed government under the Constitution had the duty to prevent exploitation of labor and commerce and the prerogative to act for the benefit of all. She stood firmly for government regulation. She considered government social projects as evidence of changing public attitudes and a realization of civic responsibility. She believed that concepts of liberty were redefined with every generation and that it behooved every citizen to vote for candidates who best defined his or her concept of liberty.

Allen sent copies of her book to a host of lawyers, judges, and influential people. Several expressed the wish in their thank-you letters that high school students would read it for the patriotism it inspired. Allen sent a copy to Eleanor Roosevelt, referring to it as a "non-technical" book on the Constitution. Roosevelt replied that she was delighted with it and thought it was "just what we need."[19] A radio reviewer thought it warmed the Constitution into life and praised the "sensitive poetic temperament" of Judge Allen. Other commentators found it refreshingly Jeffersonian. The *New York Times* reviewer found her elucidations "calm and often brilliant" but noted that the Constitution was not devised as a safeguard of individual liberty but as an instrument of legislative and executive power and that the elected representatives were not expected to be obedient to popular mandates but to use their own judgment.[20]

This Constitution of Ours was, as many reviewers said, clearly written and eloquent in phrasing. It idealized the Constitution rather than analyzing it. It was written to appeal to the heart and mind of the average citizen and not for an audience of legal scholars. It added no new interpretations to constitutional law; most of the content was seasoned and familiar. Clearly the author cherished the Constitution with a feeling of confidence and pride that carried over to the reader.

Bert and Florence prodded the publisher to send more examination copies. Mary supplied names of organizations and publications of educators, and the publisher sent a thousand copies to school principals. In spite of all sales were not sufficient to justify a cheaper textbook edition. Bert was crestfallen at the size of the first royalty check and the paltry number of copies sold. Reviewers had praised it as a good high-school text but educators were not buying it, and Bert and Florence were convinced that the reason could only be insufficient advertising. The publisher, Bert thought, was treating the book like a stepchild.[21]

The fact of the matter was that most of the reviewers who praised the book as a text were not classroom teachers. A teacher might well find the book interesting and inspirational, but reflect that it would not carry the burden of explaining the framework of government to the students. Judge Allen repeatedly said and wrote that every American schoolchild should memorize the Declaration of Independence, the Preamble of the Constitution, the Gettysburg Address, and the First Amendment of the Constitution. American schoolchildren were no longer being taught government through memorization and inspiration.

149

Work on the autobiography dragged on from a snail's pace to nothing at all. Mabie was eager and persistent in searching for means to motivate her subject. She continued to propose conferences and meetings, not wishing to "badger" Allen or hurry her, but suggesting that it all might be easy and very relaxing with her collaboration. She did not give up the idea of serialization, although Allen had told her she would not even think of serialization or any arrangement for it. Mabie reduced the enticement to the hard relevant fact that the $15,000 that might result from serialization in the *Saturday Evening Post* would relieve Allen's troublesome financial affairs. She aimed at the judge's heart through the dogs, remembering such details as Star bouncing through the woods wagging her tail so estatically, or Kip's beautiful color, or Top's sweet baby face. Mabie worried that the publisher would expect some progress since they had advanced money to her and would want it back if nothing materialized.[22]

What can I do? How can I work with you, Mabie asked. She presented the autobiography as a cause. Allen's life would have a heartening effect on readers, it would be a fine example of a way of life that was tottering, it would "offset some of the garbage" on the market. Nothing worked. Allen saw no time when she could do it, but told Mabie not to worry about the money advanced for it was all within the contract.

Three and a half years after the original contact a letter came from the publisher's office, asking for word on the autobiography, and informing her that they had advanced Miss Mabie a thousand dollars. The writer said they were still interested and thought it would be "a highly profitable venture."[23] Allen replied that she had no time to work on it, but that Miss Mabie had worked very hard and deserved compensation. Using illness as a pretext, she explained that she had been sick most of the winter, although the doctors couldn't find much wrong with her except exhaustion. She noted "in passing" that she had been greatly disappointed in their handling of the book on the Constitution. She didn't know why she should work on the autobiography when there was an enormous opening for the Constitution book which the publisher had failed to take advantage of.[24]

A year later another letter came from the publisher asking when they could expect delivery. The letter said they had advanced funds to the collaborator but had lost touch with her. They were insistent that we have paid and we can expect delivery. Allen replied with a concise legal explanation as to why Mabie did not need to return the money and said she had no idea when she might write an autobiography. Apparently she had second thoughts, for the letter was never sent.

Another year later, a letter came from the publisher's lawyers informing her that the publisher was "decidedly anxious" to publish her autobiography but that nothing could be done if she didn't reply to letters.[25] Allen replied in a letter that she didn't send that she had been ill, didn't have time to write, and that it didn't increase her interest to have the matter handled by attorneys. In a second letter, which she sent, she regretted that she had been unable to write, but that no date of completion was set in the contract.[26] About the same time Bert had a call from the publisher, and in spite of her explanation that Florence had been sick and that being a federal judge was a full-time job, the caller had become "testy." Bert wished that she had the money to buy a release on the Constitution book because she was sure it had a great future.[27]

Obviously the book on the Constitution had failed to appeal to a wide audience as Allen hoped it would. American readers had reacted with indifference and apathy to her idealistic interpretation. Florence Allen really cared about the Constitution in the way her forefathers cared; most people did not care in that way any more.

Why was she so reluctant to publish an autobiography? Surely it would have been profitable, but she was never motivated by money. Did she fear that it would reveal her inner self and destroy the public image of noble selflessness and dedicated purpose that she had worked so many years to create? She was a very private person about herself; her public image predominated.[28] An autobiography would have extended her name and fame, which appeared to be one of her motives in pushing the Constitution book, but an autobiography would have extended her name and fame as a woman. She was more desirous of being known as a lawyer, jurist, and authority on the Constitution, for she had learned from experience that being a woman was a serious handicap in elective politics and judicial appointments. How frustrating it was that the public was not interested in her expertise on the Constitution but only in her as a woman! No autobiography of Judge Allen appeared for another twenty-five years, after the flame of ambition had subsided.

FOOTNOTES

[1] First notations about publishing a book appear in her diary in January 1939 when she talked with friends about the autobiography and with DeLo about the contract. Correspondence and contracts (February-March 1939) are in Allen papers, WRHS, container 6, folder 6. This sort of publication was a Putnam specialty. Harriot Stanton Blatch, daughter of Elizabeth Cady Stanton, founder of the Women's Political Union, suffragist and peace advocate, told her story to Alma Lutz and it was published as *Challenging Years: The Memoirs of Harriot Stanton Blatch*, G.P. Putnam's Sons, New York, 1940.

[2] According to her diary, Allen read Beard in October 1938.

[3] Philadelphia *Evening Bulletin,* February 24, 1939, Allen papers, WRHS, container 27, folder 4.

[4] Thomas's spirit loomed over the campus still in 1974-1975, according to Dobkin, p. 1.

[5] Philadelphia *Evening Bulletin,* February 24, 1939.

[6] Letter from Bertha Miller to Allen, January 3, 1940, Allen papers WRHS, container 7, folder 1.

[7] From correspondence and diary entries.

[8] From Allen papers, WRHS, container 6, folder 6 and container 27, folder 5.

[9] Letter from Allen to Kennett Rawson, April 4, 1939, Allen papers WRHS, container 6, folder 6.

[10] letter from Rawson to Allen, Allen papers, WRHS, container 7, folder 1.

[11] Letter from Janet Mabie to Allen, September 30, 1939, Allen papers, WRHS, container 6, folder 6.

[12] Florence E. Allen, *This Constitution of Ours,* New York: G.P. Putnam's Sons, 1940, p. 4.

[13] *Ibid.,* Summarized and paraphrased from pp. 8-17.

[14] *Ibid.,* p. 117.

[15] *Chicago Daily News,* September 6, 1939, Allen papers, WRHS, container 27, folder 4.

[16] *This Constitution . . . ,* pp. 114-115.

[17] *Ibid.,* p. 124.

[18] Letter from Harrison B. McGraw to Allen, February 29, 1940, Allen papers, WRHS, container 7, folder 1.

[19] Letter from Allen to Roosevelt, February 20, 1940, Eleanor Roosevelt papers, RL, ER correspondence, 1940. Letter from Roosevelt to Allen, March 20, 1940, Allen papers, WRHS, container 7, folder 1.

[20] All reviews are in Allen papers, WRHS, container 27, folder 5. John Corbin was the *New York Times* reviewer.

[21] Letter from Miller to Allen, November 1, 1940, Allen papers, WRHS, container 7, folder 1.

[22] Letters from Mabie to Allen January 15, February 6, and 21, 1940, Allen papers, WRHS, container 7, folder 1.

[23] Letter from Earle H. Balch to Allen, July 23, 1941, Allen papers, WRHS, container 7, folder 1.

[24] Letter from Allen to Blach, September 29, 1941, Allen papers, WRHS, container 7, folder 1.

[25] Letter from lawyers to Allen, February 12, 1943, Allen papers, WRHS, container 7, folder 1.

[26] Letter from Allen to Balch, March 16, 1943, Allen papers, WRHS, container 7, folder 1.

[27] Letter from Miller to Allen, March 12, 1943, Allen papers, WRHS, container 7, folder 1.

[28] Casual acquaintances and colleagues, and occasionally news reports, observed that they knew very little about Allen's personal feelings. Her diary is revealing only in her younger years. When she finally wrote an autobiography, at the age of 80, she did not reveal her inner self.

Chapter 12

FEDERAL JUSTICE

The federal courts have jurisdiction in a wide variety of cases arising under the Constitution, the statutes enacted by Congress, and the decisions of administrative boards and bureaus. In the court system the appellate courts are intermediate courts. They review decisions of the district courts and are bound to follow the decisions of the Supreme Court. Most questions never go to the Supreme Court and are settled at the appellate or district level. The expansion of government services in the reforms of the thirties caused an expansion of the work of the courts in the following years. More than ever before, the federal court system and its judges became the final arbiters of social policy.[1] The legal problems brought to the courts of the Sixth Circuit were a good sampling of the problems with which the national courts were struggling.

Judge Allen believed that the law is the ethical and moral basis of society and that "the attainment of justice is the highest human endeavor."[2] She considered it a privilege to be a judge and in that capacity she served humanity to the utmost of her ability. Law school graduates Robert Toepfer and Richard Kuhn were her law clerks in the forties; later Mary Welles, although not a lawyer, served in that capacity. Their help in research was indispensable, but Judge Allen always wrote her own opinions.[3] She studied the cases conscientiously, always kept up with her docket, and over the twenty-five years of her service wrote several hundred opinions. She was naturally hard working, and zealous in her determination to make a woman judge acceptable. As a result, she could be counted on to volunteer to take for opinion the cases with the most enormous records and complicated issues.[4] In contrast to her colleagues in the Ohio Supreme Court, she found her federal brethren high-minded men and the judges of the Sixth Circuit were welded into a finely coordinated team. Allen was regarded as a good judge and she made important contributions to her profession in the areas of constitutional law and patent law. Her opinions were commended for their direct attack on the heart of issues, their closely reasoned discussions, full documentation, and clear writing style.[5]

In the middle thirties there was a great constitutional collision between proponents of the New Deal and the conservative courts over national power and the economy. The crisis began when the Supreme Court refused to extend its definition of commerce among the several states and knocked out such measures as the National Industrial Recovery Act of 1935 and the Bituminous Coal Conservation Act in 1936.

By 1937 the Supreme Court justices were becoming more sympathetic to extension of the commerce powers, and in a line of cases expanded the federal power to regulate the economy. The culminating case originated in the Sixth Circuit. The case, *Filburn v. Helke,*[6] involved the constitutionality of wheat crop controls and was heard by Judge Allen and two district judges. The Court decided against wheat crop controls, but in a dissenting opinion Judge Allen reasoned:

> . . . regulation of the supply of wheat that normally moves in interstate or foreign commerce must be upheld as an appropriate means reasonably adapted to the regulation of interstate commerce. Since regulation of the supply of wheat available for sale in interstate commerce but actually used within the state of its origin is drawn into a general plan for the protection of interstate commerce in the commodity from the interferences, burdens and obstructions arising from excessive surplus and the social evils of low values, the power of Congress extends to it as well.[7]

The Supreme Court reversed the Sixth Circuit decision, generally following Judge Allen's dissent. The case attracted little attention because it occurred during World War II, but, according to Sixth Circuit historian Judge Harry Phillips, it is considered a landmark case because it was the last of the major cases on New Deal economic regulation and marked a "crest" in the constitutional reach of the federal commerce power. It was relied on by the Supreme Court in both the leading cases upholding the Civil Rights Act of 1964 as a valid exercise of the commerce power.[8]

In the Ohio Supreme Court Judge Allen had participated in affirming workmen's compensation and alleviating exploitation of employees by employers. In the Federal Court of Appeals she participated in the next advancement of labor rights, the right to unionize and engage in collective bargaining. The Wagner Act of the New Deal gave workers the right to bargain collectively and prohibited employers from interfering with union organizational activities. The Fair Labor Standards Act established a maximum work week of forty hours and a minimum wage with time and a half overtime for all workers in interstate commerce. Women workers particularly benefitted from the minimum wage law which eliminated the differential between men's and women's wages.

The role of employers in unionization and collective bargaining created thorny problems. The manager of a Midland Steel Plant, for instance, wrote a letter to employees explaining the Wagner Act and ending with an invitation to drop into his office at any time to discuss future policies for making the plant a happier and better place in which to work. The National Labor Relations Board regarded the last part of the letter as an appeal for individual bargaining and interference with collective bargaining. The Court set aside the decision of the NLRB, Allen's opinion stating that the letter had not violated the statute, had exerted no pressure, and was in fact an effort to secure cooperation between the front office and the workers, one of the objectives of the legislation.[9]

Decisions of the NLRB very often were not enforced until the courts affirmed or set aside the decision. It was the courts that forced reluctant employers to recognize unions, to bargain collectively and in good faith, and to cease threats to fire union members, reduce their pay, withdraw vacations, or close down plants. The plant manager of the Hopper Manufacturing Company, for example, refused to bargain collectively with the employee's union and said no raises were possible. Later some of the employees were reclassified and given raises without consulting the union. The Court and Allen's opinion supported the NLRB decision that the management must recognize the collective bargaining agent.[10]

Sometimes it was difficult to distinguish employers from employees. Foremen at Packard Motor Company for many years were considered employers and not eligible to join a group for collective bargaining. When the number of foremen doubled or tripled during the war they became interested in collective bargaining just as employees of the rank and file had. Judge Simons vigorously dissented on the grounds that foremen are employers by reason of their duties and if they join a union it becomes a company union.[11]

Automation brought new questions of classification. In the older electric generating plants operators worked close to the equipment in the boiler rooms, the turbine rooms and the pump rooms and were union employees. In a new automated plant these employees were replaced by a small number of supervisors who worked in a control room removed from the machinery. Were the new supervisors eligible for union membership and collective bargaining? The NLRB said yes, but the Circuit Court said no, Allen writing that the supervisors worked full-time directing operations in the interest of the employers.[12]

Among the cases testing "good faith" vis-á-vis the unions was that of the *NLRB v. Salant and Salant,* a New York Corporation that had been urged by seven towns in Tennessee to come and build plants in their area. The corporation was granted substantial concessions in exemption from taxation and availability of land and buildings, and a community of interest had developed between Salant and the towns. When unions came the townspeople opposed them and formed civic committees to discourage them. Among other things, store owners refused credit to union members. The NLRB decided that Salant had violated the principle of good faith. The local committees were ordered dissolved and the Court upheld the NLRB.[13]

The Fair Labor Standards Act applied only to companies engaged in interstate commerce, but cases questioning the boundaries between intrastate and interstate commerce were numerous. Were Ford auto retail sales agencies, for example, engaged in interstate commerce? Branches of chain stores, such as Montgomery Ward and gasoline stations operated by oil companies had been required to comply and the NLRB petitioned that Ford agencies by required to do the same. Allen wrote for the Circuit Court that Ford agencies were not integral parts of the auto manufacturing company and need not comply.[14]

Must a company that makes asphalt for roads, streets and highways in only one county comply with the Fair Labor Standards Act in the payment of overtime? The Court said yes, reasoning that roads are instrumentalities of interstate commerce used by agencies of interstate transportation.[15] On the other hand, a local road repair crew was found not to be involved in interstate commerce and not eligible for time and a half overtime.

Domestic liberalism abated as the war and international problems diverted the nation's attention. The expanding power of labor unions suffered a set-back in the mid-forties with the Taft Hartley Act and Administrative Procedures Act. The new laws provided, among other things, that decisions upholding charges of unfair labor practices must be supported by evidence from the record as a whole. In the case of the *NLRB v. The Pittsburgh Steamship Company* the NLRB charged the company with firing Howard Shartle for union activities; the company claimed he was discharged for incompetency. In view of the Taft-Hartley Act Allen's opinion reasoned that there was no "reliable, probative, and substantial evidence" that the employee was discharged because of union activities, that the company had permitted a union organizer on each of its 73 ships and Shartle was the only one discharged, and that based upon "the record considered as a whole" the company had not engaged in anti-union conduct and Shartle need not be reinstated. The case was reported in several newspapers, and lawyers and businessmen wrote Allen commending her excellent opinion.[16]

Women were encouraged to work during the war — Rosie the riveter was the ideal — often in violation of the laws protecting women. In Cleveland, again, more than 300 women were hired as street-car conductors and motormen in spite of the fact that the Ohio General Code specified that women could not work more than four hours without a half-hour break and street-car conductors were expected to work a longer shift with a ten-minute break at the end of each run. The General Code was relaxed to permit women to occupy jobs formerly held by men. Neither the earlier restrictions on women working nor the new relaxation was challenged in the courts.[17]

Although Judge Allen condoned restrictive legislation for other working women, she continued to object to special classification for herself. In the Common Pleas Court she had refused to preside over a special division of the court for cases concerning women and children, not wanting to be channeled into this specifically women's area. In her first months in the federal court she noticed that she was not being assigned cases about patents. She objected, saying that her background and experience qualified her to write patent opinions as capably as the men on the bench.[18] Surely her main motivation was to prove that a woman judge could handle a patent case as well as a man, but she also found these cases intriguing. She liked to know how things worked and to investigate the mechanism of the patent's application. The brethren did not object to sharing the cases, and Allen wrote many patent opinions. Justice Potter Stewart, who was a Sixth Circuit judge from 1954 to 1958, read most of her opinions in doing research necessary to decide patent cases and said that "few students have ever found a more helpful teacher than I found in her."[19]

After 1952 the Supreme Court no longer took patent cases for review and final adjudication was in the courts of appeal. In the fifties the U.S. patent system became the subject of lively debate. Critics claimed that the system hindered industrial growth rather than encouraging it. About six out of every ten patents were granted to corporations and were jealously guarded by huge monopolistic trusts, sometimes to prevent competitive challenges to their standardized production methods. The system, it was charged, no longer stimulated invention or protected the rare individual genius who had a new idea. The organized patent bar was resistant to change in the system.[20]

In this milieu patent cases became enormously complicated and prolonged by litigation. The Sixth Circuit included the heartland of the machine tool and automobile industry where patent control was critical to production and profit. Judge Allen could be counted on to volunteer to take for opinion the most difficult cases and to prove that a solution to the complications could be found.

Illustrative of some of the issues involved in patent problems was the case of *Great Lakes Equipment Company v. Fluid Systems, Incorporated.* The patent in question was a system for electrically heating a viscous fluid, in this case oil, so that it could be transported through pipes from storage to burners. It permitted the use of heavy fuel oil instead of light oil, resulting in considerable economy for the user. The user claimed to have been able to duplicate the patented system, with modifications, from information existing in prior literature on the art. It was further claimed that the patent holder had "induced" the Patent Office examiner to allow claims of invention through misrepresentations, and then had established a monopoly on the system in violation of antitrust laws and forced users "to pay tribute" for its use. The Court of Appeals found, with Judge Allen writing the opinion, that the user's system included "substantially the same devices, performing precisely the same offices, with no change in the system," and that the patent was valid and had been infringed.[21]

A much more complicated case, involving many issues, was that of the *Cold Metal Process Company v. Republic Steel Corporation.* The case had

157

been in the courts for nearly twenty years. Republic, and other Steel companies, had found that cold-strip rolling produced metal cheaper, better, and faster than hot-strip rolling and made metal of exact and uniform thickness suitable for the specifications of the auto industry. Republic had purchased a series of mills from Cold Metal Process Company in 1927 under a licensing agreement. Over the years Republic had replaced the original four-high rolling mills with three-high or two-high mills which worked better, had added oil-sealed roller bearings, tension devices, flood cooling and lubricants and other modifications. Cold Metal claimed patent infringement, but Republic argued that the patent had been overclaimed. The Court found that there had been no misuse of patents or abuse of the licensing agreement, and Judge Allen wrote a lengthy opinion, carefully reasoning the decision with many technical ramifications and citing literally dozens of cases in support.[22] The case was settled; there was no appeal.

Patent lawyers were "aghast" when Judge Allen, a woman, was appointed a federal judge,[23] but over the years they did an about face and were among her most conspicious advocates. One of her most interesting and carefully-prepared speeches was for their benefit. "Invention American Style" traced the history of invention from the wheel to modern times. After commenting on the restraints on early English inventors she continued:

> When the United States of America was founded the inhibitions and traditions of the old world to a large degree were done away with. Men who came to American no longer worked for kings and lords. They were no longer members of crafts which controlled their wages, their occupations and their employment. Here they were free and initiative was released. It was released in a country which . . . as part of its basis doctrine announced a belief in the dignity and rights of the individual. Inevitably, it followed that men worked as never before for themselves, for their families, and for the comforts and convenience of their individual surroundings.[24]

The talk concluded with ringing praises for the incentives which had resulted in a remarkable profusion of American inventions. The speech was in no way controversial, but it provided ample food for thought on the current status of invention American style.

Allen found very interesting the case of the Koch Laboratories, a patent medicine company, that had been in the courts for ten years and remained unsettled. The company sold through the mail under several names medicines that promised to cure almost everything: cancer, heart disease, multiple sclerosis, arthritis, syphilis, psoriasis, allergies, insanity. The Federal Trade Commission found the advertising false, misleading and deceptive. Thirty-three physicians and scientists testified for the Commission that the products had no therapeutic value. Thirty-six witnesses, including twenty-nine physicians testified for the company, some having miraculous testimonies to prove the wonders of the medicines. But the

Commission concluded that the evidence against the medicines was better tested and ordered their sale prohibited. The Court agreed, but defended Dr. Koch's right to publish and send to doctors his book and scholarly papers on the basis of the First Amendment guaranteeing free speech.[25]

The building of the TVA installations brought several cases to court involving eminent domain as the agency condemned easement strips for erection of steel towers and power lines. A widening range of claims were considered in compensation for the easements: the price of the land as valued at its most advantageous use, damages from erosion caused by deforestation, the effects of the increases in river currents caused by deforestation, damage to the productivity of the soil, damage to asthetic values. In the case of Hunter Giers Hicks the district judge had awarded $7,500 for the easement. Hicks claimed this was too little; the TVA said it was too much. Witnesses for Hicks testified that the land was worth about $600 an acre, but that the easement would reduce its value by at least $100 an acre. An expert on soil erosion testified that the cutting of trees and breaking of retaining walls would cause erosion making it impossible to use the strip for farming; evidence indicated that tons of debris had already washed into the strip from higher up the line. TVA witnesses made much lower estimates of value and damages. The court was convinced by the owner's proofs, and Allen wrote the opinion awarding Hicks $15,090 for the easement with 6 per cent interest retroactive to the date of condemnation.[26] A new breed of liberals would soon say that the TVA project was a tragic disturbance of the ecology of the Tennessee valley.

Judge Allen pondered long and seriously over the case of *Stefana Brown v. United States of American.* The case was one of many around the country resulting from cold-war efforts to root out communist plots and punish or deport the offenders and rested on a body of laws to suppress communism. Leaders of the American Communist Party were jailed under the Smith Act which made it illegal to advocate or teach the overthrow of the government by force or to belong to an organization with this objective. The McCarran Internal Security Act made it unlawful to combine with any other person to contribute to the establishment of a totalitarian dictatorship. Communist front organizations were required to register with the attorney general; aliens who had ever been members of a totalitarian party were denied admittance. In the Sixth circuit, Detroit was thought to be a hotbed of communism, and one of the major anti-communist cases was there. Six leaders of the Communist Party were sentenced to prison for conspiring to overthrow the government by force.

Judge Allen was personally very opposed to communism, believing it a challenge to "the conception of right and justice which lies at the basis of civilization."[27] The case she pondered was an effort to denaturalize Stefana Brown, who was believed to be part of the Detroit communist circle. The case revolved on the issue as to whether Brown could refuse to answer

159

incriminating questions on the basis of the Fifth Amendment, and had come to court on the grounds that at the time of her 1940 registration as an alien she had knowingly falsified her membership in the Communist Party. Later it was proved that she had been a member of the Young Communist League from 1933 to 1937. She was quite willing to testify that she did not nor ever had believed in anarchy or overthrow of the United States government. In fact, she said, "I like this country. I never told anybody I didn't. I believe in fighting for this country . . . . I believe in helping the country and helping the people." In cross examination, however, she refused to answer questions as to whether she knew other members of the Communist Party, as to whether she had had meetings at her house, as to whether she had attended a celebration of the birthday of William Z. Foster or a memorial for Lenin sponsored by the Communist Party.

The Circuit Court found, with Allen writing the opinion, that Brown was in contempt of court for her refusal to answer questions put to her and stated that because she had at one time falsified her membership in the Communist Party the right of protection under the Fifth Amendment was waived. The opinion rested on decisions of the Supreme Court, but Judge Allen chose to conclude her opinion with a quotation from Judge Learned Hand,[28] perhaps the most respected judge in the country, but one who, like Allen, was never promoted from the appellate court to the Supreme Court in spite of his excellent qualifications.

Harbingers of the new egalitarian reforms of the sixties and seventies followed the 1954 decision of the Supreme Court in the case of *Brown v. Board of Education of Topeka* finding that separate educational facilities for black students are inherently unequal. Tennessee law before 1954 made it unlawful for any teacher, professor, or educator in any college, academy, or school of learning to allow the white and colored races to attend the same school or be in the same classroom. The state Board of Education had decided to integrate gradually, in the first year admitting qualified black students to graduate classes, and in succeeding years to the next lower class. The district court had accepted this plan, but the appellate court, with Allen writing the opinion, found this not in compliance with the Supreme Court order requiring all deliberate speed in school desegregation.[29] The case did not settle problems of desegregation in Tennessee but was one of a series of cases bringing it about.

The Sixth Circuit's most significant case in desegregation concerned housing. The Detroit Housing Commission had followed the practice of limiting certain public housing to whites only and other facilities to blacks only. Complaint had first been filed in 1950 and by 1954 there were twenty times as many black applicants as white and many vacancies in the white housing and none in the black housing. The district court had ordered the Commission to bring about integration forthwith, but the

Commission said time was needed for orderly integration and appealed the case. The following year, after the Supreme Court decision in *Brown v. Board of Education*, Allen wrote for the Circuit Court:

> The order of the District Court does not contemplate an immediate change of all or the greater number of occupants in any housing project. It contemplates that the applications for occupancy shall be considered and acted upon in order of their filing without reference to whether the applicants are white or colored . . . . and if plaintiffs should accuse defendants of obstruction and illegal delay, the defendants are entitled, under the doctrine of *Brown v. Board of Education of Topeka* . . . . to apply to the United States District Court for hearing and decision as to whether defendants are in good faith implementing the governing Constitutional principles.[30]

It was the first federal court ruling calling for desegregation in public housing.[31]

Missing from the dockets were cases advancing the cause of women's rights. The exception was in the area of minimum wages, for state legislatures had found a way to circumvent the decision of the Adkins case finding minimum wages for women unconstitutional. Judge Allen was pleased to have participated in the 1936 decision finding minimum wages legal for women and minors in dry cleaning, laundry, restaurant and hotel services and retail selling.[32] The following year the Adkins decision was reversed by the Supreme Court "in one of the most celebrated reversals" in its history,[33] and minimum wages for women (and men) came about. Otherwise during Judge Allen's entire judicial career there were no great landmark decisions affecting women's rights, indicating there was no pressure of cases in the lower courts. The fifties, in particular, witnessed an ebb in the flow of women's rights.

Appointment as a United States Supreme Court Justice is the ultimate honor that can come to a successful lawyer or judge. Innumerable men have aspired to such an honor, but only a few have received it. Judge Allen, her friends, and women's organizations aspired to such an honor for her for more than twenty years.

Unusual recognition and publicity came to Judge Allen during most of her career because it was so unusual for a woman to be a judge. There were virtually no sisters among the brethren, and the media found her interesting and newsworthy. She was also the darling of women's organizations. She was too busy to hold offices in such groups as the League of Women Voters, the National Association of Women Lawyers, and others, but she was regularly consulted by their executive boards and asked to speak at their conventions. She was removed from the internal politics of these groups but revered as their model and mentor.

Progress in women's equality with men had not advanced since the good old days of the suffrage movement, and the links in the movement had weakened.[34] But stalwarts in women's groups cherished the illusion of progress and continued their great expectations. Because the epitome of career for a judge was appointment to the Supreme Court, that became their aspiration for Florence Allen.

Her credentials were very convincing of her potential for such a position. Except for her sex, her background was typical of that of Supreme Court justices: from white Protestant, English stock, born in the professional upper middle class, from an urban or small-town environment, with a good education, and often from families with a very deep sense of social responsibility and political involvement[35] At the county and state level she had mounted three successful campaigns for judgeships with surprising, indeed amazing, support from the electorate. Her appointment as a federal judge had met with acclaim; she had served well and the ultimate goal seemed attainable.

The first efforts in 1937, 1938, 1939 were disappointing, but not discouraging, for the men who were appointed were better qualified. Roosevelt made four more appointments before his death, and Allen's nomination was repeatedly proposed to him. Several newspapers supported her candidacy,[36] as well as individuals. Ohio Congressman Stephen M. Young, a staunch, life-long supporter, wrote to Roosevelt recommending Allen as "the outstanding woman jurist in the United States," and added the new thought that since women were making such great wartime sacrifices it would be fitting to appoint a woman.[37] Women's groups were most persistent. Among them was Pilot International, an organization of 116 women's clubs in 23 states which urged Roosevelt to appoint Allen.[38]

Roosevelt's last appointments were again outstanding men with experience a woman would not have. Frank Murphy was an ardent and active liberal Democrat, who had become a national figure through his settlement of labor problems in the auto industry in his home state of Michigan. James F. Byrnes, a southern Democrat, had a thirty-year record of voter support in Congress. Robert Jackson of Pennsylvania was a strong New Dealer whose experience was primarily as United States Attorney General. Not one of them had a background of judicial experience comparable to that of Judge Allen. Each of them reflected in some way a voting constituency with some semblance of voting unity: labor, southerners, liberals.

Women were less optimistic about their appointment possibilities when Harry Truman became president upon Roosevelt's death. There was no organized support for Allen to fill the vacancy which occurred in 1945. Truman chose an Ohioan, Harold H. Burton, a prosperous Cleveland lawyer, a reform mayor of that city, and a U.S. Senator at the time of his appointment. If Allen felt a twinge of disappointment she did not reveal it.

The following year, with another vacancy pending, Allen's supporters tried to organize a campaign to write to the president on her behalf and many did. Carrie Chapman Catt, who had supported her vigorously in 1934, wrote Allen that she was not writing to the president because "you hold the highest court appointment of any woman in the world, and if we should conduct a lively campaign and fail you would lose a good deal of the prestige you have."[39] Allen replied that she agreed and had not lifted a finger to encourage a campaign. Oh the other hand, she did nothing to discourage the campaign, but it seemed unlikely that another justice from Ohio would be appointed soon. Truman appointed Fred M. Vinson of Kentucky in 1946.

When Truman was elected in 1948 India Edwards became executive director of the Women's Division of the Democratic National Committee. Edwards was a dynamic and effective woman and had a close personal relationship with the president. Shortly after the election columnist Dorothy Thompson wrote that the possibility of appointment of women to high posts in the coming administration was slim, and that although Edwards had a list of women to propose even she was not very hopeful. Thompson chose to highlight Allen's name as the best prospect.[40] Eleanor Roosevelt added her voice to those proposing Judge Allen for the Supreme Court.[41] The brightest spot on the political scene for women in 1948 was the election of Margaret Chase Smith, the first woman to be elected to the Senate without first having been appointed to fill a vacancy.

Every Supreme Court vacancy continued to inspire media speculation that Judge Allen would be appointed. A reporter for the *Detroit News* took advantage of the opportunity to question judges in convention in his home town when a vacancy occurred in 1949. He asked the judges if they felt Allen was capable of doing the job. He found their response "quick and unanimous" in approval, saying that she had a fine legal mind and years of experience. They all agreed — for the benefit of the reporter — that they had no prejudice against women in high positions, that having a woman judge would not alter anything and that "a good judge is a good judge."[42]

There were two vacancies in 1949 when justices Frank Murphy and Wiley Blount Rutledge died in office. On the day Murphy died India Edwards promised to talk to Truman immediately. She made it plain to news reporters that Judge Allen was the first choice of Democratic women. She said that after Truman's election the previous fall she had submitted a list of women she would like to see appointed and that Judge Allen's name was at the top of the list, adding that "If the President should decide to appoint a woman, I don't think there's any doubt it would be Judge Allen."[43] Stephen Young also said that he was going to see Truman and suggest Allen.

The president did not decide to appoint a woman. In her memoirs Edwards wrote that she "begged" him to consider Judge Allen and that

President Truman assured me he thought it a good idea to have a woman, especially one of "Sister" (as her fellow judges called her) Allen's reputation and capability as a Supreme Court Justice, but that he would have to consult Chief Justice Fred Vinson to find out how he and other Justices would feel about having a woman in their august group. My disappointment and unhappiness were great when the President sent for me a few days later to tell me that the Chief Justice and his conferees would not willingly have a woman as a Justice. She would make it difficult for them to meet informally with robes, and perhaps shoes, off, shirt collars unbuttoned and discuss their problems and come to decisions. I am certain that the old line about their being no sanitary arrangement for a female Justice was also included in their reasons for not wanting a woman, but President Truman did not mention this to me.[44]

Theoretically members of the Supreme Court have nothing to do with the appointment of colleagues, but theory and practice in this case evidently diverged. And Truman's interest in appointing a woman wasn't great enough to override the superficial objections of the brethren.

Truman appointed Tom C. Clark and Sherman Minton. Truman's Supreme Court appointments generally were not of the caliber of Roosevelt's and Minton's appointment in particular provoked controversy. In his home state of Indiana, the editor of the *Fort Wayne News Sentinel* found the appointment disappointing. It overlooked a number of better qualified jurists, the editor wrote, mentioning specifically Judge Learned Hand and Judge Florence Allen. The editor believed that Minton was appointed not because of any long and distinguished career on the bench but because he was one of Truman's cronies and a chore boy for the party. "Most thinking Americans will recognize the appointment for what it is — very mediocre," the editorial concluded.[45]

Except for a few diehards, women of the Democratic Party at this point seemed to give up and be resigned to the fact that Truman was not going to appoint Allen to the Supreme Court. Vadae Meekison refused to give up and prevailed upon Edwards until the end of Truman's term to bring about Allen's appointment. She told Edwards that if Allen was not appointed "history would say that there was still discrimination against women."[46] History confirmed that statement. Meekison also told Edwards that there was not a man in the whole United States who was as well qualified as Florence Allen. Although that statement was doubtful, it did seem that Allen was as well qualified as some of those appointed.

Meekison was tireless in her efforts. Her daughter Virginia worked for the government and Vadae made frequent trips to Washington. In her later years she wrote to the publishers of Allen's autobiography that "most of the people in high places in government" thought that appointment of a woman to the Supreme Court was long past due, but that "something held it back." In Meekison's view that something was that the judges did not want a woman.[47]

Maud Wood Park was another who refused to give up. Although Park was in her dotage, she still had connections in Washington from her days of political action for the suffrage amendment. Park sent a messenger to Truman in 1951 to talk with him personally about Allen's appointment,[48] but it was too late for Truman to make make appointments.

President Truman was not insensitive to demands to end the white male domination of the court system.[49] In October 1949 he appointed a black male judge to the Federal Court of Appeals for the Third Circuit and an active feminist, Burnita Shelton Matthews, to the District Court for the District of Columbia. Although Matthews and Allen were both in the women's movement, their viewpoints diverged. Matthews had been active in the National Woman's Party, a party that encouraged women to create their own voting bloc and fight for all kinds of equalities. Matthews had acted as attorney for the Woman's Party, much as Allen had acted as attorney for the Ohio Woman Suffrage Party. Matthews was one of the women who picketed the White House during World War I, believing democracy at home to be just as important as making the world safe for democracy. The NAWSA was embarrassed by the activities of the pickets and supported the war effort. Matthews had defended the Equal Rights Amendment in a hearing before a Senate Judiciary Committee, reciting a long list of legal and economic discriminations that handicapped women.[50] Allen never defended the Equal Rights Amendment. Matthews was President of the NAWL in 1934-1935 and stood for more energetic support of the ERA. She had helped to write many laws to better the position of women, including equal pay for equal work,[51] rather than a minimum wage.

The District of Columbia Bar Association, of which Matthews was a member, endorsed her appointment because she was a woman with a demonstrated feminist viewpoint. A member of the Association told India Edwards that they had endorsed Matthews so as not to be considered anti-female and would probably never endorse another woman.[52] Truman appointed her primarily because she was a woman and secondarily because she had good qualifications. Allen based her hopes in the premise that she must excel in qualifications and downplay her feminism. At the time neither method was potent enough for appointment of a woman to the Supreme Court.

Judge Allen considered it a sad fact that there weren't more women in the judiciary and worked for the appointment of other women, particularly Marion Harron. Dr. Harron was appointed by Roosevelt to the U.S. Board of Tax Appeals in 1936. The Board was later transformed into the U.S. Tax Court and when Harron's appointment expired in 1948 her reappointment was very much in doubt. A poll of lawyers in the American Bar Association tax section voted 104 to 57 against her appointment.[53] It was said that Judge Harron did not have the proper judicial temperament, and, as might be expected of a woman, was not in complete control of her emotions. Rumor had it that on one occasion she had lost her patience with a lawyer who irritated her in the course of a case and in a fit of temper had thrown an ink well at him.[54] Marion's friends were certain that the charges were fabrications to remove a woman judge, and the sisterhood rose to her defense.

Judge Allen worked fervently but inconspicuously to clear Harron's name and promote her re-appointment. She solicited the aid of the Cleveland women lawyers' organization to alert their sisters all over the country of Marion's perdicament and to encourage them to write to the Senate Judiciary Committee favoring the appointment.[55] She made several trips to Washington to discuss the matter with her network of friends and wrote to Eleanor Roosevelt about the matter. Marion visited Hyde Park and Mrs. Roosevelt wrote supporting her. Finally her re-appointment was confirmed. India Edwards called what happened to Judge Harron "a nasty incident,"[56] and Allen and her correspondents agreed.

In the process Marion and Florence became devoted friends. Marion visited at the Briar Patch frequently and treated Florence royally when she came to Washington. Marion's attitudes toward Allen were much like those of an adoring daughter that Florence never had. It would not have been appropriate for Marion to address Florence as "Dear Mom," but she and several other younger women did address the judge affectionately as "Dear Cap." Many younger women remembered Allen with small deeds of thoughtfulness and kindness. Younger women's dogs sometimes sent greetings to Allen's dogs and remembered them at Christmas with such gifts as little red sweaters and pretty green ribbons.

The ideal of political abstinence by judges has perhaps been more observed in its breach than in its adherence. Most judges have publicly renounced politics when they entered the marble halls of justice and donned official robes. Privately, however, many have found it impossible to give up a life-long addiction to the fascinating game of politics.[57] Florence Allen adhered to the ideal religiously. The tragedy of her conscientiousness was that she gradually lost her interior political connections which might have cracked the door to the Supreme Court. Her political past was as a Democrat, however, and it would seem that hopes for her appointment would be laid to rest when the Democratic Party lost its twenty-year domination of politics in 1952 with the election of Dwight D. Eisenhower.

What actually happened was that the torch of aspiration passed to a new generation of women, many of them Republicans, and was rekindled with bright new flames. The first vacancy passed without action on the part of women. Eisenhower's appointment of Earl Warren was brilliant. Warren, a few years younger than Allen, had passed the bar exams in California in 1914, the same year Allen passed them in Ohio. Warren had gone on to be a successful lawyer and a dynamic governor of his home state. His leadership of the Supreme Court justified Eisenhower's confidence and resulted in many landmark decisions in civil rights and "individual liberties that made great changes in American society.

Meantime Allen was joining a new network of sisterhood, many of the women younger than she and many of them active in the International Federation of Women Lawyers. The new sisterhood at first fancied Allen as a judge at the international level. In 1953 when a vacancy occurred in the International Court of justice the Federation petitioned the United States government to nominate Judge Allen. Allen realistically predicted that such a nomination would not be made for another generation, but she was enormously pleased by the confidence placed in her.[58] The projected campaign was blasted in the bud within a few days by the reappointment of the incumbent judge for another nine-year term.

The following month there was a vacancy on the International Law Commission. The women lawyers immediately thought of Allen, and she responded to their inquiry that she was indeed interested in this appointment.[59] But again a man was appointed before the campaign could get under way.

Superficially it appeared that the proposal for a world judgeship had failed for lack of a campaign. Federation President Rosalind Bates did not plan to have that happen on the national level. Her newsletter to the membership in 1954 contained a helpful suggestion: "Would it not be wonderful if President Eisenhower is sufficiently overwhelmed by wires to realize the value of Judge Florence Allen on the Supreme Court!"[60] Eisenhower did not feel overwhelmed and appointed a male justice in 1955 and another in 1956. Allen noted in her diary that she felt "depressed about the Supreme Court."[61]

Justice Stanley F. Reed retired in 1957 because of age. He was 72; Allen was 73. Newspapers forecast that Eisenhower would very likely appoint a Republican from Ohio. It was also hinted that he might shatter precedent and appoint a woman. The *Cincinnati Enquirer* wrote that it would most likely be Florence Allen and that she was a Republican.[62] The idea that Allen was a Republican was probably based on her connections with Senator Bricker and his U.N. treaty amendment. Allen shortly identified herself as a "split-ticket" voter.[63]

Marion Harron initiated the drive for the Supreme Court in 1957. Marion could not act openly because she was a judge, and it was Neva B. Talley, President of the NAWL, who visibly led the campaign. The campaign got under way in mid-February when the NAWL voted a resolution recommending Allen's appointment.[64] A telegram was sent to Eisenhower, followed by a letter suggesting that the whole country would benefit from Allen's incisive legal mind and the women of the country would be complimented. The judge herself became very busy supplying information, making contacts, bringing her supporters together for this last campaign.[65] Success or failure is "in the lap of the gods" she told a reporter in Chicago.[66]

Women all over the country sent letters to the president, the attorney general and senators of the Judiciary Committee. The Business and Professional Women's Clubs joined the NAWL in spearheading the drive; hundreds of other organizations joined in. Rosalind Bates persuaded more than a hundred women's organizations in California alone to endorse Allen's candidacy. To Eisenhower Bates wrote that they were voicing the hopes not only of the women of California and the women of the United States but "the hopes of women of the free world."[67] To Allen she wrote, "Cap, dear, we would be so honored if the president has the wisdom to appoint you."[68] Neva Talley made a trip to Washington to talk with Attorney General Herbert Brownell. Brownell told her that Allen's age was the biggest obstacle to her appointment.[69]

Viola Smith, representative of the International Federation of Women Lawyers to the United Nations,[70] spread the word in New York, Massachusetts, Illinois, and Texas. Encouraging radio and TV newscasts whetted the enthusiasm and Viola wrote Cap that the news was glorious and that she hoped the appointment would come to Allen's crown of honor.[71] A new generation of Ohio women joined the old timers in acclaim. Bertha Adkins, assistant chairman of the Republican National Committee, promised that the requests would be delivered to the right people.

Support from men was notably slight in 1957. Presumably they thought she was too old for the appointment. Some women refused to join on the grounds of age. Her advocates countered that even if she served only for a year or two because of her age it would still be a great victory for women.

Clearly Allen had worked and hoped for this appointment, but her diary on March 2 recorded only "[Charles E.] Whitaker of Kansas City appointed to Supreme Court." Whitaker's credentials, except for his age, were not better than Allen's. A graduate of the University of Kansas City in 1924, in private law practice for several years, he had been a judge in the U.S. District Court and the Eighth Circuit Court of Appeals. Although conscientious and hard working, he was a poor choice for the Supreme Court because he lacked intellectual capacity and had difficulty making decisions.[72]

Presidential Assistant Robert Gray said that Eisenhower had considered all applications and endorsements. Senator Bricker wrote that Allen was considered too old, having passed the informal age limit set by the Justice Department. Bricker noted, however, that there were "special circumstances" in the case of Judge Allen which he would try to bring to the attention of the Justice Department.[73]

Olga Jones, a Washington newswoman and close friend of Allen who had an undisclosed "court friend," wrote Allen that she thought she knew what happened but that she should not write it and would tell her when she saw her. Olga thought that the future might be different if Allen was willing to go through the trying ordeal again. The pot was still boiling, Olga said, and the next time it was necessary to find someone close to the president "to personally talk with him" and encourage him to invite Allen for an interview.[74]

The pot was indeed boiling and in 1958 Eisenhower nominated an Ohioan, Potter Stewart. Aside from being 30 years her junior, a graduate of Yale Law School and from a distinguished Republican family, his credentials were very similar to Allen's. His judicial experience was as her colleague on the bench of the Federal Court of Appeals of the Sixth Circuit; his opinions, like hers, were based on a strict application of the law. Stewart was apparently surprised, for he told a reporter that he was "bowled over" by the appointment and that "it was like being knocked off the Christmas tree."[75] Fifteen years later Justice Stewart joined in writing the Supreme Court decision finding abortion constitutional,[76] a landmark decision in the history of women's rights, written at a time of rapid social change in attitudes toward women.

When Judge Allen was asked what she thought of the appointment of Justice Stewart she shrugged it off with a comment that judges don't talk about such things.[77] The next year she retired from the bench.

Why wasn't Florence Allen ever selected for the Supreme Court? Was it just a matter of luck? William O. Douglas wrote in his autobiography that ". . . the chances of being on the Supreme Court, even for a male Caucasian, are one in a million."[78] At any given time there is a plethora of male Caucasians with acceptable qualifications available and eager for promotion. No merit system of selection exists; no campaign is conducted to sift out the winners and the losers. The president in his wisdom or with his inner circle choses one from many.

Good fortune does not necessarily fall to the best. Judge Learned Hand, ranked "unquestionably first among American judges" by the *Harvard Law Review*,[79] was never appointed to the Supreme Court and spent a long and honorable career in the lower courts. Luck kept him for 37 years in the Court of Appeals. In his youth he was too progressive; in his middle years he was from New York and there were too many justices from New York; in his later years he was too old. Allen's fate had similar vagaries.

One of Judge Hand's biographers wrote that the overriding reason why he was never appointed was most likely because he had not been a faithful party stalwart.[80] Allen, like Hand, was not a party stalwart. Her great campaigns were non-partisan campaigns. In fact, the suffrage ideal was to shift emphasis from party loyalty to a consideration of issues and candidates. Only in the 1932 campaign against Bolton had she been a party stalwart, and then she piled up a few chips and received her reward. After

169

1934, she lost her connections in the Democratic party. She was politically too independent. Judge Allen herself believed that this was why she was never appointed to the Supreme Court.[81] Judicial appointments have customarily gone to faithful members of the president's party.[82]

Granted there was a plethora of male candidates. But there was no plethora of female candidates; Allen was *the* female candidate. Roosevelt, Truman, and Eisenhower appeared to have no prejudices against a qualified woman per se, but for the president and his party, appointment of a woman had no political advantages. Women were not voting as a bloc. It was believed that women voted with their husbands or fathers. Judge Allen said this was "just another political generalization with little or no basis in fact," and that many men asked their wives how to vote because their wives knew more about issues and candidates than they did.[83] Either way, as far as the presidents were concerned the women's vote did not count for getting programs through Congress or winning another term in office.[84]

Since there was no political advantage, the presidents chose not to antagonize the male judicial establishment. The chief hazard to her appointment in 1934 to the Federal Court of Appeals was that she was a woman, not wanted by the male establishment. The Supreme Court was even more rarified. Whether one interprets the Supreme Court of Allen's time as an exclusive men's club, a monastic order, the high priesthood of the marble halls of justice, or a fraternity of the brethern, women were surely not expected. There weren't even any women among the law clerks, except for one who had worked for Justice Douglas for a year in the forties.[85] Bathroom facilities would have been a problem because the justices' robing room was directly connected to the men's room. The selection of candidates was made by men who respected the feelings of other men.

Allen's chances were vastly overrated by the women's organizations. They wanted to believe that women were acceptable in public life. Frustrated by their failure to achieve political equality, they had almost a neurotic fixation on Allen as the symbol of what they wanted and had not attained. Time was passing and prospects for the future weren't much better. The number of women moving up in the ranks was pathetically small.

Florence Allen wanted the appointment for herself and for women. She would have accepted the responsibility as a conscientious duty and performed to the best of her ability. Both her conscience and her ability were thoroughly reliable and superbly good. On the other hand, she knew enough about the system and was realistic enough not to dwell on the possibility. Privately she came to feel that she had been "in a hot spot" about it for more than twenty years. Perhaps after a number of years and a number of disappointments she would have preferred to withdraw, although there is no evidence of that. She could not withdraw for she was the leader and the symbol of a cause to which she had devoted most of her life. To withdraw would be to admit defeat and to disappoint her loyal admirers.

"The thing that you hope for will never happen," she wrote Vadae at one point, "but that you still hope for it touches me very much."[86]

FOOTNOTES

[1] Friedman, pp. 567-568; John R. Schmidhauser, *Judges and Justices: The Federal Appellate Judiciary*, New York: Little Brown, 1979, p. 11.

[2] *To Do Justly*, p. 150.

[3] From personal interviews.

[4] So Judge McAllister remembered in a letter to Allen, January 6, 1966, Allen papers, WRHS, container 10, folder 4. According to her papers she had written 457 opinions as of September 30, 1959, Allen papers, LC, container 2.

[5] According to Maureen H. Abernathy, President NAWL, 288 F 2d. 7 (1959).

[6] *Filburn v. Helke*, 43 F Supp. 1017 (S.D. Ohio 1942).

[7] Quotation from *Filburn v. Helke*, p. 1023.

[8] Summary from Harry Phillips, *History of the Sixth Circuit*, Bicentennial Committee of the Judicial Conference of the U.S., 1976 pp. 80-82. The Supreme Court case affirming Allen's findings was *Wickard v. Filburn*, 317 U.S. 111 (1942). According to Herbert Wechsler, *Principles, Politics and Fundamental Law*, Cambridge: Harvard University Press, 1961, p. 106 *Filburn v. Helke* was the final case in a series confirming broad federal commerce power.

[9] *Midland Steel Products Co. v. National Labor Relations Board*, 113 F 2d. 800 (1940).

[10] *NLRB v. Hopper Mfg. Co.*, 170 F 2d. 692 (1948).

[11] *National Labor Relations Board v. Packard Motor Company*, 157 F 2d. 80 (1946).

[12] *Ohio Power Co. v. NLRB*, 176 F 2d. 385 (1949).

[13] *NLRB v. Salant and Salant, Inc.*, 183 F 2d. 462 (1950).

[14] *NLRB v. Bill Daniels, Inc., NLRB v. Gilbert Motor Sales*, 202 F 2d.

[15] *Emulsified Asphalt Products Co., Appellant v. James P. Mitchell, Sect. of Labor, Appellee*, 222 F 2d. 913 (1955).

[16] *NLRB v. Pittsburgh Steamship Co.*, 180 F 2d. 731 (1950); newspaper clippings, Allen papers, WRHS, container 28, folder 1; letters container 7, folder 2. Judges McAllister and Simons congratulated her on the decision and its affirmation by the Supreme Court.

[17] Cleveland *Plain Dealer*, undated, 1943, Allen papers, WRHS, container 27, folder 8.

[18] *To Do Justly*, pp. 102-103.

[19] From speech for Cleveland Patent Bar Association, October 10, 1959.

[20] Summarized from *Business Week*, December 29, 1956, p. 36 and January 26, 1957, pp. 149-150, 152.

[21] *Great Lakes Equipment Company v. Fluid Systems, Incorporated*, 217 F 2d. 613 (1955).

[22] *Cold Metal Process Company and the Union National Bank of Youngstown, Ohio, Trustee, Appellants v. Republic Steel Corporation. Republic Steel Corporation v. The Cold Metal Process Company*, 233 F 2d. 828 (1956). *To Do Justly*, p. 103.

[23] Letter of Allen to Mary Dewson , December 4, 1959, Dewson papers, RL., container 1.

[24] "Invention American Style," *Journal of the Patent Office Society*, v. 40, No. 5, May 1948, pp. 312-321.

[25] *Koch et al. v. Federal Trade Commission*, 206 F 2d. 311 (1953).

[26] *Hunter Giers Hicks, Appellant v. United States for the Use of TVA, Appellee*, 266 F 2d. 515 (1959).

[27] *To Do Justly*, p. 152.

[28] *Stefana Brown, Appellant v. United States of America, Appellee*, 234 F 2d. 140 (1956).

[29] *Ruth Booker, an infant, by Davie Booker, Her Mother and Next Friend, et al., Appellants v. State of Tennessee Board of Education, et al., 240 F 2d. 689 (1957).*

[30] *The Detroit Housing Commission v. Walter Arthur Lewis et al., 226 F 2d. 180 (1955).*

[31] *Cleveland News*, October 27, 1955, Allen papers, WRHS, container 28, folder 5, identified it as the first court ruling for housing desegregation.

[32] *Columbus Citizen*, November 20, 1936, p. 1, Allen papers, LC, container 8. Letter of Allen to Josephus Daniels, December 8, 1936, Allen papers, LC, container 1.

[33] According to Jennifer Friesen and Ronald K. L. Collins, "Looking Back on *Muller v. Oregon*," v. 69, *American Bar Association Journal*, April 1983, p. 477. The case was *West Coast Hotel v. Parrish*, 300 U.S. 379.

[34] Ryan, p. 219.

[35] Schmidhauser, pp. 96-97.

[36] Clippings from *The New York Post, The New York Sun*, Cleveland *Plain Dealer, Akron Beacon Journal, Syracuse Post Standard, Cincinnati Enquirer*, and many others are among Allen papers, WRHS, container 26, folders 3, 4, and 5.

[37] According to the Cleveland *Plain Dealer*, October 19, 1942, Allen papers, WRHS, container 27, folder 7.

[38] *Columbus Journal*, January 31, 1941, Allen papers, WRHS, container 7, folder 1.

[39] Letter from Catt to Allen, May 10, 1946, Allen papers, WRHS, container 7, folder 1.

[40] Cleveland *Plain Dealer*, January 8, 1949, p. 26.

[41] Tribute to Allen at NYU banquet, Allen papers, WRHS, container 18, folder 1.

[42] *Detroit News*, August 1949, Allen papers, WRHS, container 27, folder 11.

[43] *Cincinnati Enquirer*, July 21, 1949, Allen papers, WRHS, container 27, folder 11.

[44] India Edwards, *Pulling No Punches: Memoirs of a Woman in Politics*, G. L. Putnam's Sons, New York, 1977, pp. 171-172.

[45] *Fort Wayne News Sentinel*, September 16, 1949, Allen papers, WRHS, container 27, folder 11.

[46] Letter from Meekison to Allen, January 14, 1952, Meekison papers, OHSL.

[47] Letter of Meekison to Western Reserve University Press, March 29, 1966, Meekison papers, OHSL.

[48] Letter of Park to Allen, March 3, 1951, Allen papers, WRHS, container 7, folder 2.

[49] By 1945 the idea of having a woman on the Supreme Court was much more acceptable than it was in 1938, probably as a result of women's war efforts. A public opinion poll in 1945 showed that 52% of women and 42% of men approved of the appointment of a woman to the Supreme Court. Cantril, p. 1053.

[50] Kraditor, *Up From the Pedestal*, pp. 293-294.

[51] *History of the NAWL*, p. 61.

[52] Edwards, p. 186.

[53] *Ibid.*, p. 189.

[54] Personal interview.

[55] *Ibid.*

[56] Edwards, p. 189.

[57] See Bruce A. Murphy, *The Brandeis-Frankfurter Connection*, New York: Oxford, 1982; Jack W. Pelterson, *Federal Courts in the Political Process*, New York: Random House, 1955; Bob Woodward and Scott Armstrong, *The Brethren*, Austin: S. and S. Press, 1980.

[58] Correspondence between Bates and Allen, September 8 and 14, 1953, Allen papers, WRHS, container 7, folder 4.

[59] Correspondence Between Bates and Allen, October 1953, Allen papers, WRHS, container 7, folder 4.

[60] Newsletter October 14, 1954, Allen papers, WRHS, container 7, folder 4.

[61] Diary, June 18, 1956.

[62] *Cincinnati Enquirer*, undated 1957, Allen papers, WRHS, container 28, folder 7.

[63] Cleveland *Plain Dealer*, undated 1957, Allen papers, WRHS, container 28, folder 7.

[64] *History of NAWL*, p. 239.

[65] Diary January 1, 1957 ("planning many things" with Marian Harron) to March 2, 1957. All from personal interviews.

[66] *Chicago Daily Tribune*, February 16, 1957, Allen papers, WRHS, container 28, folder 7.

[67] Bates letter to Eisenhower, February 1, 1957, Allen papers, WRHS, container 8, folder 2. Among her many responsibilities Bates was legislative chairman of the California Presidents Council of Women's Organizations. By 1957 five countries, including West Germany and Turkey, had women on the supreme court.

[68] Handwritten on copy of Bates' letter to Eisenhower.

[69] *History of NAWL*, p. 240.

[70] In 1920 Viola Smith was the first woman to be given an office in the foreign field by the Department of Commerce. She was named clerk to the American Commercial Attache in Peking. Breckinridge, p. 307.

[71] Letter from Smith to Allen, February 11, 1957, Allen papers, WRHS, container 8, folder 2.

[72] Diary, March 2, 1957. Bernard Schwartz, *Super Chief: Earl Warren and His Supreme Court — a Judicial Biography*, New York: New York University Press, 1983, pp. 216-217.

[73] Bricker letter to Neva Talley, March 14, 1957, Allen papers, WRHS, container 8, folder 2.

[74] Letter from Jones to Allen, March 6, 1957, Allen papers, WRHS, container 8, folder 2.

[75] The reporter was Lowell K. Bridwell, staff reporter for Scripps-Howard newspapers, Allen papers, LC, container 6.

[76] Justice Blackmun wrote the majority opinion in which Chief Justice Burger and Justices Douglas, Brennan, Stewart, Marshall and Powell joined. *New York Times*, January 23, 1973, p. 1.

[77] Cleveland *Plain Dealer*, undated 1958, Allen papers, WRHS, container 28, folder 8.

[78] William O. Douglas, *Go East, Young Man: The Early Years*, New York: Dell, 1974, p. 455.

[79] G. Edward White, *The American Judicial Tradition: Profiles of Leading American Judges*, New York: Oxford, 1976, p. 263.

[80] Kathryn Griffith, *Judge Learned Hand and the Role of the Federal Judiciary*, Norman: University of Oklahoma Press, 1973, p. 5.

[81] From personal interview.

[82] Sheldon Goldman, *The Federal Courts as a Political System*, New York, 1971, pp. 57-58. Susan Ware (op. cit.) thought Allen lost her interior connections with political women because they were mostly in Washington and she was in Cincinnati.

[83] Cleveland *Plain Dealer*, September 7, 1960, Allen papers, LC, container 3.

[84] This is the view of Beverly B. Cook in "Women as Supreme Court Candidates: From Florence Allen to Sandra O'Conner," *Judicature*, v. 65, No. 6, December-January, 1982, pp. 314-326.

[85] Lucille Lomen of the University of Washington Law School.

[86] Letter from Allen to Meekison, January 17, 1952, Meekison papers, OHSL.

Chapter 13

THE BRIAR PATCH

The Kellogg-Briand Pact of 1928, for which Florence Allen had worked so zealously, outlawed war. It was followed by a decade of unprecedented international lawlessness as aggressors moved into Manchuria, the Rhineland, Ethiopia, Austria, and Czechoslovakia. Only when it came to Poland did the powers rise in protest, and then by means of armed combat and not by means of law, marking the beginning of a second world war. The first world war had been a highly emotional experience for Allen, especially as it involved her brothers, but she took little note of the events that shattered Europe. In the second world war no one close to her was in uniform, but she followed events avidly: the collapse of France, the departure of British troops from the continent, the agonizing destruction of eastern Europe, the accumulation of Soviet power and the inexorable rolling back of the Nazi tide. Lowell Thomas and Hans Kaltenborn were her favorite informants and their names appeared regularly in her diary like family friends.

With the coming of the war there were no more trips to Colorado or jaunts to Europe. More time was spent at home. Precisely where home was to be was a question for some time. Esther resigned as Dean of Women at Ohio State and the family home there sold and the possessions divided.

Mary Pierce had interviews at several private schools after her release from Park School during the depression, but as no jobs materialized she was free to move with Florence. They looked at houses and apartments in Cincinnati, but didn't settle on anything permanent. They thought about building a new house, but didn't. Finally they settled on fixing up the shack in Lake County, partly because it was affordable. Florence owned the property; it could be made livable with a small investment and improved over the years.

It was a plan that had something for everyone. Florence could walk in private among the trees and gullies she loved. Mary could be the farmer she had always fancied she wanted to be. For the dogs it was paradise. It would involve a good deal of driving, but Mary was willing, and more and more she became the chauffeur who drove Florence to the bus or the train or even to Cincinnati, or transported visitors to and fro. It would involve an hour's bus ride each way to her Cleveland office for the next twenty-five years, but Florence came to cherish that time as time when she could concentrate on her briefs far from friends, telephones, or

175

interruptions.

The Briar Patch was Mary's baby. During the summer of 1942 she spent her days at the shack. Getting water in and out of the house was the first step, starting from a well and ending in a cesspool. The well and pump forever after caused endless trouble. The cesspool, once built, was never heard of again. With water a bathroom was soon ready. The old roof was torn off, a second story added with new bedrooms. Mary cemented up the chimney, painted the bedrooms and Florence wrote in her diary that it looked "sweet," and that Mary had achieved "great things upstairs." Downstairs a study was set aside for Florence, which she evaluated as "a sweet little room."[1]

In September they officially moved to the Briar Patch. It had been too much for Mary and she was confined to the hospital for three weeks, leaving Florence to arrange for the furnace, for building the garage, for entertaining the steady stream of friends, and for figuring out how income would cover expenses. Bert came the middle of September and stayed until court started. Bert and Florence walked with the dogs in the autumn woods, shucked walnuts and picked grapes. The dogs, especially Star, liked to pick grapes, according to their mistress.

The first winter was a new experience in learning to cope with the snow and ice. Sooner or later it seemed that everyone skidded a car into the ditch or was stuck in the driveway, including a policeman whom Mary had to push out. Curtains went up all over the house, the birds found a refuge around Mary's bird feeder, and great plans were made for spring gardening.

Mary's gardening plans went far beyond the ordinary victory garden that many families toyed with during the war. Over the years her gardening expanded to provide most of their food supply and there were orgies of canning and freezing, making grape juice and jam and jellies. Meals were varied and delectable with the produce of her efforts. Landscaping and flowers galore beautified the pleasant country home. Eventually two sheep and two pigs were added to the estate and Mary could truthfully define her vocation as that of a farmer. Correspondents often referred to the Briar Patch as Miss Pierce's farm.

Miss Pierce was a lady farmer. She had many helpers — gardeners, cleaning women, handymen and experts, farmers to do the plowing, plumbers to deal with the water problem. In the long run a couple of helpers was the most satisfactory arrangement. The lady farmer herself was a handsome, well-groomed woman, active in church and community affairs, serving on the local library board for many years, graciously at ease and conversant with the judge's associates and friends, and a never-failing source of kindness and thoughtfulness to everyone. Her primary concern, however, was always the comfort of the judge.

The judge's role at the Briar Patch remained the same as it had been at the shack. The dogs were hers, right down to the ticks and fleas and broken legs and trips to the veterinary. Anything to do with the trees was hers: gathering fruit and nuts, trimming, sawing and splitting wood. By all accounts she was handy with a saw and swung an axe with accuracy and determination. She proved by her example that women as well as men could saw wood. There was a growing surplus of wood. Eventually the pile became so large that visitors were utterly astonished at its size.[2] She fought a continuing battle with the briars that claimed the land as rightfully theirs.

Occasionally she liked to feed the animals, and in a pinch helped to prepare vegetables for canning and freezing. She wrote to a friend that Mary from time to time threatened to teach her to cook so that her help would be available in emergencies,[3] but as far as is known neither teacher nor student ever appeared for lessons. One reporter found that "culinary arts are mysteries to the judge, but she is highly and vocally appreciative of the results."[4]

There were two pianos in the house, an upright and a grand, and at times both must have been in use. Florence revived her skills with frequent practice. Mary took up playing the piano seriously, Bert played Chopin when she came, and Mary Welles played the violin. Other guests brought their instruments and music was often the evening's entertainment. Mary took up photography and sometimes showed her slides.

Florence and Mary were seldom alone at the Briar Patch either for meals or overnight. Ordinarily from one to four guests were present. Some guests stayed overnight, some stayed for a week or a month, and a few stayed for a year or more. Florence and Mary's hospitality and generosity were infinite and it was inevitable that a few beneficiaries would hang on too long and settle into a state of dependency.

Nieces had a special place in Florence's heart and thoughts. Keenie went to college with Aunt Florence's help. Like the overwhelming majority of the young women of her generation, she did not aspire to have a great career. She married Lon Hill when she was very young and settled down to have children: two boys, Jack and Tom, and a sweet little girl, named Florence Allen, with a halo of red curls. Keenie's family was often in Judge Allen's thoughts, and although they were always very cordial to their famous maiden aunt, they did not respond with the overflowing warm intimacy that Aunt Florence felt for them.

Weebie's daughters Betty, Barbie and Lucie were very dear to Aunt Florence. She thought Betty's wedding was beautiful and Betty and Ted were always welcomed. Barbie lived in Columbus with Esther for some years and Aunt Florence liked to talk with her about colleges. Barbie had several serious illnesses. In 1947 she came to stay with Aunt Florence for a month before going to Mayo Clinic for an operation, where she died. "I loved Barbie as if she were my own child," Florence wrote to a friend[5] as she left to visit Weebie in San Diego to share her grief. Lucie often visited the

Briar Patch and so did Emir and Elise Gaw. Mary had nieces and nephews too, and they were equally welcomed.

Old friends and new friends met at the Patch. Most were women but men visitors were frequent. Women friends collectively were called "the girls" in a connotation of friendship and intimacy rather than naivete or immaturity. Several were old-timers from the suffrage campaigns, women in their fifties or more.

The public image of Judge Allen was that she exhibited great strength of mind and body — that she was as sturdy as a tree. In private life she was very frequently ill and worried all the time about her health, to the point of hypochondria. One acquantance remembered that she ordered pills in bulk at wholesale, sorted them out by color, and took them frequently, seemingly also by color.[6] Amazingly, her illnesses never seemed to interfere with her schedule of court obligations and incessant travel for conventions of women's organizations and bar associations and speaking engagements.

Florence and Mary lived strenuous lives and suffered the consequences of broken bones, sprained joints, aching muscles and exhaustion. Each was very attentive to the others illnesses, and now and then Mary laid down the law to Florence that she must take it easier, without apparent effect. They explored the ranks of women doctors in Cleveland, Columbus, and Cincinnati, usually taking given advice. When her niece died after an operation by a male surgeon, Florence was very critical of him for never coming to see his patient after the operation, implying that a woman doctor would not be so uncaring.[7] It was only in their old age, when specialists were needed, that Florence and Mary brought themselves to rely on male doctors.

Before the war ended plans were under way to replace the discredited League of Nations and an organizational meeting was scheduled for San Francisco. Allen wanted to participate, as did many other women who had been active in the peace movement in the twenties. Friends proposed Allen's name to the president and the state department, but no place was found for her. Judge Thomas F. McAllister of the Federal Court of Appeals, who wrote on her behalf, received a reply that the number of women advisers at San Francisco would be rather limited.[8] Once again decisions about keeping the peace were relegated not to women and young men, but to middle-aged and older men. Allen made many speeches, however, for the United Nations and for peace with justice. The United Nations did not become a controversial political issue as the League of Nations did and as a judge Allen was free to speak about it.

She thought the United Nations charter a stronger instrument for peace than the League of Nations covenant because it expressly outlawed war. She said we should demand that our government never bypass the United Nations, that we should demand compulsory jurisdiction of problems in the new United Nations court. The machinery of the United Nations is useless, she told her audiences, unless it is used to put into force the fundamental ethical principles of the Ten Commandments. She condemned peace making at summit conferences of world leaders. "Never again should men, however great, be allowed to meet in an Oriental capital and give away with a nod or an ok the rights of lesser nations."[9] The Pottsdam agreement she found in violation of all our traditional regard for human rights because it included wholesale transfer of populations.

Our obligation to build world peace dwarfs all other issues, she told a New York audience. She told women especially that they had "the duty and the power, through the great force of public opinion, of helping to prevent the moral bankruptcy among governments which led directly to the second world war."[10]

In the light of political facts, Allen's call to women to enforce peace had more potential after the second world war than after the first. Women were voting in larger numbers after World War II than in 1920, and in the next generation the number of women voting would exceed the number of men voting. Women did not find unity in a voting bloc, but there was one issue on which women demonstrated a voting pattern in contrast to men — the issue of war and peace. During the Viet Nam war distinctly more women than men were "doves" rather than "hawks." By the late seventies a clear pattern had emerged: women were more opposed to the use of force and to the support of warlike policies than men.[11]

After World War II for the first time in history men who had instigated war and committed crimes against humanity during war were tried before an international tribunal in the Nuremberg trials. More than twenty nations agreed to a charter setting up an international military tribunal and identifying the crimes over which the court had jurisdiction. Three American judges, including Justice Robert Jackson of the U.S. Supreme Court, participated along with judges from England, France and the Soviet Union.

Judge Allen was gratified that finally war criminals were to be brought before a court of justice, but many lawyers and judges were adamant that the trials were unfair. They said the rules had been written after the crimes were committed, ex-post facto, a condition which the U.S. Constitution specifically declares unconstitutional.

Allen vigorously defended the trials. In speeches and articles she argued that the law making wars of aggression a crime had existed in the Kellogg-Briand Pact since 1928 and had been signed by 63 governments. The Geneva Protocol of 1924 had also declared a war of aggression an international crime and it had been signed by 48 countries. The 1927 assembly of the League of Nations had passed a similar resolution unanimously. The crime had therefore been defined before it had been committed and the trials were legal. The Nuremberg trials was the first time the law had been enforced, but that did not make it less legal. She believed the horrifying evidence of Nazi treatment of the Jews was, in itself, proof of aggression of nation against nation.[12]

At its inception Florence Allen was among the most enthusiastic supporters of the United Nations, but soon she began to view with alarm some of the treaties proposed by it and its related agencies, which, if ratified by the U.S. Senate, would become the supreme law of the land. She studied the draft Covenant of Human Rights, which dealt with the traditional rights included in our Bill of Rights, but proposed added new rights: the right to social security, the right to work, the right to medical care, the right to education, and many others. She studied the proposed Genocide Treaty which defined genocide as intent to do serious bodily or mental harm to members of an ethnic, racial or religious group and provided for the perpetrators to be punished by an international penal tribune. She studied the proposed conventions (treaties) of the International Labor Organization, which included recommendations on specific aspects of labor and social regulations. These were not treaties as the term was used by our forefathers who drafted the Constitution, Allen thought, and many Americans agreed with her. These treaties concerned essentially domestic affairs and had the effect of legislation which must be enforced by the courts.

When Kappa Delta Pi, the national education honor society, in 1951 asked her to write an essay on a topic of her choice, the essay to be published as a book and abstracted as a lecture for the society's national convention, Allen decided to tackle the problem of the treaties.[13] She mulled it over in her mind, firm in her conviction that the treaties if ratified would interfere with the American way of doing things, but fearful that her exposition would brand her as an opponent of the United Nations and an obstructionist of its work.

She consulted Frances Kellor, whose judgment she trusted implicitly. "I realize fully," she wrote, "that any opposition in this country to ratification of treaties submitted by the United Nations is going to be viewed with alarm and result in recrimination for the person raising the objection. I wish to ask you especially if you think I should engage in this controversy at all." Kellor replied that it might well be worth doing.[14]

The first draft went to Elizabeth Hauser, who responded with a very thorough criticism. "The article is terribly important," she wrote Florence, adding, "I come away with the feeling that it exposes fundamental weaknesses in the whole U.N. system." Although she felt "very much depressed" by the situation, Hauser had, as usual, suggestions for improvement. The United Nations should agree on limits. Treaties should be limited to international matters: boundaries, fishing rights, trade agree-

180

ments and so forth. Other matters should be simply declarations of principles. Otherwise a constitutional amendment should be proposed separating international treaties from domestic ones.[15]

Virginia Meekison — the baby in the buggy in the 1912 suffrage campaign, now grown and a lawyer working for the government in Washington — and several of her friends worked very hard finding information to send and making suggestions for Allen. They also read and approved the finished manuscript, but asked that their work not be acknowledged in view of their government connections.[16]

Florence was completely absorbed in her subject for months, limiting her travel to trips in connection with the manuscript. In November she wrote a letter to "Dear Girls" explaining her seclusion, and commenting that she had spent more money on research books, long-distance calls and consulting trips than she would be paid for the work. She read aloud sections of the manuscript to her family and friends at the Briar Patch, and, of course, Bert read the whole thing. She delivered an abstract of the book as a speech as a formal banquet of Kappa Delta Pi at Michigan State University in March, 1952.[17]

The book, *The Treaty as an Instrument of Legislation*, dedicated to her brothers Emir and Jack, was published by the Macmillan Company in 1952. At Allen's request more than a hundred complimentary copies were sent. A representative of the company wrote that it was "not customary to distribute so many free copies," but that they felt the world-wide implication of it justified this exception.[18]

Reviewers were unanimous in agreeing that the writing was erudite and scholarly and that she had presented the ramifications of a very serious topic with clarity, although most did not comment on the substance of the book. The reviewer for *The Annals of the Academy of Political and Social Science* found her legal discussion "not enlightening," but did not think that too important for "the problem is not a legal problem but a political problem. The issue is whether it is wise to make the protection of human rights an international issue . . . ."[19]

Senator John Bricker, Republican of Ohio, took up the burden of introducing a constitutional amendment denying U.N. conventions the authority of international treaties. Bricker was much more conservative than any of Allen's previous associates. "This is the only country in the world," he wrote her, "that recognizes human rights as God-given." He thought the draft Covenant of Human Rights lower than our standards and reflective of the ideas of "the Godless and Socialist" members of the United Nations.[20] Bricker quoted from Allen's book on the floor of the Senate in support of his amendment and saw to it that several other senators received copies.

Support trickled in slowly from other sources. W.L. McGrath, an employer delegate to the ILO, wrote Allen that the technical assistance program of the organization had very little to do with teaching or introducing labor skills in underdeveloped nations. but was more concerned with labor relations and advancing socialism. He thought the Russians had taken over the ILO and supported the Bricker amendment.[21] The amendment, however, failed to survive the attacks made on it in Congress.

Allen was saddened by the news that Eleanor Roosevelt, who had served on the Human Rights Commission, had the impression that Allen had turned against the United Nations.[22] Florence hastened to write Mrs. Roosevelt that she had hoped to consult with her personally while writing the book but never got there. She carefully explained her views and emphasized that it in no way affected her enthusiasm for the U.N.[23] Eleanor replied that she was glad to know Allen supported the U.S. and invited her to come for a visit the next time she came east, which Allen did.[24] Although the treaty book was a scholarly endeavor, Allen spoke and wrote of it apologetically as her "little book," especially when writing to Mrs. Roosevelt. Writing it seemed a distasteful task that must be done to defend the American way.

During the war American destruction had been very slight and production had been enormous. The United States emerged after the war as a seeming new colossus of world power, with an industrial complex of a size and productivity such as the world had never seen, agriculture that could feed its own population abundantly and provide surpluses to sell or give away to the rest of the world, a military complex that had suffered little in comparison to other wartime powers, a navy that was in undisputed control of the seas and could go wherever it chose, and a frightening new atomic weapon that no one else had. American attitudes were exuberantly international, in sharp contrast to the isolationist attitudes following World War I.

Affluent Americans wanted to travel, to observe the rest of the world with their own eyes, to join international organizations, and to participate in world decision making and problem solving. American lawyers were in the forefront in creating international organizations. The Inter-American Bar Association was organized and Judge Allen delivered a major address on human rights and the International Court of Justice at their meeting in Detroit in 1949. She spoke of the need for a juridical world order. Violations of treaties after World War I were either not referred to the World Court or its decisions were not enforced. Again after World War II, she argued, the same thing was happening in the United Nations and questions of human rights did not go beyond resolutions in the Assembly of the United Nations.[25]

The International Bar Association began on a small scale with a meeting in 1946 in New York, a second on a larger scale in The Hague in 1948, with 500 representatives from 51 countries, and thereafter met biennially in London, Madrid, and Monte Carlo.

Woman lawyers were organized into the International Federation of Women Lawyers by Rosalind Goodrich Bates, a lawyer from Los Angeles, and eventually women lawyers in 65 countries joined. In 1948 Allen represented the women's federation at the International Bar Association at The Hague and presented an address on "Peace through Justice." She called upon lawyers of the world to participate in the peace-keeping process much as she had called upon women thirty years earlier to participate in the political process:

> In this formative period lawyers have a significant part to play. They understand the need of governmental structures that will offer both legal and other more flexible methods of amicable adjustment for international disputes. They know, for instance, that the informal processes of the arbitral tribunal are of great assistance where rights of nations are involved. Lawyers, therefore, should see to it that the Hague Tribunal (the Permanent Court of Arbitration) should be fitted into the international system and increasingly used than with the International Court of Justice. Lawyers know that executive bodies tend to usurp even judicial power, that the usurpation of judicial functions is possible in the United Nations and that lack of judicial safeguards when an executive acts judicially is bound to create injustice. They know that the Security Council may by-pass the International Court of Justice and that governments may and on occasions have by-passed the United Nations. Lawyers must guard against and help to prevent these dangers. The system of private warfare was abolished by the upgrowth of law. The upgrowth of the international judicial process will eventually eliminate war. The lawyer is an indispensable instrument in this process. For it is not an emotional exaggeration to say that atomic time is running out. In a vital sense what this group does to erect the standard of peace through justice may determine the future of the race.[26]

For Allen the international organizations presented a wonderful opportunity to travel for a purpose. She became a globe-trotter with the best of them but she never lost sight of her goal to advance the causes of women and peace. She delighted in exploring the usual tourist routes and expanding her acquaintance to the worldwide sisterhood.

The International Federation of Women Lawyers was very responsive to the pleas and invitations of women around the world. Visits were scheduled to combine with other international meetings. Rosalind Bates and Judge Allen became friends and traveling companions; Mary Pierce went along to take care of travel arrangements and join in the sightseeing.

In 1950 Florence and Mary met Rosalind in Madrid where they were guests of Spanish women lawyers. The purpose of the visit was to tour prisons where women political prisoners, victims of the fascist winners of the Spanish Civil War were still incarcerated without trial. With dictator Franco's friends as guides, they found the prison conditions superb but the prospects of release or trial dim. They also found the holdings of the Prado museum superb.

They drove to Rome along the Mediterranean coast, admiring the pope's palace at Avignon and the Roman ruins in the lovely mountains behind Monte Carlo along the way. In Rome they attended a bar association meeting and an organizational meeting of women lawyers. It seemed to Rosalind and Florence that the Latin women lawyers were holding their meetings in turmoil with complete disregard for parliamentary procedure, but with Judge Allen presiding elections were held and resolutions passed.

There was only time for a quick tour of the Roman forum and an opera before flying on to Israel, where they had been invited by Israeli women lawyers who felt that women were suffering legal restrictions in their new homeland. Before independence Palestine had operated for two decades under the British common law. For many centuries before that the country had been under the laws of Islam which relegated women to a special secluded sphere. In the new homeland the rabbinical establishment remembered the even more ancient Mosaic Code. Israeli women lawyers found the rabbinical laws in regard to family matters less liberal than the British or Islamic codes and felt that they discrimnated greatly against women.[27] Rosalind and Florence spoke about women's rights with men of the bar associations in Jerusalem and Tel Aviv. In their spare moments the visitors took a tour of holy Jerusalem, visited Bethlehem, the Mount of Olives, a modern kibbutz and several courts before boarding the plane to London. After Allen returned to Cleveland she was pleased to hear that some things had improved for Israeli women after their visit and that one of them, at least, regarded her as a prophet.[28]

In London Allen was interviewed on a British Broadcasting Corporation show and talked about the home as the source of everything good and the need for women to take part in the solution of public problems. The International Federation of Business and Professional Women's Clubs was meeting in London, and for the first time ever women were permitted to use the Guildhall. At the banquet the King's health was toasted in port wine, and Allen gave the address of the evening, lauding men and women working together. The chairperson called it "a truly magnificent speech."[29]

The most memorable trip was in 1952 when Rosalind, Florence and Mary visited women lawyers around the world. They flew from Los Angeles to Honolulu, putting up in the "lovely and snooty" Royal Hawaiian Hotel and visiting Waikiki and Diamond Head. At Tokyo they were greeted by many reporters and engulfed by the hospitality of the Japanese "girls," who had only been permitted to practice law since the American occupation of their homeland. A Japanese supreme court judge was their official host and kept them so busy with sight seeing that Florence had to get up at 5:30 in the morning to work on the speech which she was to deliver in the supreme court chamber. Judge Allen felt honored that she was also

184

asked to speak to law students on her patent cases. The visitors' hearts were warmed by the courtesies extended to them by their Japanese hosts and by the excellence of the programs arranged for them. One of the most interesting and touching visits was to an orphanage where they saw unwanted children of a variety of colors and racial combinations, one of the sad results of war.

From Tokyo they flew to Okinawa and Manila, where they were officially welcomed by the minister of justice. Florence made a speech at a luncheon for women lawyers and the next day at Centro Escolar University. On Wednesday they were in Hong Kong where Mary had a gorgeous day shopping, and on Thursday they were in Thailand for tea with the prime minister and sightseeing of wonderful old temples and modern prisons and medical clinics. They were surprised to find in this gentle country that women lawyers could not rise above positions as clerks. Rosalind and Florence chided the judges they met about this injustice and later were gratified to learn that two Thai women were promoted as lawyers after their visit.

In New Delhi they arose at four in the morning to see the sunrise at the Taj Mahal. Unfortunately it was cloudy and since they had no time to wait for the sun they flew on to Karachi. The found their meeting with Moslem Pakistani women very interesting and different, and enjoyed an elegant tea with Begum Ali Khan, but had no talks with men of importance.

It was a beautiful flight from Karachi to Istanbul, over the Euphrates and Tigris, lovely snowy mountains, Cyprus and the beautiful Bosphorus. Among the resolutions passed at the International Federation of Women Lawyers meetings in Istanbul was one to nominate Judge Florence Allen for the next vacancy in the International Supreme Court. Rosalind and Florence found the Turkish women lawyers very sophisticated and well informed. Their conversation ranged far beyond the position of women in Turkey and the visitors were queried about Negroes and human rights in the united States. Entertainment for the guests was magnificent, with luncheons overlooking the Bosphorus, tours of mosques, viewing the sultan's jewels, and receptions by public officials. Women lawyers in Turkey seemed to be doing very well, and shortly one was appointed to the supreme court bench. The meetings of the International Bar Association in Madrid were something of an anticlimax after the glamorous and stimulating meetings in Istanbul.[30]

Judge Allen's niche in the International Bar Association was in the realm of human rights. She was appointed co-chairman of the Human Right Committee, a large committee representing several nations of the world. She presided over section meetings in London in 1950, Madrid in 1952 and Monte Carlo in 1954. The main task of the committee was an assessment of the draft Covenant of Human Rights. A lengthy report of the co-chairmen in 1950 reflected the unsolvable problems of defining human

185

rights. Many said the draft covenant of the United Nations created a sort of supernational supervision of relations between a state and its citizens. No harmony could be found among the delegates on such issues as the right of every citizen to a job, the limits of private property, the right to use native languages and many other issues. In spite of the disharmony, a session on human rights was put on the agenda for the Madrid meeting in 1952 with Allen as chairperson. Even the seating arrangement at the meeting caused disharmony. When Allen went to the assigned room she thought the chairs were too formally arranged and the speakers too far from the audience. She laboriously moved the chairs so that speaker and audience would be closer to each other. When the meeting began a Spaniard arose to protest that the seating arrangement was too informal and stalked angrily out of the room.[31]

The meeting was successful, in Allen's opinion, but no agreement was reached on human rights. When arrangements were made for the 1954 conference the subject of human rights was omitted from the agenda, although the section met, and Allen agreed it should be omitted. "Personally," she wrote to the chairman, "the whole question seems to me in something of a state of flux at this time."[32]

FOOTNOTES

[1] Diary entries August-October 1942.

[2] From personal interviews.

[3] Letter from Allen to Vadae Meekison, August 7, 1952, Meekison papers OHSL.

[4] Cleveland *Plain Dealer*, Pictorial Magazine, August 1, 1948, article by Grace Goulder Izant.

[5] Letter to Vadae Meekison, August 14, 1947, Meekison papers, OHSL.

[6] From personal interviews.

[7] According to diary, June 21, 1947, "Barbie died alone." Feelings about surgeon in letter to Meekison, August 14, 1947, OHSL.

[8] Letter from Mrs. Tillett to Judge McAllister, April 17, 1945, Allen papers, WRHS, container 7, folder 1.

[9] Cleveland *Plain Dealer*, July 11, 1946, Allen papers, WRHS, container 27, folder 6.

[10] *New York Times*, July 12, 1946, Allen papers, WRHS, container 27, folder 6.

[11] Sandra Baxter and Marjorie Lansing, *Women and Politics*, Ann Arbor: University of Michigan Press, 1980, pp. 58-59.

[12] Reprint from *The Educational Forum*, May 1947, in *To Do Justly*, pp. 163-175.

[13] Allen's explanation of the content in *To Do Justly*, pp. 131-142.

[14] Letter from Allen to Kellor, April 19, 1951; letter from Kellor to Allen, April 25, 1951, Allen papers, WRHS, container 7, folder 2. Kellor regarded the finished manuscript as excellent.

[15] Letters from Hauser to Allen August 15 and September 13, 1951, Allen papers, WRHS, container 7, folder 2.

[16] Copies of their information, undated, in Allen papers, WRHS, container 7, folder 2.

[17] Letter from Allen to Dear Girls, November 1, 1951, WRHS, container 7, folder 2.

[18] Letter of Mary Clint Irion to Allen , June 17, 1952, Allen papers, WRHS, container 7, folder 3.

[19] Quincy Wright, *Annals of the Academy of Political and Social Science*, July 1952, Allen papers, WRHS, container 28, folder 2.

[20] Letter from Bricker to Allen, September 15, 1952, Allen papers, WRHS, container 7, folder 3.

[21] Letter from W. L. McGrath to Allen, December 28, 1955, Allen papers, WRHS, container 8, folder 1.

[22] Diary April 4, 1954, from conversation with Marian Harron.

[23] Letter of Allen to Eleanor Roosevelt, April 16, 1954, Allen papers, WRHS, container 7, folder 4.

[24] June 14, 1954, according to her diary. No conversation noted.

[25] "Human Rights and the International Court: The Need for a Juridical World," published in *American Bar Association Journal*, v. 35, September 1949, pp. 713-716, Allen papers, SMITH, box 1, folder 10.

[26] *To Do Justly*, pp. 121-123.

[27] From letter of Allen to Sidney L. Harold, September 15, 1950, Allen papers, WRHS, container 7, folder 2.

[28] Diary, September 18, 1950.

[29] Letter from Dame Caroline Haslett to Allen, August 11, 1950, Allen papers, WRHS, container 7, folder 2. Information about 1950 trip from diary June 18 to August 24, 1950, and *To Do Justly*, pp. 121-130, unless otherwise indicated.

[30] Information about 1952 trip from diary June 3 to August 6, 1952, and *To Do Justly, pp. 121-130.*

[31] Incident from *To Do Justly*, pp. 126-127.

[32] Allen letter to Edward V. Saher, undated, Allen papers, WRHS, container 7, folder 4.

Chapter 14

FIRST LADY OF THE LAW

Florence Allen turned 70 in 1954 but her public and private life continued to be packed with activity. Her popularity on the lecture circuit continued until physical disabilities ended her acceptance of invitations. Preparation of speeches was a labor of love, including preparation in her study, criticism by friends, and practice on listeners at the Briar Patch. Nothing was ever perfunctory about her public appearances, whether it was for the New Lyme alumni association, which she never refused, or the multitude of college functions, bar associations, women's organizations, civic groups, international organizations, or memorial services for departed associates.

Her court load increased as cases multiplied in the fifties. The number of judges was increased to six to handle the pressure of work, but, although her colleagues were congenial, she felt overworked. And the years had numbed the social consciousness that had originally attracted her to the law.

In September 1958 Allen added another first to her long list of firsts by becoming the first woman chief judge of a federal court. A new law was to take effect in the following year prohibiting judges over seventy from being chief judges. Chief Judge Simons stepped down so that Allen could be chief judge before the law took effect. In February 1959 Chief Judge Allen stepped down so that Judge Martin, also over seventy, could have a chance to be chief judge before the law took effect.[1]

The Briar Patch was her refuge, her private kingdom, where she could do as she pleased, with whom she pleased. In an unusually revealing moment she wrote to the girls in 1957, "I really lead two lives, a court life and a Briar Patch life. The court life is hectic and unsatisfactory; the Briar Patch life is hectic and satisfactory." Sometimes, she said, when she thought she had struck a blow for truth and justice in a court case, it turned out to be just another lawsuit. But when she cut down brush at the Briar Patch the improvement was obvious and permanent.[2]

Local police kept a benevolent eye on the ladies at the Briar Patch, ostensibly to help with the car and the driveway, but undoubtedly aware that they were protecting an important person who wanted privacy. Florence did not drive any more, and so it was Mary who navigated the Olds or the Lincoln. Other drivers found Judge Allen a nervous rider.[3]

189

The house itself never completely shed its origin as a shack and kept Mary busy with structural problems. Inside it was furnished with big, old, comfortable furniture and the accoutrements of hospitality. Neighboring women were friendly and some of them joined "the girls." One magnanimously left Florence a bequest which eased her always worrisome financial problems.[4] It was not that a judge's salary was inadequate, but that her expenses were great and she was generous to a fault, always giving a worthy cause or a friend in need priority over the exigencies of her budget, sometimes borrowing money for special needs.[5]

Entertainment centered in the Briar Patch. The girls no longer went to concerts, plays and movies. Television took their place. Favorite shows — Halls of Ivy, most of the westerns, and Perry Mason — were regularly rated as "good" or "not so good." Sometimes the judge slept through her favorite show, more frequently as the years went by. She read "whodunits" by the score and exchanged copies with her friends. The *Saturday Evening Post, Colliers, The Reader's Digest,* and *U.S. News* were regular reading fare, although the classics never gathered dust. Her interest in politics continued and she liked to talk about political affairs with guests.[6] Even though she had lost her political connections, she lived vicariously in that realm from which fate had excluded her.

Her political and social outlook became more conservative, surpassing the conservative milieu about her. Her ideas about women remained those of the suffrage movement, almost fifty years past. By the late fifties the Equal Rights Amendment had gained respectability and was promoted not only by the NAWL and the NFBPWC but also by other organizations that spoke for other than professional women. When asked to make a statement about it in 1956, Judge Allen declined, claiming judicial restriction.[7] Neutrality in this instance, amounted to opposition, although possibly she thought her example sufficient evidence of its viability.

She bemoaned the decline of society's spiritual values, values which she steadfastly retained from her "Puritan sense of right." She lost her optimism about peace and believed the United States should be fully armed to meet the communist threat.[8] She saw no inconsistency in silencing communists while constantly praising American freedom of thought and expression. She worried about the breakdown of our moral standards,[9] blamed parents for juvenile delinquency, and condemned pornography and vulgarity on the stage. What was needed, she thought, was to get back to the ideals that had been accepted by civilized mankind before World War I.[10]

Her appearance was old-fashioned. In an era when women's tresses had again become long and curling, she clung to the boyish style of the twenties. She never gave up her corsets, which were always fitted by her favorite corsetier. In the days when bosoms, tiny waists and frills and ruffles had returned and hemlines were prescribed in inches, the judge clung to her simple dresses of undetermined length. She no longer worried about her weight because she lost fifty pounds after the age of 65 with no crash diet whatever.[11] Judging from photographs, her height also declined perceptibly. She approached old age with grace and without regret, but she was aware that the years showed. When her older sister, Esther, came for her retirement ceremonies she noted that "Esther looks fine and young and full of beans. Younger than me, for fair!"[12]

Florence and Mary's life style was less common than in former times. It was a household, a family, of women who depended on each other for companionship and emotional support. It harked back to the generation of Florence's mother, the days when unwed women social reformers and others lived together in a benign pre-Freudian society. Those days were gone; only individuals of opposite sex were supposed to live together. Some municipalities enforced it by ruling that only persons tied by bonds of marriage or blood might share a residence. Finding a husband was the most important thing in a young woman's life; being unwed was a calamity. The "heterosexual imperative"[13] demanded a couples society. Perhaps Florence sensed that her living arrangements might be considered odd, for she invariably explained that Mary, with whom she lived for more than thirty years, was a cousin, emphasizing, but never explaining, the blood relationship.

There was a clear division of labor between Florence and Mary, not unlike that of husband and wife in a conventional household . Florence was the one with the public career, the commuter with the briefcase, the breadwinner and billpayer, the one who did the outdoor chores. Mary was the homemaker and hostess, the dispenser of care for the sick, the chauffeur and community activist, the typical suburban housewife. She was as well organized as the women's magazines said every housewife and mother should be. It was Mary who packed the suitcase when Florence travelled. "It is quite a task for me," Florence wrote the girls, "to fold and pack up all my dresses. Mary does it beautifully when I go, but when I come home I wrestle with it quite a while, and it takes me twice as long as it takes her."[14] So completely was the household Mary's realm that Florence called her "the Cap." An elderly couple, Obie and Florence, helped Mary with the house and garden. Everyone had an identity in the household.

Although the Briar Patch family provided satisfying relationships, it was far from the ideal family Judge Allen often described in her speeches as the root of everything good. Her ideal family was a replica of that of Corinne and Emir Allen: a mother and father dedicated to the proper formation of their children, and a mother especially who, although always at home to encourage and guide her children, found time to contribute to civic affairs and work for progressive causes. She must have reflected with some sorrow that among the Allen children only Weebie and Harry approached that kind of family life. Florence invariably went out of her way to be kind to children of families among her acquaintances, and in moments of confidence counselled parents to cherish their children in what she called a "real" family relationship.[15]

Several of the girls helped with the judge's work at home. Elizabeth Hauser, Frances Kellor, and Bertha Miller had for years been her trusted advisers and critics. Lois Mook and Nina Schoeflin were added to the number in the fifties. DeLo died in 1949 and Lois came often with her sons or brothers to visit. Soon Lois was coming by herself, almost every day, to type, edit, and retype Florence's speeches. Nina helped with editing, proofreading and literary advice. Florence was dearly loved by the girls around her, some of the younger women thinking of her as "a great old girl."[16]

The judge's homecoming to the Briar Patch after trips was always a joyful occasion. The Judge never spoke for herself, but invariably noted that the little dogs greeted her with frenzied joy, sometimes going "crazy with delight." Whether the dogs or the judge were more delighted is hard to say.

The dogs and the judge shared their love for the field and woods of the Briar Patch. Florence wrote to the girls:

> The Spring and Fall are particularly lovely in Ohio because of the woods and the great variety of trees. But the Winter also is extremely beautiful . . . . We go back into the large field and see ourselves ringed about everywhere with woods leading up to the ridge of the mountain, all of the trees a lovely brown, and not a house in sight, with the expanse of snow bringing out the color of every trunk and limb of the trees.
> A Winter day like Saturday or Sunday when I am not downtown begins with a whoop from the little dogs. I let them out, do the various chores, and then we start off for a walk in the darkness. I carry a lantern so that I will not slip or fall down . . . . The moon is out, maybe, or perhaps the very bright morning star . . . .
> The loveliest part of a winter day at the Briar Patch is the afternoon when we all walk together . . . . We trail off, Mary and three dogs in the lead, and up in the large field we see the glory of the sunset. The sky is massed with blue-black clouds that are shot with light, lying across the black woods and at the horizon is the golden sunset. As we come down past the little gulley the clouds ahead of us have taken on a variety of colors. Sometimes we can see the blue line of the lake underneath, but above it is lilac, turquoise, and delightful shadings of gray. Toward the lake the line of the woods is almost purple — a lovely scene not to be surpassed in far more famous and distinguished places.
> This is Winter in the Briar Patch and I wish you could see it.[17]

Along with the enjoyment of its beauties went the endless work of caring for the woods and field. Arthritis in her feet and legs made it increasingly difficult for her to care for her beloved trees, but her indomitable spirit prevailed over the pain and she trimmed and sawed until her legs would no longer take her to the woods.

Florence Allen was a very exceptional woman and an individual of great accomplishments regardless of sex. She received many honors and accepted them all with pleasure and modesty. She was the recipient of twenty-five honorary degrees,[18] a record seldom matched. Ohio colleges, Oberlin, Western Reserve, and Otterbein gave the first honorary degrees; New York University, Rutgers, Smith, and others followed. Perhaps it helped that she could be counted on to give a substantive and inspirational speech in reciprocation, but honorary degrees are not based on speech making alone.

Among universities, her alma mater, New York University Law School was most generous in its praise. As a result of the liberal policy of encouraging women students there were 800 active alumnae by 1948. Judge Allen was a living demonstration of their expectations and dinner was planned in her honor. The affair was arranged by Judge Dorothy Kenyon, a 1917 graduate, a New York City municipal court judge and great admirer of Judge Allen.[19]

Eleanor Roosevelt was honorary chairman for the banquet for 1000 at the Waldorf-Astoria. Mrs. Roosevelt was in Paris and unable to attend but she sent a fine tribute to her "good friend," including the thought that if the president should decide to nominate a woman for the Supreme Court it should be Judge Allen. Harold M. Stephens, now a federal judge, gave the major testimonial of the evening, praising Allen as the embodiment of truth, honor, integrity, stability and courage, and at the same time being kind, gentle, sympathetic and understanding. Dean Elizabeth Lee Vincent of the Cornell University College of Home Economics honored her as "a symbol of great strength in a world of wavering purposes."[20] At the dinner Judge Stephens sat on one side of her and Judge Learned Hand on the other side.

Allen was especially pleased that a scholarship fund had been established in her name and that thirteen Florence Allen scholars were seated at a special table.[21] Again NYU was ahead of its time, in granting professional scholarships to women. Most universities were wary about granting graduate or professional scholarships to women who, it was assumed, would only marry and never have a career. The judge's honor was further perpetuated by dedicating a room in the new Law Center as the Florence E. Allen Room. Allen accepted the honor graciously, saying she owed the supreme gift of a fine legal education and generous encouragement to NYU. The whole affair was "marvelous," she wrote the girls.[22]

New York Univesity honored her again in 1960 with its Albert Gallatin Award, an award granted for outstanding service to humanity. It had been awarded to such distinguished men as Dr. Jonas Salk and Ralph Bunche, but this was the first time it had been awarded to a woman. At a dinner at the Hotel Pierre a bronze medal was bestowed on her for her accomplishments in the field of law and the cause of women. Again the company was very distinguished. In her response she admonished women for not using the power of the ballot and for the lack in this generation of women leaders with intelligence and courage to work unselfishly for all women. Florence wrote the girls that "it was the loveliest thing I ever attended."[23] One thought was repeated in every speech she made acknowledging honors: that she owed everything she was to her parents. Over and over she wished that her father and mother could be with her to share the honors.

One of the most personally moving events in Allen's life was the honor of speaking at the dedication of the bust of Susan B. Anthony to the Hall of Fame for Great Americans.[24] She worked with tender loving care on the speech for weeks in the privacy of her study and it was one of her masterpieces. Allen was much too modest to note the similarities between Anthony's life and her own: the tutelage of a male parent, the study of law, the courage to speak out in the face of adversity, the faith in truth, justice, and the ballot, the humility, the unbounded energy, the willingness to sacrifice the usual amenities of womanhood for the cause. Anthony sought nothing for herself, Allen said, no honor, no advantages, no fame.[25] Some of her listeners, or possibly the committee that extended the invitation, must have thought of the similarities between Anthony and Allen.

Another great honor was that of being invested with honorary membership in the Order of the Coif at George Washington University. The Order of the Coif was a very old organization, originating among English lawyers and judges, and including such famous members as Blackstone and Coke. The coif was a cap that did not have to be taken off even in the presence of the king. The day of the investiture was a busy one for Judge Allen. The Washington Chapter of Kappa Beta Phi, society for women lawyers, honored her at a luncheon at which she spoke, and she delivered the address of the evening at the Order of the Coif. She wrote the girls that it was a very great honor, adding, "When I heard the names of justices and chief justices of the Supreme Court and men of similar distinction read out as being honorary members I thought it really was quite amazing that this distinction should have been conferred on me."[26]

Her retirement from the Court of Appeals in 1959 was accompanied by honors reserved for only the most distinguished retirees. The Cleveland Patent Law Association began the celebration with a dinner for 200 at the Hotel Sheraton-Cleveland with Justice Potter Stewart heading the speakers. In the course of his talk he quoted Judge Allen's philosophy about law:

> I believe in the ethical purpose of law. After all, law is an outgrowth of faith. At first law was the effort of the race to hold brutality in leash. It began as a series of 'don't's —' Thou shalt not kill,' 'Thou shalt not bear false witness.' But in its broader development, law expresses the desire of mankind to erect and maintain positive standards of right: 'Thou shalt regard the rights of others,' 'Thou shalt love thy neighbor as thyself.' Where has mankind attempted anything finer than the attainment of justice through evidence based

194

on fact, illuminated by moral principle? This is part of my fundamental faith. 'What doth the lord require of thee,' said the prophet, 'but to do justly, to love mercy, and to walk humbly with thy God?'[27]

There followed a portrait unveiling at the Court House in Cincinnati with Senator Lausche, all the Sixth Circuit judges, representatives from several bar associations, women's organizations and others present. Nieces Betty and Keenie were there, the latter with namesake Florence Allen Hill. Sister Esther unveiled the portrait. Senator Frank Lausche presented the portrait in a very heartfelt speech. Her accomplishments, he said, added "glory to the Allen name." He praised her fidelity to the "ancient virtues that made this country so great" and predicted that "judges and lawyers yet unborn will read the words she has written in the endless, ever-old and ever-new quest for justice." Chief Judge McAllister accepted the portrait for the court dubbing Judge Allen "The First Lady of the Law," a title which she undeniably deserved.[28]

Other affairs followed. The NAWL presented her with a plaque honoring her unprecedented judicial career. The audience gave her a standing ovation as she walked slowly out of the banquet hall leaning heavily on her strong wooden cane. The Press Club of Ohio gave a great ball at the Neil House in Columbus honoring her as a great woman, a great jurist, and a great personality.

Letters of congratulation came from all over the country. A fan from Kentucky wrote that she had heard Allen speak for Wilson in Billings, Montana in 1916 and Allen had been her ideal ever since. Another remembered a speech in Millersburg, Ohio in 1919 that had left a permanent impression. Several from the class of '04 remembered her with their tribute. President Eisenhower had fine words of praise. Judge Simons wrote with regret about their sharp disagreements in the early years and, now, with sadness that their finely coordinated judicial group was breaking up. Judge Martin was saddened by the departure from the court of his sister in law. Senator Lausche wished there would be among people today "a greater spirit, as exemplified by yourself and your ancestors." One letter was from a retired dining car waiter who remembered that although their stations were so far apart she always called him her friend and said nice things to him.[29]

Vadae Meekison, quite unknowingly, sounded the most prophetic note. Saddened by the news of Allen's retirement, she wrote "It is the end of an era. The curtain is coming down."[30] It was, indeed, the end of an era in women's history, an era that took root at the turn of the century, reached full bloom in 1920 and then declined. By 1959 when Allen retired its ideas had been badly eroded by social change and were so moribund they were rapidly laid aside in the new feminism of the sixties and seventies.

Federal judges are appointed for life. When they retire they become Senior Judges, free to participate or not participate in cases as they

195

wish and are needed. Judge Allen continued to work on a few cases in which she had been involved, but rather quickly dropped out of the judicial routine. Chief Justice Warren wrote asking if she would like to be included in the roster of judges available.[31] Allen replied favorably, but her doctor emphatically recommended no work — a recommendation which she did not follow in regard to cutting brush and sawing wood. Actually retirement came as a relief from the burden of court work, for during the last years she had been overburdened.

During her years as a judge she had taken care not to express her views on controversial or political questions. She sometimes apologized to groups she knew well, saying that when she was a young lawyer she wondered why judges chose such dull topics for speeches, but now she knew why. When she retired she planned to cast off judicial seclusion and speak out on current issues. All her life she had talked about the power of public opinion and urged men, and especially women, to be informed and speak out. Now, after many years of silence, she could speak her mind about women's rights if she chose, support the ERA, take a stand on discrimination against women in the professions or on equal pay for equal work. She chose none of these issues. Instead of joining the new feminist movement, she chose to follow the suffragist dictate of promoting societal reform generally. She perceived communism as being the greatest threat to American society and became as obsessed with the threat as her mother before her had been obsessed with the threat of sexual promiscuity. Judge Allen's first foray was in the area of education.

When the Soviet Union launched the first space craft Americans were shocked and immediately began to question the excellence of their own education system. Allen read an article in the *Saturday Evening Post*, "Can Ivan Read Better Than Johnny?" the essence of which was that Ivan could read better and that Soviet schools were educating their children to be better communists than we were to be better Americans. Allen found the article a terrible indictment of our education and wrote the *Saturday Evening Post* commending it. The magazine printed her letter.[32] She ordered many reprints of the article to send to leaders of the educational world with a covering letter recommending, among other things, that the content of elementary readers be changed to include the classics of civilization. Children might better have the old McGuffy readers, she said, than the current texts.[33] Most of the recipients thanked her kindly and promised to pass the article along to those directly concerned with elementary education.

A number of educators eventually responded, hotly defending their methods of teaching reading. The classics, one said, were not designed to teach children to read. Others said the Soviet Union had demonstrated accomplishment in only one scientific field, space, but that American students were taught to be good citizens, not just good scientists. Another defended the American system because it taught students to think and discuss, and argued that simple rote learning might result in scientific success but would not teach students the freedoms of speech, thought, and press. A *Post* reader from Peoria, Illinois liked her letter and suggested that she start an organization to "lead the countrie's [sic] schools out of this ridiculous situation. How about it? Will you?" the letter pleaded.[34] A librarian from Texas asked for permission to reprint her letter to pass out to the public. It must have been of some satisfaction to Allen to find that her talent for inspiration to action was still intact.

Communism continued to be a frightful bug-a-boo to Allen even after popular paranoia about it had declined. By the end of 1963 she began to feel that the courts were emasculating the statutes designed to protect the nation from communism. In December of that year the District of Columbia Appellate Court reversed a conviction of the Communist Party for failing to register as an agent of the Soviet Union. The problem was that no one in the Communist Party would register for it on the grounds that he would thereby incriminate himself. The court said the party could not be forced to find someone to sign and that the Smith Act did not apply in this case. Judge Allen protested with all her might that communism would revive, that there was now nothing to stop the Party from holding conventions and nominating candidates. She feared the decision would pass unnoticed and spent much time and effort alerting her many connections of the dangers, including women's organizations and bar organizations. Most correspondents replied favorably, but one bar correspondent replied that such things as committees on communist tactics had become controversial and that liberal members either opposed them or had them abolished.[35]

The decision in the communist case was appealed to the Supreme Court, as Allen hoped it would be, but to her great disappointment it affirmed the decision of the lower court. As a last resort, she wrote to Esther Peterson, head of the Women's Bureau and member of the Commission on the Status of Women, telling her that now new anti-communist legislation was needed and that women must be organized to agitate for it. Peterson replied politely, but not encouragingly, saying this was out of her purview.[36] She did not express surprise that this distinguished and renowned leader of women had written to her not about the status of women but about the threat of communism. To Allen it was not strange because her conception of women was that of the suffrage movement when an important part of women's role was to keep a watchful eye on the public virtue.

In her late years Senator Lausche proved to be her most sympathetic link in Washington. Although of different ethnic backgrounds and different generations they were joined in their idealization of America. Lausche was on the Senate Foreign Relations Committee and Allen wrote him often encouraging and commending his stand against the slightest concession to "Red Russia."

Allen also hoped that Lausche would be able to use his influence to have more women appointed as federal judges. On this score the Senator, although very sympathetic, found that this word received "only secondary consideration" and thought that success in that area required "a greater devotion . . . to political partisan machine service" than he was able to give.[37]

In 1965 Lorna Lockwood was selected by her brethren to be Chief Justice of the Arizona Supreme Court. *Time* magazine found the appointment as being equivalent to the selection of a female coach for the Cleveland Browns football team,[38] but Allen was pleased and wrote congratulating her. Lockwood replied that Judge Allen had always been her ideal.[39]

During her retirement she became increasingly alarmed about the growing crime rate. Her first perception of it was to note the increase in sex crimes, the fact that the streets were not safe for women alone at night. She thought the cause was the terrible influence of war and "the inordinate emphasis on sex which is characteristic of our modern life. Women are taught today," she wrote to a *Plain Dealer* correspondent," that their function is primarily that of sex. When even the clothes that are exhibited to us to buy . . . accentuate the physical form of women . . . the race begins to forget that women are human beings first and women second."[40]

Her alarm quickly widened to include all kinds of crime. She thought the courts themselves were helping to free the guilty and failing to protect the public, and she exhorted lawyers everywhere to take up the burden of enforcing criminal law. The NAWL was most reponsive to her plea and asked her to wrote an article for the *Women Lawyers' Journal*. She wrote on the impact of recent Supreme Court decisions on the administration of justice which had expanded the rights of criminals and slowed down the wheels of justice.[41]

Other causes came in for their share of Allen's support: stopping the indiscriminate use of insecticides, restoration of prayer in the schools, preservation of the redwoods, compensation to the Indian nations for use of their reservation lands. Without compensation to the Indians, she said, we were behaving just like Russia. She liked Stewart Alsop's articles and wrote to tell him of her approval. Locally she used her legal skills and speaking talents to prevent the East Ohio Gas company from running a line through Chapin Forest, which bordered the Briar Patch, and the Holden Arboretum.

The only activity from which she actually resigned after her retirement was as chairperson of the Outer Space Committee of the International Bar Association.[42] She had been appointed to the committee in 1958, after the Committee on Human Rights foundered on definitions and Sputnik was launched. Knowing very little about outer space, the Committee had little difficulty in agreeing on resolutions that no part of outer space could be appropriated by any nation, that exploration was to be jointly undertaken, and that space shall not be used for other than peaceful purposes.

Allen resigned immediately after her retirement, preferring to devote her time to people on earth rather than to problems of space.

She continued to make speeches into her eighties, some audiences responding with near reverence. The media reported her to be a "pert" and "peppery" little lady, who walked stiffly, or with a cane or taking someone's arm. Her speaking technique was perpetuated in a textbook on public speaking by a writer in Kansas City who first heard her in 1923 and considered her his "favorite American speaker." He asked permission to quote her speeches as illustrations of effective techniques.[43]

Interesting invitations never ceased. In 1960 Radcliffe College celebrated the fortieth anniversary of woman suffrage and asked Allen to speak. She used the opportunity to reiterate her belief that suffrage had liberated women and that today the college woman stands forth a full partner in community and national affairs. She said that ever since women secured the suffrage there had been a debate as to whether they used it well. For three decades she believed women had used the vote to improve the morality of politics. Women's work in political reform seemed to her most important. Women's groups, especially the League of Women Voters, initiated reforms which men and women then took up. Women in many states had been active in revising state constitutions, in working against political machines, in promoting civil service examinations, workmen's compensation and equal pay for equal work. In international affairs, the Kellogg-Briand Pact, implemented in the Nuremberg trials "owes its very existence to women and they have repeatedly demonstrated their eagerness to outlaw war."[44]

The record for women in the fifties Judge Allen found not so notable. Women have grown slack morally: "We do not teach responsibility to the coming race, and we do not willingly accept it ourselves." Critical dangers at home and abroad give women an opportunity to give "intelligent and vigilant thought" to the grave problems that challenge us and then to act.[45] She continued to attribute the inactivity to the lack of young women leaders who work unselfishly for all women.[46]

She emphasized the theme of women's moral responsibility again in 1960 in a major address at the National Convention of the General Federation of Women's Clubs in Washington. She had been invited to speak on the topic of opportunities for women in the legal and judicial field. Instead she decided to speak on "the broader opportunity" which faces women lawyers in teaching youth "our glorious traditions." Unless we inspire the coming race with a conception of the ethical basis of the law our freedoms will be destroyed, she warned, concluding "This for women lawyers is at once our challenge and our mighty opportunity."[47]

The University of Utah granted Judge Allen her last honorary degree in 1960. She delivered the commencement address on "Challenge to the Citizen," warning that today we face a crisis greater than ever before in the advancing tide of communism all over the world. The cause she said was a crisis in faith in our own values. We must revitalize our own faith in the Declaration of Independence and the Constitution. We can promise other nations greater material benefits than communism and "assure the oppressed of their place as a free people in a free world."[48]

In the spring of 1963 Allen was anticipating two unusually pleasant events, one in Utah and one in Massachusetts. Cleveland composer Arthur Shepherd had written an instrumental and choral arrangement entitled "A Psalm of the Mountains," based on her poem of that title from *Patris:*

> Know ye the mountains and their wondrous peace
> Ye who from worse than trial crave release;
> From bitter questioning of heaven and earth,
> Suspects of gladness save for children's mirth,
> Callous to sorrow save for children's tears,
> Stung by injustice that will never cease,
> Know ye the mountains and their nameless peace.
> Surely there dwells not anywhere such calm,
> Such silence musical, a very psalm
> Of majesty to pierce the doubt of years.[49]

It was to be premieried by the Utah Symphony Orchestra in May and Allen's presence was much desired.

In the same month the Smith College Library was having a festival honoring its beginnings and its first students. Florence had much correspondence with the archivist about her mother, the first student to matriculate, and was looking forward to the event. Unfortunately she sprained her hip and was unable to attend either event.[50] Smith College postponed its celebration, hoping that she could come later, but her infirmities continued to limit her travel. She did manage with difficulty and Mary's help to go to New York to attend her fiftieth reunion at the NYU Law School and to enjoy one more time the honors which its alumni so generously bestowed on her. It took two men to raise her from her chair after dinner, and she knew that trips to Utah and Massachusetts were impossible.

In the fall of the same year the Women's City Club of Cleveland gave her its Margaret Allen Ireland Award, the first time it was given. It was remembered that Allen was a charter member of the organization and had made the keynote speech 41 years earlier at the cornerstone laying ceremony for its building in downtown Cleveland.[51]

The dogs were always a joy as well as the field and woods of the Briar Patch, but as navigation became more difficult Florence's study became the center of her life. She began to think about the disposition of her papers. Radcliffe College was eager to have them for its Women's Archives, the largest and most important collection in women's history in the country. Allen was honored and sent copies of speeches and articles. Copies also went to the Library of Congress, which very much wanted the whole collection. Allen declined the request, writing that she thought her papers were really the property of the women of Ohio who had made her what she was.

Her friends insisted that she must write her memoirs, if not for her own satisfaction then for the inspiration of women everywhere. At least three authors, including Catherine Drinker Bowen, who had written a best-selling biography of Judge Oliver Wendell Holmes, were much interested in writing a biography of Florence Allen, but all stopped short of publication. She began to go over and over her papers, selecting this for her memoirs, burning that. She wrote sections and read them to the Briar Patch audience, asking for criticism and advice. Advice flourished, most of it contradictory. She should or she shouldn't discuss the Alcazar; she should or she shouldn't go into legal details; she should or she shouldn't have a collaborator. Relatives she rarely saw came and had opinions, but most of the real collaborators in her life had already passed on: Susan, Helen, Elizabeth, Rose, Nina, Bert, Rosalind. Esther and Weebie lived far away in California. Keenie had moved out of the state. Florence wrote Viola that she did not overestimate the value of the memoirs or consider herself a good writer, but that "as a record of the history of the woman movement I feel compelled to complete them."[52]

The title, *To Do Justly*, was no problem for it came from a passage from the Old Testament prophet Micah that she knew by heart and had quoted innumerable times: "He hath shewed thee, O man, what is good; and what doth the Lord require of thee but to do justly, to love mercy, and to walk humbly with thy God." The autobiography was published in 1965. Reviewers found it interesting, charming, and "calmly unemotional," but were sorry that it did not reveal the inner woman.[53] Actually the public image of Florence Allen had absorbed the inner woman; self had been sublimated into a worthier cause. Neither did the memoirs reveal the range and depth of difficulties she had encountered as a woman in her rise to success. Even for the historical record she heeded Maud Wood Park's advice to avoid confrontation on issues of discrimination or prejudice.

Moving about became more and more difficult as trouble with her feet, knees, and hips increased. One day as she walked out of her study a leg gave way, her hip was broken. After a short stay in the hospital she returned home to the loving care of Mary, Obie and Florence, but she did not recover. Her heart failed and she died in September, 1966.

Mary settled the judge's small estate, sold the Briar Patch which was deeded to her, organized the papers for disposition to the Western Reserve Historical Society, and left for the east to live with a cousin there. Only the little dogs remained, at home with kind neighbors or at rest in the beloved earth of the Briar Patch.

The suffrage era, which was coincident with Florence Allen's adult life, was marked by a "diffused preoccupation of the differences between the sexes."[54] Ideologically woman's realm was in the private sphere of the home and man's realm in the public sphere of business and politics. Those women who, because of some misfortune, worked outside the home were protected by legislation. The right to vote was insurance of a voice in government.

The conventional image of women was set aside temporarily during World War II. They were encouraged to work, protective legislation was set aside if it interferred. Millions of women responded. Most of the jobs were in industry and many of them were menial; professional and executive opportunities did not open to women during the war.

After the war it was expected that women would return to the home, and many did willingly. In 1947 popular writer Fannie Hurst wrote that women preferred to keep it a man's world while they snuggled cosily at home. Women didn't want to be taken seriously in industry, in government, in the judiciary. Women do not go in for politics because they don't want to, she wrote, and they don't vote for other women because they don't trust them. Hurst used the example of Florence Allen to prove that women can succeed if they want to, but she didn't think most of them wanted to.[55]

The traditional image of women was refurbished and reinforced in the fifties. Women's magazines dwelt on fashion, food, and furniture and never hinted that women might have careers other than homemaking. Women spent more time shopping than ever before. By 1960 the number of hours spent shopping, including transportation, was about seven and a half per week, compared to about two hours in 1920.[56] Courts and social workers presumed that mother's place was in the home in custody of the children for better or worse. Government policy shored up the image by cancelling funding for day care centers at war's end and funding a woman's bureau that monitored women's protection. Political parties funneled women through their women's divisions, gave them no decision-making power, and presidents were expected to make a token gesture by appointing a few women to high office. Women's organizations continued to be more interested in self-fulfillment than in public reform. Many universities continued unpublicized quotas for women in graduate and professional schools, not wanting to waste their resources on students who would never use the education. But most of all the image was reinforced by middle-class men and women who accepted the conventional wisdom.

At the same time social change was eroding the old life style. Married women, mothers of young children, middle-class women were going to work. Between 1940 and 1960 the number of working wives doubled and the number of working mothers quadrupled.[57] They were very quiet about it, not demanding good jobs or equal pay, rationalizing that they were merely "helping out" the family budget. It was the husband's work that determined the family social status and credit rating, and was the family topic of interest, conversation, and pride. There was almost no public interest or agitation for women's rights in the fifties.

Women were not following Florence Allen's lead into the law profession or any other profession except those traditional for women. The number of women lawyers had increased rapidly, as Allen often pointed out, but the number of men lawyers also increased rapidly. At the time of Allen's retirement the proportion of women in the profession of law was about three per cent, not significantly larger than in 1920. Most law schools, including Yale and Harvard, admitted women in a token fashion, but the proportion of women in law schools was only four per cent.[58]

Also quietly, a debate was going on about the position of women in American society. Shortly after the war the American image of motherhood was attacked and condemned by exponents of "momism." They claimed the whole thing had been overdone, warping women's lives and emasculating their sons. Sociologists, anthropologists, and psychologists joined the fray, some scientifically proving that "true womanhood" was merely the result of social conditioning and not necessarily natural for women.[59] College alumnae protested often that their education had not prepared them for changing diapers and doing housework, but could not agree on solutions.

Also quietly, without any public forum millions of individual women were wrestling with their problems. They were living much longer and faced years when motherhood and home making could not possibly occupy their time. All kinds of inventions had shortened the time really needed for housework. Many were secluded in lovely homes in suburbs that husband and children only occupied evenings and week-ends. By 1957 Max Lerner would write that the American woman held an ambiguous and frustrating place in our civilization, torn between trying to compete with men for jobs, careers, business and government and finding her identity as wife, mother, and woman. Psychically and socially, he wrote, she was caught in a society still dominated by masculine power and standards. Lerner found women's dilemma the result of social conditioning rather than biological differences.[60]

The stage was set for the "third incarnation" of the women's rights movement.[61] Puzzled by the dichotomy between the image and the reality of women and the argument between ERA supporters and protectionists, President John F. Kennedy established a Commission on the Status of Women in 1961. The Commission reported the existence of discriminations against women and proposed remedies to eliminate them. In a more emotional way, the civil rights movement, like the abolitionist movement more than a century earlier, brought attention to the inequalities suffered by women as well as black people. Public participation in the civil rights movement created a corps of women experienced in taking action for black people and ready to take action for women.[62]Betty Friedan capsulated in popular readable form the scholarly findings of the previous decade that women were trapped in "the feminine mystique."[63] Millions read it and believed it.

Change came quickly with the surge of a new feminist movement that did not focus on one issue or define men and women as different, as Florence Allen and the suffragists did, but demanded a broad range of equal rights. One of the most presistent demands of the new feminism was for women in the professions traditionally reserved for men. Law was one of the most responsive. By 1980 the proportion of women in law schools had risen to thirty-three per cent.[64] After 1964 more women than men were voting and there were faint perceptions that they were beginning to vote together on some issues.[65] So important had the women's vote become, and so much had the social climate changed, that President Ronald Reagan found it politically expedient in 1981 to appoint a woman, Sandra Day O'Conner, to the Supreme Court.[66] But this was beyond the times of Florence Allen.

Florence Allen was a living model of the suffrage movement, where it came from, what it did, and what it hoped to do. Coming from an English, Puritan background, she believed in the power of the vote and in the social responsibility of individuals. Raised during the progressive era, she was taught by her family to seek causes that would promote improvement of the human condition. She lived in the new industrialized society that rewarded men with economic and political control and compensated women with honors to their moral purity and motherly skills.

Florence Allen found her cause in the women's crusade that brought the right to vote in 1920. The crusade glowed with promises that women would be liberated to participate in and reform the political process and find equality in economic life. Having chosen law as her profession, she was elected a judge in 1920 and 1922 by the power of the sisterhood, just as the crusade promised. Her work in the cause of women, court reform, and peace confirmed her image as a woman reformer. Campaigns for the U.S. Senate and House of Representatives demonstrated her willingness to work within the framework of a political party. Presidential appointment to the highest judicial position ever held by a woman was the next natural step. She had the qualifications and was in the pool for selection as a Supreme Court justice, "probably the only woman judge who might have been considered."[67] Women's organizations supported her every step of the way with unflagging loyalty.

Although she never married and had no children, she was a remarkable mother. Her conception of motherhood was much broader than that of the average homebound woman, and included care and affection for all to whom society had been unjust and especially to women, finally extending to women of the whole world. She combined the qualities of social motherhood and the liberation of a splendid career in the world of men, a career of the type for which women were supposedly now eligible. She was modest about her accomplishments, acknowledging that she was the beneficiary of the woman movement. She made contributions to her profession in constitutional and patent law; she made contributions to the cause of women as a role model of what a woman could do. As Marion Harron said in memoriam, "Judge Allen went forth and did the things which women had claimed they were entitled to do."[68]

Other women were not doing these things. Florence Allen was one in a million, an exception to the rule, a woman ahead of her time. She would probably have been an exceptional woman at any time in American history and in a variety of careers. She had outstanding intelligence, good common sense, great ambition, incredible energy, personal pride, sensitivity, integrity, and, not the least, constant good humor. She was bound to succeed at something. She might have been an outstanding musician, or teacher, or news correspondent. In men's clothing she might have been a remarkable actor or an inspirational minister or a successful politician.

In addition to her outstanding capabilities, she had an extra ingredient which sustained her in excellence. That was faith in her ideals: faith that justice is real and achievable, faith that peace can be attained, that human rights can be defined, that women can achieve equality with men. It was the faith of her forefathers, from the Old Testament and the Puritan sense of right, embedded in the Constitution, expressed in the American way. She was a great woman and a great American.

FOOTNOTES

[1] Letter of Chief Justice Earl Warren, October 14, 1958, asking if she was willing to accept chief judgeship. Letter of Allen to Warren, January 10, 1959, stepping down for Judge Martin. Allen papers, LC, container 1.

[2] Letter to the girls, June 22, 1957, Allen papers, WRHS, container 8, folder 2.

[3] Personal interviews.

[4] Personal interviews.

[5] Diary January 7, 1952, she borrowed $300 to visit Helen who was ill. Helen died in 1953.

[6] Personal interviews.

[7] Letter of Allen to Nina Horton Avery, National Woman's Party, October 24, 1956, National Woman's Party records, LC, microfilm reel 103.

[8] From speech to New Lyme alumni reunion as reported in *Warren Tribune Chronicle*, August 3, 1953, Allen papers, WRHS, container 28, folder 3.

[9] From speech to AAUW in Athens, Ohio, April 3, 1950, Allen papers, WRHS, container 15, folder 5.

[10] First noted in 1949 when she spokle at a meeting of the Cleveland Bar Association on "A Rebirth of Justice" calling for a return to the ideals accepted by mankind before the two world wars, *Cleveland News*, March 8, 1949, Allen papers, WRHS, container 27, folder 11.

[11] Diary December 21, 1950 recorded that she weighed 205; on December 21, 1960 she recorded that she weighed 153 3/4.

[12] Diary November 11, 1959.

[13] Ryan's phrase, pp. 169-177.

[14] Letter to the girls, June 20, 1955, Allen papers, WRHS, container 8, folder 1.

[15] Personal interviews.

[16] Personal interviews.

[17] Letter to the girls, February 1, 1955, Allen papers, WRHS, container 8, folder 1.

[18] Judge Allen had LLD honorary degrees from Western Reserve University, New York University, Ohio State University, Oberlin College, Smith College, Western College, Otterbein College, Beloit College, Toledo University, Berea College, Marietta College, Ohio Wesleyan University, Wittenburg College, Mt. Holyoke, Pennsylvania State College for Women, Rockford College, University of North Carolina, Wilson College, Russell Sage College, Lindenwood College, Rutgers University, Washington College of Law, Washington University, Lake Erie College, and the University of Utah.

[19] Programs, speeches, etc., in Allen papers, WRHS, container 18, folder 1; *To Do Justly*, pp. 143-145.

[20] NAWSA papers, LC, container 37, reel 25.

[21] The Ohio Federation of Business and Professional Women also had a Florence Allen Scholarship Fund, established in 1924. By 1959 55 girls had used the fund. *Forty Years of Progress and Service, 1920-1960*, Columbus: OFBPWC, 1960, p. 30.

[22] Letter to the girls, November 12, 1948, Allen papers, WRHS, container 7, folder 1.

[23] Letter to the girls, November 29, 1960, Meekison papers, OHSL; *To Do Justly*, p. 145.

[24] *Ibid.*, pp. 145-146.

[25] Speech in Allen papers, WRHS, container 15, folder 5.

[26] Letter to the girls, June 20, 1955.

[27] From Justice Potter Stewart's speech to the Cleveland Patent Bar Association, October 10, 1959. Originally written for Edward R. Murrow for inclusion in his book *This I Believe*. Murrow did not include Allen's statement in his book.

[28] Accounts of retirement in *To Do Justly*, pp. 147-150; speeches in 278 F 2d. 5-15 (1959).

[29] All letters in Allen papers, WRHS, container 8, folder 5.

[30] *Ibid.*

[31] Letter from Chief Justice Earl Warren to Allen, October 22, 1959, Allen papers, WRHS, container 8, folder 4.

[32] Arthur S. Trace, "Can Ivan Read Better than Johnny?" *Saturday Evening Post*, v. 234, No. 21, May 27, 1961, pp. 30, 67-68. Allen's letter to SEP July 1, 1961, p. 6.

[33] Letter of Allen to William G. Levenson, June 14, 1961, Allen papers, WRHS, container 9, folder 2.

[34] All letters in Allen papers, WRHS, container 9, folder 2.

[35] Letter of Frank E. Holman to Allen, January 14, 1964, Allen papers, WRHS, container 10, folder 2. Holman replied that the Committee on Communist Tactics had been criticized as a "witch hunting" committee.

[36] Correspondence between Allen and Peterson, 1964, Allen papers, WRHS, container 10, folder 2.

[37] Letter of F. J. Lausche to Allen, October 2, 1961, Allen papers, WRHS, container 9, folder 2.

[38] *Time*, January 29, 1965, p. 41.

[39] Letter of Lorna E. Lockwood to Allen, February 18, 1965, Allen papers, WRHS, container 10, folder 3.

[40] Allen letter to J. F. Saunders, November 8, 1961, Allen papers, WRHS, container 9, folder 2.

[41] *Women Lawyers' Journal*, v. 51, No. 1, Winter 1965-1966, pp. 3-7, 27-29.

[42] According to her resignation letter she resigned because she did not expect to attend the Bar Association Conference in Manila in 1960. Allen papers, WRHS, container 9, folder 1.

[43] Correspondence with Loren D. Reid, January-February 1962, Allen papers, WRHS, container 9, folder 3. The book was published in 1962 under the title *Speaking Well*, New York: McGraw Hill.

[44] Reprint of "Participation of Women in Government," *Annals of th eAcademy of Political and Social Science*, May 1947, Allen papers, SMITH, box 1, folder 10.

[45] NAWSA papers, LC, container 37, microfilm reel 25, from speech at Radcliffe, November 10, 1960.

[46] *World Telegram Sun*, November 23, 1960, Allen papers, WRHS, container 28, folder 10.

[47] Allen papers, SMITH, box 1, folder 10. This message is also in *To Do Justly*, pp. 151-152.

[48] Allen papers, SMITH, box 1, folder 10.

[49] *Patris*, p. 10.

[50] It was premiered May 26, 1963, without her. The Cleveland *Plain Dealer*, May 26, 1963, Allen papers, WRHS, container 25, folder 11.

[51] Diary, November 18, 1963, noted Louis Seltzer among the guests. Seltzer, editor of the *Cleveland Press*, was the young newsman with the suffragists on the trolley trip to Medina in 1912. Lucia McBride, her old suffrage friend, was chairman of the selection committee, according to the *Cleveland Press*, November 6, 1963, Allen papers, WRHS, container 28, folder 11.

[52] Allen letter to Viola Smith, February 14, 1964, Allen papers, WRHS, container 10, folder 2.

[53] *Dayton Journal Herald*, January 8, 1966 and *Youngstown Vindicator*, January 2, 1966, Allen papers, WRHS, container 28, folder 11.

[54] Erik H. Erickson, "Inner and Outer Space: Reflections on Womanhood," *Daedalus,* Journal of the American Academy of Arts and Sciences, Spring 1964, p. 582.

[55] Fannie Hurst, "Women Prefer to Keep it a Man's World," International News Service, June 7, 1947, Allen papers, LC, container 1.

[56] Joann Vanek, "Time Spent in Housework," *Scientific American,* v. 231, No. 5, November 1974, p. 119.

[57] Chafe, *The American Woman,* p. 218.

[58] Information from Cynthia Fuchs Epstein, *Women In Law,* New York: Basic Books, 1981, pp. 4-5.

[59] For further exposition of the debate see Chafe, *op. cit.,* pp. 199-255.

[60] Max Lerner, *American as a Civilization,* New York: Simon and Schuster, 1957, pp. 599-611.

[61] So-called by Chafe, *Women and Equality,* p. 117.

[62] Jane De Hart Mathews, "The New Feminism and the Dynamics of Social Change," in Linda K. Kerber and Jane De Hart Mathews, *Women's America,* New York; Oxford, 1982, pp. 397-425.

[63] Betty Friedan, *The Feminine Mystique,* New York: Norton, 1963.

[64] Epstein, pp. 4-5.

[65] Baxter and Lansing, p. 2 and pp. 58-59.

[66] According to Cook, *Judicature,* op. cit.

[67] Beverly Cook, "The First Woman Candidate for the Supreme Court," in Supreme Court Historical Society, *Yearbook, 1981,* p. 19.

[68] Marion J. Harron, "In Memoriam: Honorable Florence Ellinwood Allen," *Women Lawyers' Journal,* v. 52, No. 4, Fall 1966, p. 145.

Bibliography

Archival Material

Corinne Tuckerman Allen papers, Arthur and Mary Schlesinger Archives of Women's History, Radcliffe Institute.

Corinne Tuckerman papers, Smith College Library Archives.

Florence E. Allen papers: diaries, correspondence, speeches, articles, newspaper clippings, court notes, scrapbooks, etc., Western Reserve Historical Society, Cleveland, Ohio.

Florence E. Allen papers, Library of Congress, Manuscript Division.

Florence E. Allen papers, Schlesinger Archives.

Florence E. Allen papers, Sophia Smith Collection, Smith College Library.

Mary Dewson papers, Franklin Delano Roosevelt Library, Hyde Park, New York.

Mary Elizabeth Drier papers, Schlesinger Archives.

Bernita Shelton Matthews papers, Schlesinger Archives.

Vadae G. Meekison papers, Ohio Historical Society Library, Manuscript Collection.

National American Women's Suffrage Association papers, Library of Congress, Manuscript Division.

Belle Sherwin papers, Schlesinger Archives.

Women's Rights Collection, Schlesinger Archives.

Newspapers
Cleveland News
Cleveland Press
Cleveland *Plain Dealer*

Periodicals
Woman Citizen
The Woman's Journal
Women Lawyers' Journal

Judicial Opinions
Federal Reporter, Second Series
Reports of Cases Argued and Determined in the Supreme Court of Ohio

Books

Abbott, Virginia Clark, *The History of Woman Suffrage and the League of Women Voters in Cuyahoga County, 1911-1945*, Cleveland: LWV, 1949.

Adams, Elizabeth Kemper, *Women Professional Workers*, Chautauqua, N.Y.: Chautauqua Press, 1921.

Allen, Florence Ellinwood, *Patris*, Cleveland: World Publishing Company, 1908.

———, *This Constitution of Ours*, New York: G. P. Putnam's Sons, 1940.

_____, *To Do Justly*, Cleveland: Western Reserve University Press, 1965.

_____, *The Treaty as an Instrument of Legislation*, New York: Macmillan, 1952.

_____ and Mary Welles, *The Ohio Woman Suffrage Movement*, Cleveland: Committee for the Preservation of Ohio Woman Suffrage Records, 1952.

Allen, Frederick Lewis, *Only Yesterday: An Informal History of the Nineteen-Twenties*, New York: Harpers and Brothers, 1931.

_____, *Since Yesterday: The Nineteen Thirties in America*, New York: Harpers and Brothers, 1940.

Anthony, Susan B. and Ida Husted Harper, *The History of Woman Suffrage*, v. 4, published by S. B. Anthony, 1902.

Aumann, Francis R., *The Changing American Legal System: Some Selected Phases*, New York: Da Capo Press, 1969.

Baker, Leonard, *Back to Back: The Duel Between FDR and the Supreme Court*, New York, Macmillan, 1967.

Baxter, Sandra and Marjorie Lansing, *Women and Politics*, Ann Arbor. University of Michigan Press, 1980.

Bennett, Helen C., *American Women in Civic Work*, New York: Dodd Mead, 1915.

Blair, Karen J., *The Clubwoman as Feminist: True Womanhood Redefined, 1868-1914*, New York: Holmes and Meier, 1980.

Breckinridge, Sophonisba P., *Women in the Twentieth Century: A Study of Their Political, Social and Economic Activities*, New York: McGraw Hill, 1933.

Cantril, Hadley, Ed., *Public Opinion, 1935-1946*, Princeton: Princeton University Press, 1951.

Chafe, William Henry, *The American Woman: Her Changing Social, Economic, and Political Roles, 1920-1970*, New York: Oxford, 1972.

_____, *Women and Equality: Changing Patterns*, New York: Oxford, 1977.

Chambers, Clarke A., *Seedtime of Reform: American Social Service and Social Action, 1918-1933*, Minneapolis: University of Minnesota Press, 1963.

Conway, Jill, "Woman Reformers and American Culture, 1870-1930," in Jean E. Friedman and William G. Shade, *Our American Sisters, Third Edition*, New York: D. C. Heath, 1976.

Danelski, David J., *A Supreme Court Justice is Appointed*, New York: Random House, 1964.

Davis, Allen F., *American Heroine: The Life and Legend of Jane Addams*, New York: Oxford, 1973.

Deutsch, Helene, *The Psychology of Women: A Psychoanalytical Interpretation*, v. II, *Motherhood*, London: Research Books, 1947.

Dobkin, Marjorie Housepain, *The Making of a Feminist: Early Journals and Letters of M. Carey Thomas*, Kent: Kent State University Press, 1979.

Doerschuk, Beatrice, *Women in the Law*, New York: Bureau of Vocational Information, 1920.

Douglas, William O., *The Court Years 1939-1975: The Autobiography of William O. Douglas*, New York: Random House, 1980.

_____, *Go East Young Man: The Autobiography ...*, New York: Dell Publishing Company, 1974.

Edwards, India, *Pulling No Punches: Memoirs of a Woman in Politics*, New York: G. P. Putnam's Sons, 1977.

Epstein, Cynthia Fuchs, *Women in Law*, New York: Basic Books, 1981.

Faderman, Lillian, *Surpassing the Love of Men: Romantic Friendship between Women from the Renaissance to the Present*, New York: William Morrow and Company, 1981.

Filene, Peter Gabriel, *Him: Her: Self: Sex Roles in Modern America*, New York: Harcourt Brace, 1975.

Flexner, Eleanor, *Century of Struggle*, Cambridge: Harvard University Press, 1977.

Friedman, Lawrence M., *A History of American Law*, New York: Simon and Schuster, 1973.

The Gallup Poll: Public Opinion 1935-1971, v. 1, *1935-1948*, New York: Random House, 1972.

Goldman, Sheldon and Johnige, *The Federal Courts as a Political System*, New York, 1971.

Griffith, Kathryn, *Judge Learned Hand and the Role of the Federal Judiciary*, Norman: University of Oklahoma Press, 1973.

Grimes, Alan P., *The Puritan Ethic and Woman Suffrage*, New York: Oxford University Press, 1967.

Gruberg, Martin, *Women in American Politics*, Oshkosh: Academia Press, 1968.

Harper, Ida Husted, *History of Woman Suffrage*, v. 5, New York: Arno Press, 1969.

Harris, Barbara J., *Beyond Her Sphere: Women and the Professions in American History*, Westport: Greenwood Press, 1942.

Hurst, James Willard, *The Growth of American Law: The Law Makers*, New York: Little Brown and Company, 1950.

Kessler-Harris, Alice, *Out to Work: A History of Wage Earning Women in the United States*, New York: Oxford, 1982.

Kinnear, Mary, *Daughters of Time: Women in the Western Tradition*, Ann Arbor: University of Michigan Press, 1982.

Komarovsky, Mirra, *Women in the Modern World*, New York: Little Brown, 1953.

Kraditor, Aileen S., *The Ideas of the Woman Suffrage Movement, 1890-1920*, New York: Norton, 1981.

Lagemann, Ellen Condliffe, *A Generation of Women: Education in the Lives of Progressive Reformers*, Cambridge: Harvard University Press, 1979.

Lape, Esther Everett, *Ways to Peace*, New York: Scribners, 1924.

Lash, Joseph P. *Eleanor and Franklin*, New York: Signet, 1971.

Lemons, J. Stanley, *The Woman Citizen: Social Feminism in the 1920s*, Urbana: University of Illinois Press, 1975.

Lerner, Max, *America as a Civilization*, New York: Simon and Schuster, 1957.

Lindley, Harlow, Ed., *Ohio in the Twentieth Century*, v. VI of Carl Wittke, Ed., *The History of the State of Ohio*, Columbus: Ohio State Archeological and Historical Society, 1941.

Lockhart, Earl G., *My Vocation by Eminent Americans*, New York: H. W. Wilson, 1938.

Marshall, Carrington T., *A History of the Courts and Lawyers of Ohio*, New York: The American Historical Society, 1934.

Murphy, Bruce A., *The Brandeis/Frankfurter Connection*, New York: Oxford, 1982.

Murphy, Walter F. and C. Herman Pritchett, *Courts, Judges, and Politics*, New York: Random House, 1961.

National Federation of Business and Professional Women's Clubs *A History of the National Federation of Business and Professional Women's Clubs*, New York: NFBPWC, 1944.

Neff, William B., *Bench and Bar of Northern Ohio*, Cleveland: Historical Publishing Company, 1921.

Ohio Woman Suffrage Association, *Yearbook, 1916, 1917*, Warren: Ohio Woman Suffrage Association.

O'Neill, William L., *Everyone Was Brave: The Rise and Fall of Feminism in America*, Chicago: Quadrangle Books, 1969.

Park, Maud Wood, *Front Door Lobby*, Boston: Beacon Press, 1960.

Parshalle, Eve, *The Kashmir Bridge: Women*, Los Angeles: Oxford, 1965.

Peck, Mary Gray, *Carrie Chapman Catt: A Biography*, New York: H. W. Wilson, 1944.

Peltason, Jack W., *Federal Courts in the Political Process*, New York: Random House, 1955.

Phillips, Harry, *History of the Sixth Circuit*, Bicentennial Committee of the Judicial Conference of the U. S., 1976.

Pritchett, C. Herman, *The Roosevelt Court: A Study of Judicial Politics and Values, 1937-1947*, New York: Macmillan, 1948.

Redlich, Josef, *The Common Law and the Case Method in American Law Schools*, New York: Carnegie Foundation, 1914.

Reed, Alfred Z., *Training for the Public Profession of the Law*, New York: Carnegie Foundation, 1921.

Roosevelt, Eleanor and Lorena A. Hickok, *Ladies of Courage*, New York: G. P. Putnam's Sons, 1954.

Rose, William Ganson, *Cleveland, The Making of a City*, Cleveland: World Publishing Company, 1950.

Rodabaugh, James H. Ed., *A History of Ohio*, Columbus: Ohio Historical Society, 1969.

Rothman, Sheila M., *Woman's Proper Place: A History of Changing Ideas and Practices, 1870 to the Present*, New York: Basic Books, 1978.

Ryan, Mary R., *Womanhood in America*, New York: New Viewpoints, 1979.

Sapiena, Virgilia and Ruth Neely and Mary Love Collins, *Eminent Women*, New York: George Banta, 1948.

Scharf, Lois and Joan M. Jensen, *Decades of Discontent: The Women's Movement, 1920-1940*, Westport: Greenwood Press, 1983.

Scharf, Lois, *To Work and To Wed: Female Employment, Feminism and the Great Depression*, Westport: Greenwood Press, 1980.

Schlesinger, Arthur M. Jr., *The Age of Democracy*, v. 2, *The Coming of the New Deal*, Boston: Houghton Mifflin, 1958.

Schmidhauser, John R., *Judges and Justices: The Federal Appellate Judiciary*, New York: Little Brown, 1979.

Schwartz, Bernard, *The Law in America: A History*, New York: McGraw Hill, 1974.

Scott, Anne F. and Andrew M. Scott, *One Half of the People: The Fight for Woman Suffrage*, Philadelphia: Lippincott, 1975.

Sicherman, Barbara and Carol Hurd Green, Eds., *Notable American Women*, Cambridge: Harvard University Press, 1980.

Smith, Reginald Heber and Herbert B. Ehrmann, *The Criminal Courts*, Part I of *The Cleveland Foundation Survey of Criminal Justice in Cleveland*, The Cleveland Foundation, 1921.

Sunderland, Edson R., *History of the American Bar Association and Its Work*, American Bar Association, 1953.

Tompkins, Leslie Jay, *The New York University Law School*, New York: NYU, 1904.

Ware, Susan, *Beyond Suffrage: Women in the New Deal*, Cambridge; Harvard University Press, 1981.

Warner, Hoyt Landon, *Progressivism in Ohio, 1897-1917*, Columbus: Ohio State University Press, 1964.

White, G. Edward, *The American Judicial Tradition: Profiles of Leading American Judges*, New York: Oxford University Press, 1976.

Woodward, Bob and Scott Armstrong, *The Brethern*, Austin: S and S Press, 1980.

Young, Rose, Ed., *Why Wars Must Cease*, New York: Macmillan, 1935.

Zimmerman, Mary H. Ed., *75 Year History of the National Association of Women Lawyers, 1899-1974*, Lansing: NAWL, 1975.

Articles

Allen, Jane, "You May Have My Job," *The Forum*, April 1932, pp. 228-231.

Collins, Ronald K. L. and Jennifer Friesen, "Looking Back on Muller v. Oregon," *American Bar Association Journal*, v. 69, March 1983, pp. 294-298.

Cook, Beverly B., "The First Woman Candidate for the Supreme Court," *Yearbook 1981*, Supreme Court Historical Society, pp. 19-35.

————, "Women as Supreme Court Candidates: From Florence Allen to Sandra O'Conner," *Judicature*, v. 65, No. 6, December-January 1982, pp. 314-326.

Friedsen, Jennifer and R. K. L. Collins, "Looking Back on Muller v. Oregon," *American Bar Association Journal*, v. 69, April 1983, pp. 472-477.

Harron, Marion J., "In Memoriam: Florence Ellinwood Allen," *Women Lawyer's Journal*, v. 52, No. 4, Fall 1966, pp. 145, 175-176.

Kessler-Harris, Alice, "Where Are the Organized Women Workers?" *Feminist Studies*, v. 3, No. 1/2, Fall 1975, pp. 92-110.

"Five Years of the City Manager Plan in Cleveland," *National Municipal Review*, Supplement XVIII, March 1929, pp. 203-220.

Smith-Rosenberg, Carroll, "The Female World of Love and Ritual: Relations Between Women in 19th Century America," *Signs*, v. 1, No. 1, Autumn 1975, pp. 1-29.

Spencer, Thomas T., "Auxiliary and Non-Party Politics: The 1936 Democratic Presidential Campaign in Ohio," *Ohio History*, v. 90, No. 2, Spring 1981, pp. 114-128.

Trace, Arthur S. Jr., "Can Ivan Read Better than Johnny?" *Saturday Evening Post*, v. 234, No. 21, May 27, 1961, pp. 30, 67-68.

Tunis, Lucy R., "I Gave Up My Law Books for a Cook Book," *American Magazine*, July 1927, pp. 34-35, 172-177.

INDEX